Pergamon Titles of Related Interest

Amara BUSINESS PLANNING FOR AN UNCERTAIN FUTURE
Dewar INDUSTRY VITALIZATION
Elkan THE NEW MODEL ECONOMY
Fusfeld/Haklisch INDUSTRIAL PRODUCTIVITY AND INTERNATIONAL TECHNICAL COOPERATION
Fusfeld/Langlois UNDERSTANDING R&D PRODUCTIVITY
Hill/Utterback TECHNOLOGICAL INNOVATION FOR A DYNAMIC ECONOMY
Hussey THE TRUTH ABOUT CORPORATE PLANNING
Nelson GOVERNMENT AND TECHNICAL PROGRESS

Related Journals*

ECONOMIC BULLETIN FOR EUROPE
LONG RANGE PLANNING
OMEGA
SOCIO-ECONOMIC PLANNING SCIENCES
TECHNOLOGY IN SOCIETY

*Free specimen copies available upon request.

PRICES, WAGES AND BUSINESS CYCLES

PRICES, WAGES AND BUSINESS CYCLES
a dynamic theory

BURTON H. KLEIN
California Institute of Technology

Pergamon Press
New York   Oxford   Toronto   Sydney   Paris   Frankfurt

Pergamon Press Offices:

U.S.A.   Pergamon Press Inc., Maxwell House, Fairview Park,
                                    Elmsford, New York 10523, U.S.A.

U.K.   Pergamon Press Ltd., Headington Hill Hall,
                                    Oxford OX3 0BW, England

CANADA   Pergamon Press Canada Ltd., Suite 104, 150 Consumers Road,
                                    Willowdale, Ontario M2J 1P9, Canada

AUSTRALIA   Pergamon Press (Aust.) Pty. Ltd., P.O. Box 544,
                                    Potts Point, NSW 2011, Australia

FRANCE   Pergamon Press SARL, 24 rue des Ecoles,
                                    75240 Paris, Cedex 05, France

FEDERAL REPUBLIC   Pergamon Press GmbH, Hammerweg 6,
OF GERMANY   D-6242 Kronberg-Taunus, Federal Republic of Germany

Library of Congress Cataloging in Publication Data

Klein, Burton H.

    Prices, wages, and business cycles.

    Includes index.
    1.Economics. 2. Statics and dynamics (Social
sciences) 3. Equilibrium (Economics) 4. Competition.
5. United States--Industries. 6. Prices. 7. Wages.
8. Business cycles. I. Title.
HB171.K5194   1983   338.6'048   83-4218
ISBN 0-08-030126-6

Printed in the United States of America

CONTENTS

ACKNOWLEDGMENTS

There are people who believe that writing a book is a nice evolutionary process in which disorder is gradually replaced by order. But, on the basis of my own experiences, I can testify that this is not always the case. You start with some interesting ideas—and are encouraged by the reactions of friends. Indeed, the standard model seems to be working beautifully until the day you begin to look at actual data. From then on the entire process can be described as an uneven series of ups and downs, with lucky breaks occurring at random intervals to the very end of the enterprise. For example, at the time I was involved in the tedious process of preparing footnotes, several of my Caltech colleagues were very critical of a so-called final draft because, while the dynamic model made good predictions as long as initial conditions (i.e., the degree of competitive pressure) remained unchanged, when this was not the case the results were subject to widely different interpretations. Consequently, with the burning desire to find an unambiguous test directly related to the theory, I was able to have one final burst of fun.

In any event, the following are those I want to thank, because, at one point or another, their ideas created lucky breaks for me: Donald Brown (a Yale economist), Bruce Cain (a Caltech political scientist), Bo Carlsson (an economist from the Swedish Industrial Institute for Social and Economic Research), Benedict Cohn (an entrepreneur formerly with Boeing), Evsey Domar (an MIT economist), Jeffrey Dubin (a Caltech econometrician), Gunnar Eliasson (a Swedish economist from the Industrial Institute for Social and Economic Research), Edward Green (a Caltech economist), William T. Jones (a Caltech philosopher), Roderick Kiewiet (a Caltech political scientist), Simon Kuznets (Professor Emeritus, Economics, Harvard University), Ralph Landau (a chemical entrepreneur, Listowel Incorporated), Marvin Litvak (physicist, Jet Propulsion Laboratory, California Institute of Technology), Carl J. Lydick (a Caltech graduate student in economics), Edwin Mansfield (an economist, University of Pennsylvania), Stephen R. Selinger, (a Caltech graduate student in economics), Robert Solow (an MIT economist), Myron Tribus (an MIT thermodynamicist), and Leon Trilling (an MIT aerodynamicist).

I also owe special thanks to about two dozen executives from American and Japanese business firms for greatly increasing my understanding of the nature of dynamic efficiency.

Finally, my greatest stroke of good luck occurred in September 1981, while aboard a Norwegian mailboat traveling from village to village amidst the majestic fjords, at which time I met a British banker. His contribution consisted of telling me about the experiences of some firms with which his bank dealt. This turned out to be a decisive clue for unraveling a statistical mystery of utmost importance.

Needless to say, none of the aforementioned, including the British banker, are to be held responsible for the conclusions which finally emerged.

Special thanks also go to Madeline Haddad, my secretary, who is an absolute whiz in the use of the word processor.

Finally, I am most grateful to my wife, Cecelia, who must be regarded as an integral part of the "system" involved in writing this book. Although formally trained as an English teacher, and not as an economist, Cecelia has an uncanny ability to perform the function of an editor in the large, that is, of assuring that first priority is given to the thoughts and not the words. Moreover, by working with me on a quick succession of drafts, she helped prevent my attachment to earlier ideas. The cleverness of our ideas is not necessarily a monotonic function of the length of time we dwell on them.

PREFACE

What motivated the writing of this book? And how does it differ from my book, *Dynamic Economics?*

As an unrepentant Keynesian, I not only accept Keynes's prescription for dealing with very serious economic downturns, but also share his skepticism about the usefulness of classical microeconomics as a predictive theory. This is not to say that classical economics cannot make good predictions. For example, it can make amazingly good predictions about the outcome of auctions, even when the auctioneer does not know beforehand the prices necessary to clear a market. Moreover, the classical law of supply and demand can make very good short-term predictions; for example, if OPEC restricts the supply of oil, gasoline prices will surely rise. But longer-term predictions—predictions about the rates of progress in various industries or the size of economic downturns—it cannot make. It cannot, because it does not contain the needed parameters.

To be sure, I am not the only unrepentant Keynesian economist. In Great Britain, George Shackle can be described as a leader of this movement; though my ideas differ substantially from his, I nonetheless regard myself as part of a tradition which he started.[1] This is not to say that the coming revolution in economics is being plotted only by unrepentant Keynesians. While reading some material for an economic conference to be held in the spring of 1983, I was amazed to learn that Frederick Hayek can be considered the father of dynamic competition models— models based on firms employing mutually consistent policies, rather than mutually consistent decisions.[2] Moreover, with the notable exception of the University of Chicago, where the cardinals still retain strict discipline over the thinking of those who would like to enter the priesthood,[3] young game theorists in both the United States and Britain are busily engaged in the construction of dynamic models. On the other hand, in Sweden, Gunnar Eliasson has taken the lead by constructing a model in which microbehavior and macroperformance are directly related.[4] Although such models do not resemble those of the neo-Keynesians, nonetheless they can be described as outgrowths of Keynes's ideas; that is, while he was interested in the manner in which individual savings and business investment decisions affect the macrostability of a country, Eliasson has been working toward the establishment of a wider connection between microbehavior and macroperformance.

One novelty in my own work is the construction of a dynamic model containing a wide range of parameter values with respect to the degree of competition. This approach gets us away from looking at firms and industries as if each had like characteristics. Another novelty consisted of developing a way to relate the degree of dynamic competition to the longer-run performance of a variety of industries. And by looking at the weighted average of various industries, classified in terms of their degree of competitiveness from a dynamic point of view, a more aggregate relationship between microbehavior and macroperformance can be devised.

The modeling employed was adapted from that used by biologists and physicists in the investigation of similar evolutionary issues. When I attended a conference on dynamic modeling several years ago in Berlin, I learned from a paper presented by two chemists from the Prigogine Institute, Belgium, that the basic commonsense thinking behind their model, which concerned the behavior of ants when progressively denied a food supply, was essentially that which is presented in this book. I later found that model has much the same flavor as modern population genetics.

What will become of these diverse efforts to make economics into a "predictive science" is, of course, a debatable matter. Nevertheless, it is my conviction that, while the monetarists and neo-Keynesians will continue to engage in a desperate effort to sell their diamonds to each other, and the classical economists will continue to pretend that short-term equilibria are no different from long-term equilibria (for example, as when searching for suitable matrimonial partners), over the next twenty years we dynamic economists will be engaged in a genuine interchange of ideas that will ultimately revolutionize economics just as taking dynamic considerations into account revolutionized the fields of physics, chemistry, and biology.

In contrast with the highly empirical character of this book, in which statistical hypotheses are developed and tested, my previous book, *Dynamic Economics*, can be described as "economic poetry." To be sure, it was verbal and not mathematical poetry; but which kind is to be preferred is entirely a matter of taste.

What, then, is involved in going from poetry to making statistical predictions? I began this task by obtaining the U.S. Bureau of Labor Statistics's four-digit breakdown for manufacturing, including data on price, wage, productivity, and output changes, initially for the period 1958 to 1967. Computer plots were then made, one for each industry, of price, productivity, and output changes. If I had originally known what I later ascertained, I would have separated the computer printouts into three neat groups: "pretty nice," "not so nice," and "hopeless." For those in the "pretty nice" pile the rates of output and productivity gains did, of course, turn down during recessions and up during recoveries. That, however, was no surprise. To be sure, not many of the graphs could be described as "models of steady-state progress"; that is, while in some cases the long-term rate of productivity gain accelerated, in others it declined. However, as of the time that David Feinstein and I were working on a steady-state dynamic model, we felt that dealing with such cases would be mere child's play. The "not so nice" stack, on the other hand, included some important industries in which rates of productivity advance dipped not only during an economic downturn, but the charts also indicated a continuous cycling process at work, with the curve almost always either climbing or falling. Moreover, the relationship between productivity gains and output changes was not that of the same beautiful waltzing partners included in the first group. For some strange reason, the curves always moved out of step with each other. As for those that were considered "hopeless," at first glance they might have been easily included in the second division. But, upon closer inspection, their productivity rate cycles were more irregular and, in almost all cases, bore little or no relation to the nationwide business cycles.

This led to an argument in which I was wrong and David Feinstein turned out to be right. My argument: Let us simply draw trend lines through cycles, and ignore them. Economists do that all the time. Moreover, inasmuch as the third pile contained only very small industries, why not ignore them? We economists do that too. His argument (as best as I can reconstruct it): How do you know that the cycles and trend lines are caused by independent forces? And how can you say that we should ignore the seemingly unimportant observations when we physicists are taught never to do that? Then came his more general lecture which all modern physicists and chemists, young and old, love to give. To understand any phenomenon you cannot dissect it into component parts; you must try to understand it as a whole.

Though I tried to take his lecture to heart, without the clue from a British banker I was distraught. In fact, at the time that I was provided with this clue I was so busy enjoying the Norwegian scenery that its relevance completely escaped me; and, were it not for still another stroke of good luck, the relevance of the clue might have eluded me to this date. In one of my classes was another gifted student, Mark Foster, majoring in both physics and computer science who, because of plans to go into the computer software business upon graduation, had a burning interest in trying to understand what made the U.S. economy tick, or fail to tick as well as it might.

The exercise Mark Foster and I first embarked upon can be described as "Bayesian fishing with weak or nonexistent prior probability distributions." By "fishing" I mean that when a computer run did not come up to our expectations, we did not dismiss the observation as being irrelevant, but tried to come up with a good explanation, even if it contradicted the accepted orthodoxy, say, with respect to the relationship between price and wage changes. When arriving at what we thought was a good explanation, and additional computer runs were made which confirmed our suspicions, that was like catching a twenty-five pound albacore! Though this fishing was concerned with explaining decade-to-decade changes in the rates of productivity advance in various industries, we did learn that rather than trying to make predictions across industries, the model worked far better for explaining how particular industries reacted when confronted with the same, greater, or lesser pressures to restrain price increases. In other words, we learned not to think in terms of the first, but the second, derivative of productivity indices.

As it turned out, explaining the productivity performance of particular industries during the 1960s and 1970s also provided the beginning of an explanation for the unusual cycles. And it was only then, when we were trying to decide which computer run to make by Friday (we never gave ourselves more than a week to make the next run), that the relevance of the clue provided by the British banker became clear enough to generate a new set of hypotheses. Consequently, what seemed at first like an almost impossible task turned out to be easy, and what seemed to be relatively easy turned out to be enormously difficult.

PREVIEW

Dynamic economics consists of two principal ingredients: a dynamic concept of competition and a quite explicit way to relate such competition to the overall performance of an industry. Dynamic competition is rivalry to generate advances in technological inputs (e.g., semiconductors, robots, and organic cellulosic fibers) or to bring about productivity advances (e.g., lower input costs per unit of output in final products such as computers, Japanese automobiles, and dolls). This is a dynamic definition of competition because it assumes that firms involved in such competition must compare two risks: the risk of being unsuccessful when promoting a discovery or bringing about an innovation versus the risk of having a market stolen away by a competitor: the greater the risk that a firm's rivals take, the greater must be the risks to which it must subject itself for its own survival. By contrast, in static economics there is a hidden hand to pull firms (i.e., the possibility of making higher profits) toward a static equilibrium, but no hidden foot to push them to change the boundaries of their technologies and markets. In the former case, a system operates under given initial conditions, in the latter, it changes them. And this distinction is the heart of the difference between a static and a dynamic system.

To devise a more realistic theory, the concept of a static equilibrium is replaced by the concept of a dynamic equilibrium. A sink with no stopper, but with fresh water running at a steady rate to keep the water level from dropping, can be likened to a dynamic equilibrium. The spigot consists of continuous challenges, whether from newly created firms, firms in another industry, or foreign competition.

Longer-run technological performance is measured in terms of rates of change in either improving the performance (i.e., quality and reliability) of technological inputs relative to their costs or providing more cost-effective final products. When the spigot is turned on sufficiently to prevent the water level from declining, the rate of technological progress will not fall. When the degree of risk taking increases—and with it the flow of fresh ideas—the water level and the rate of technological performance will rapidly rise; when risk taking declines, products become more and more alike, and the rate of technological performance will decline.

On the other hand, a sink fitted with a stopper and half-filled with stale water can be likened to a static equilibrium. Were it possible to pass a worldwide law preventing entrepreneurs from changing their production functions and consumers from changing their tastes, such an equilibrium would be highly stable. But in the real world this condition is seldom, if ever, approximated. Consequently, because they lack the ability to deal with new challenges, industries approaching this type of equilibrium are likely to be highly unstable, unless protected by the government. And, if only a modest proportion of all industries is in this position, their actions may result in the sink draining at a more rapid rate than it can be refilled.

As was already pointed out, when firms engage in risk taking to either make a discovery or bring about an innovation, they simultaneously impose risks upon their competitors. In terms of this concept, an industry like the steel industry can be described as one in which the average propensity to engage in risk taking (PERK) is relatively low. On the other hand, the computer and semiconductor industries can be described as industries in which PERK is relatively high; that is, firms take significant risks and, when successful, pronounced changes in market positions result. In chapter 1 it will be shown how risk taking and longer-run technological performance can be measured in the same kinds of units, which is the first step involved in the construction of a mathematical theory.

Mathematics is employed to obtain the statistical relationship between PERK and longer-run technological progress because it provides a means to an end, namely, the formulation of a testable theory (i.e., a theory that can be proven wrong). Once the relationship is ascertained, we can reason either from changes in the degree of competition to changes in the rate of progress or vice versa. However, the technical discussion of the model is confined to chapter 6, and the entire argument is made in terms of relatively simple diagrams that depict situations in which the underlying microbehavior can be observed.

It must be emphasized, however, that the rate of progress not only depends on the degree of risk firms impose on each other. It also depends on the ability to play the game by generating changes in products or production functions to provide the consumer with more competitive products. This ability is described as a firm's dynamic efficiency; and a high degree of dynamic efficiency presupposes a high degree of flexibility in both R&D activities and production processes. A high degree of flexibility in R&D involves conducting it in such a manner that risky projects which turn out to have disappointing results, as many of them do, can be weeded out at minimal cost. A high degree of flexibility in production is required so tested ideas can be rapidly incorporated into the production process (chapter 5). However, when firms impose only a small degree of risk upon each other, their flexibility is likely to suffer, with the consequence that dealing with a greater degree of risk will result in displaying a high degree of inertia.

The main difficulty encountered when developing a predictive theory is that not one but two activities are involved in bringing about productivity gains—activities which are not commonly carried on in the same firm. The first consists of bringing about advances in various types of technological inputs; and the second, of combining these advances to bring about productivity gains. This means that, while during a given time period two industries may be equally pressured by the forces of competition to reduce prices and costs, one may be luckier than the other in securing the needed technological inputs. Is there a random process for deciding which particular industries will or will not be favored by good luck, or is there a highly selective process at work, so not only good predictions can be made of the likely winners and losers, but also that sound economic arguments can be shown to underlie the predictions? Needless to say, this is the key question that must be addressed when devising a predictive theory.

At this point some important empirical conclusions will be presented, and just enough hints will be revealed to suggest the general drift of the arguments to be made in this book. *First*, let us consider a group of 145 industries, divided into A, B, C, and D groupings, which displayed either the same degree or lack of degree of restraint in raising prices in both the 1960s and 1970s. The A group of industries displayed the highest degree of restraint by raising prices one standard deviation or more *less* than the average during both periods. Conversely, the D group was composed of industries which raised their prices one standard deviation or more above the average. The B and C groups were obtained by splitting the middle of the distribution. In other words, these are industries whose relative prices remained the same during both periods; and they will be hereafter described as the *reference* group of industries: the group whose price behavior suggests that they were in a rough dynamic equilibrium.

Based on statistical observation, it can be found that not only did the A group have a higher average rate of productivity gain than the B group, but during the 1970s, the average productivity gains over the 1960s for the A group were larger. The hint to think about is the following: The variance of productivity gains for the B group can be expected to be much larger than that for the A group: to a greater extent declines in productivity performance on the part of one industry or another will offset gains in productivity performance. The key problem not only in the analysis of the reference group of industries, but others as well, was to explain why, when the incentive to restrain price increases is weaker, the variance of outcomes with respect to productivity gains in the B group increased?

It was also found that in the C and, particularly, the D groups, declines in productivity performance from the average rate of the 1960s were not nearly offset by gains in the rate of productivity advance. The hint is that a genuine discontinuity was evidently involved when going from the A and B groups, on the one hand, to the C and D groups on the other. The problem was to explain, in economic terms, why such a discontinuity was to be expected.

Second, consider two other groups of industries. One exercised a greater degree of price restraint in the 1970s than during the 1960s. In principle, this means that industries in the D group during the 1960s could have moved up three grades to the A group during the 1970s. However, as it happened, while a relatively few moved up two grades, many moved up one grade, but none moved up three grades. The principal factor at work in explaining why this group of 136 industries was forced to exercise a higher degree of price restraint is that they had to face a greater degree of foreign competition.

Conversely, there was a group of 106 industries which exercised a lower degree of price restraint during the 1970s than in the 1960s—a few of those industries actually moved down three grades. On the whole, these were industries in which foreign competition always played an insignificant role or which were increasingly protected from foreign competition during the 1970s.

By comparing the productivity gains of industries faced with greater pressures to restrain price increases with the performance of the reference group, it was found that the Bs which rose to As in price performance actually generated larger average productivity increases than the As during both periods, and the Cs and Ds under greater pressure did impressively better in increasing productivity gains than the Bs and Cs in the reference groups.

On the other hand, with respect to those industries which were under less pressure to restrain price increases, it was found that quite the opposite was true. In fact, this group of industries was mainly responsible for the productivity decline in manufacturing during the 1970s.

These results may or may not be regarded as surprising. The main point to be kept in mind is that once we understand why the theory outlined earlier can be employed to predict the behavior of the reference groups, with the same kind of reasoning we can predict the outcomes just discussed, namely, the shifts in the probability distributions of productivity gains which are likely to occur when industries are faced with a greater or lesser necessity to restrain price increases.

Third, the evidence shows that it is wrong to believe that cooling down inflation, and hence reducing the severity of economic downturns, is mainly a matter of changing workers' expectations for higher wages. Those industries that observed the greatest degree of price restraint also observed the greatest degree of wage restraint, with wage increases following rather than anticipating price increases. Generally speaking, the industries either most protected from foreign competition or late to be challenged by foreign imports were those which displayed the smallest degree of constraint in raising wages. To believe that wages and prices are determined independently in a dynamic equilibrium setting is bad theorizing. On the other hand, these findings are easy to reconcile with the argument that Keynes made with respect to wage rates in his *General Theory of Employment, Interest, and Money* (chapter 10).

Fourth, the industries in the D group during the 1960s were mainly minor industrial materials industries. They were joined by far more important industries during the 1970s, whose price behavior commonly sank from B to D. This group of industries generated serious supply shocks during business upturns, which moderated only during periods of sharp downturns. Their productivity cycles reached a low point when the price shocks were most serious.

One problem was to explain why behavior in prices and productivity gains was not a mere coincidence. Another was to explain why, when more and more industries are directly or indirectly protected from foreign competition, economic downturns will inevitably become larger. Hint: Explaining productivity gains on both a decade-to-decade and a cyclical basis are one and the same problem. The forces that influenced industries to either be lucky or unlucky in generating a larger rate of productivity gain during the 1970s also determined the size of the economic downturns (chapter 9).

The statistical data used in this book were derived mainly from unpublished U.S. Bureau of Labor Statistics (BLS) data covering all (387) four-digit industries in manufacturing (the most detailed breakdown available). In addition, foreign trade statistics were matched to the BLS data to understand the role of foreign competition in leading to a greater or lesser degree of price restraint during the 1970s. It may be noted that in an annual publication of the U.S. Department of Commerce there are published for 200 industries the same basic series which I used.[6] One reason I did not choose to use the published data is that I wanted to include *all* industries. Another is that the Department of Commerce publication does not contain data on wage rates or investment in equipment (which data play an important role in the later analysis).

A summary of the decade-to-decade results is shown in table I.1. The numbers under the column "Changes in the Degree of Price Restraint" indicate the degree to which price performance either improved (e.g., from D to B or C to A = 2; B to A or C to B = 1) or slipped (e.g., A to D = 3, B to D = 2, or B to C = 1). The last two columns in the table were included to provide the reader with additional hints.

The figures in the "constant" row represent the weighted average for the *entire* group of industries described earlier as the reference group. It must be kept in mind, however, that this group contains all of the industries under the A, B, C, and D headings discussed previously. While productivity gains for this entire group of industries were about the same in the 1970s as in the 1960s, this should be regarded as nothing more than a statistical accident. There is nothing in dynamic theory which requires the overall rate to be the same in both periods; for example, as it happened, gains on the part of A industries, such as semiconductors and computers, far offset losses on the part of D industries, such as nonferrous metals. But, if the C and D industries had been better represented, productivity gains for the constant group would have shown a significant decline.

It also can be seen that the weighted increase in the rate of productivity gain for those industries which exercised higher degrees of price restraint was about 35 percent. This is not to suggest, however, that all industries in this category increased their productivity performance by 35 percent. As a matter of fact, while some quadrupled their rate of productivity increase between the two decades, others experienced sharp declines. As already indicated, the problem was to explain why some industries were more favored by luck than others.

Table I.1. Performance of Industries Subject to Constant, Increasing, or Declining Degrees of Price Restraint Between the Periods 1959–1969 and 1969–1979.

CHANGES IN THE DEGREE OF PRICE RESTRAINT	NUMBER OF INDUSTRIES	AVERAGE ANNUAL PERCENTAGE RATES									
		PRICE CHANGES		PRODUCTIVITY INCREASES		WAGE INCREASES		INCREASE IN INPUT COSTS		CHANGE IN OUTPUT	
		Period 1	2	Period 1	2	Period 1	2	Period 1	2	Period 1	2
Increasing											
3	—	—	—	—	—	—	—	—	—	—	—
2	32	3.0	5.8	2.4	3.4	4.4	7.7	7.6	10.3	4.3	3.5
1	104	2.2	6.5	2.5	3.3	4.3	7.7	5.3	10.3	3.8	3.5
Constant	145	1.3	6.8	3.2	3.0	4.4	8.5	6.6	11.1	5.6	3.6
Declining											
1	74	0.5	8.0	3.6	2.4	4.2	8.3	5.5	12.2	5.6	3.6
2	22	0.6	12.9	3.6	2.0	3.8	9.8	3.9	15.9	3.6	1.8
3	10	-1.6	11.8	5.9	3.6	4.1	9.6	9.6	17.5	8.2	4.1

Source: Based upon unpublished data, Bureau of Labor Statistics, 1982.

On the other hand, the weighted decline for all three groups of industries subject to declining degrees of price restraint was also in the neighborhood of 35 percent; and the difference between the experience of this group of industries and those subject to increasing pressures from foreign competition is not a statistical accident; that is, while many of the C and D industries under greater pressure generated phenomenal increases, very few subject to declining pressures generated any increase in the rate of productivity gain between the two decades. As was pointed out previously, once the behavior of the industries in the reference groups can be explained, such differences in behavior are quite predictable. It also should be noted that the third group of industries contributed more to total output than the first. This is why the rate of productivity gain in manufacturing as a whole declined during the 1970s—and why there was a rapid deterioration of productivity performance toward the end of the decade (chapter 10).

As the table shows, if we compare wage increases in the periods 1959 to 1969 and 1969 to 1979, the gain for the group of industries subject to increasing pressures to restrict price increases was about 80 percent, while in all of the declining pressure groups wage rates more than doubled. Moreover, input-cost increases were smaller for the first group of industries than the second. Keep in mind that included among the 22 industries in which wages increased by 150 percent and input costs increased 300 percent were some of key importance to the American economy.

This brings up an interesting question: How do we know that price behavior explains productivity, wage, and input cost changes rather than the other way around? The answer is that causality can never be determined on the basis of statistical inference; rather, it must be determined by making sound *economic* arguments. Assume that changes in relative prices can be treated on a par with changes in actual prices. Then it can be argued that domestic rivalry will be most robust when firms in an industry act on the assumption of a positive-sum game (i.e., base their expectations on the premise that although individual firms in the industry may suffer disappointments, the quality or price elasticity of demand for the industry as a whole is likely to be relatively high). Conversely, when rivalry is weak, firms act on the assumption of a zero-sum game (i.e., base their expectations on the premise that demand elasticities are very low). Consequently, while in the first case we can expect to observe rapid growth in output; in the second, it will be slow. To be sure, when entire industries are challenged by foreign competition, particularly if the industry has been playing the second game, expectations will be disappointed. However, it is nonetheless surprising that output penalties have not been largest in those industries hardest hit by foreign competition, but, rather, in industries which, because of declining pressure from foreign imports, were the least constrained in their ability to raise prices. Thus, the 32 industries hardest hit by foreign imports moved up two steps in price performance and experienced output growth about 20 percent below the 1960s. By contrast the declines for those directly and indirectly protected from foreign imports—the last three groups shown on the table—were 35 percent for 1, and about 50 percent for 2 and 3. Also note that the penalties involved in raising prices by as much as 12 or 13 percent annually were zero; that is, prices increased far more rapidly than output rates declined. A few industries subject to increasing pressures to restrain price increases were buttons, dolls, smoking tobacco (as distinct from cigarettes), optical instruments, scientific instruments, and farm machinery; in the decreasing pressure group were industries such as cement, plywood, nonferrous metals, aluminum foundries, wood products—and *steel*. The latter group of industries acted under the assumption that the demand for their products was quite inelastic, which, in turn, greatly increased the costs of inputs for a variety of other industries. While we can agree with the monetarists that expectations for further inflation need to be dampened, is it not conceivable that the real culprit is not the expectations of workers, but, rather, firms acting on the assumption that the demand for their products is quite inelastic? And is it not also conceivable that those industries, in which firms' expectations are based on high elasticity of demand, are most likely to be favored by good luck?

However, while we dynamic economists love the concept of the elasticity of demand quite as much as do static economists, there is one very important point to be kept in mind: it does not necessarily remain constant. For example, every time a new computer comes on the market, the elasticity of demand for computers increases. This is precisely the behavior associated with a dynamic equilibrium. On the other hand, there are changes which are not quite so routine. When OPEC increases the price of oil, the price of coal increases almost as much. Or when the price of steel goes up, the price of aluminum rises almost as much (as an indirect cost of protection). Such changes, which make the elasticity of demand smaller than it otherwise would be, are not quite, but almost, as routine as the changes which increase the elasticity of demand for computers by supplying a more plentiful menu of substitutes. On the other hand, firms acting on the assumption that demand is inelastic may find their expectations disappointing. During the 1970s, newspapers came under that category, as did firms in some fairly important industries when they left Japanese firms out of account in making their calculations.

What, then, are the more general implications of the statistical and theoretical arguments to be advanced in this book?

First, it is quite apparent that, while a decline in productivity performance in manufacturing, the generation of serious price shocks, and an increasing severity of economic downturns are one and the same problem, only about two dozen industries were responsible for the worsening economic performance. This indicates that the problems involved in improving the performance of the manufacturing sector of the U.S. economy are somewhat more specific than many economists and political leaders would have us believe. For example, it is generally acknowledged that the actions of OPEC resulted in a serious supply shock. But in chapter 8 it will be seen that, during the 1970s, increased costs of steel inputs (net of increased fuel costs) had quite as important an impact on manufacturing costs as did the energy supply shock.

Second, as was indicated previously, industries contributing to either continuing low rates or large declines in the rate of productivity advance acted on the assumption that demand for their products was quite inelastic. However, to state that they behaved as if demand for their products were quite inelastic is not to suggest that, like classical oligopolists, they were engaged in making monopoly profits. Many of these industries were struggling to survive on the basis of monopoly costs. In other words, they were profit maximizers subject to information on market and technological opportunities that is ten to fifteen years old. Another difference between classical and unprodded oligopolists is this: the former create a deadweight loss to an economy in the form of a misallocation of resources equivalent to something like five percent of the GNP; the latter create a deadweight drag on an economy by continuing to bid up the prices of labor and industrial materials.

Moreover, that is not all. As already was pointed out, more or less the same industries that contributed most to inflation during the 1970s also were the first to raise prices once recovery was underway. Consequently, the even more serious cost of deadweight drag is that it increases the severity of economic downturns.

From a theoretical point of view, what is the significance of these findings? According to classical economics, a static equilibrium is as stable as the celestial system. Indeed, according to the monetarists, if only the money supply were kept stable both inflation and economic fluctuations would be banned. Yet, the same industries that were moving toward a static equilibrium—toward lower productivity gains and, hence, toward unchanging production functions—contribute most to the instability of the economy. How is this apparent contradiction between theory and observation to be explained?

Keynes observed, long ago, that the savings habits that might provide an individual with security do not necessarily contribute to the overall economic stability of the nation. And precisely the same is true with respect to the willingness of the firms to take risks. An average propensity to engage in risk taking that is close to zero in particular industries can contribute to the security of individual firms, but, at the same time, it makes an economic system less stable.

PRICES, WAGES AND BUSINESS CYCLES

Chapter 1
THE RELATIONSHIP BETWEEN RISK TAKING AT THE MICROLEVEL AND THE RATE OF PROGRESS AT THE MACROLEVEL

Firms take risks to generate technological advances or to exploit such advances to reduce costs or improve performance (e.g., speed, accuracy, and reliability). The degree of risk taking, measured in terms of either the size of the advances sought or the willingness to adopt new technologies, may be low or high. In the final analysis the degree of risk taking is determined by the robustness of dynamic competition, which mainly depends on the rate of entry of new firms. If entry into an industry is fairly steady, the game is likely to have the flavor of a highly competitive sport. When some firms in an industry concentrate on making significant advances that will bear fruit within several years, others must be concerned with making their long-run profits as large as possible, if they hope to survive. But after entry has been closed for a number of years, a tightly organized oligopoly will probably emerge in which firms will endeavor to make their environments highly predictable in order to make their short-run profits as large as possible. In this first chapter, the focus will not be on competition per se, but rather on the relationship between risk taking, measured on a microscale, and the rate of progress, measured on a macroscale.

While it is true that in many industries cost reductions and quality improvements occur simultaneously, it is impossible due to aggregation problems to combine these into a single index; that is, people or firms do not necessarily place the same value on a particular product's characteristics. In the following discussion I am assuming that improvements in the performance of a technology will be measured in terms of either cost reductions or quality improvements, depending on which will provide the most accurate representation of economic reality. Although the quality of automobiles improved during the period 1900 to 1925, progress mainly took the form of making a 1925 automobile cost only one-seventh as much as that of a 1900 automobile.[1] Conversely, if progress in the semiconductor industry during the past fifteen years were examined, the appropriate measure would be the 40% annual increase in the performance of its products, as indicated by the bits of information contained on a computer chip, while at the same time prices remained more or less constant.[2] Though not all can be measured, quality improvements should be treated on a par with cost reductions.

There are two distinct activities involved in fostering economic progress: overcoming physical limits to bring about technological advances, and making use of technological advances plus organizational innovations (e.g., quality circles) to improve productivity. Though both activities require inventiveness, the first deals with a higher degree of risk and uncertainty than the second and requires organizations with more imaginative people, who are organized differently and provided with quite different incentives.

Occasionally, both activities are combined in a single firm. For example, within AT&T, Bell Telephone Laboratories and Western Electric perform entirely separate functions and possess quite different personalities. For the most part, however, these activities are carried out by different firms, and with good reason: it is impossible for organizations to be simultaneously optimized to deal with relatively high and low degrees of uncertainty. And there must be specialization not only in making a variety of commodities, but also in dealing with diverse degrees of uncertainty.

Economic progress will be most rapid when there is dynamic competition to develop better and better substitutes in both activities; for example, semiconductors for computers and synthetic fibers for various articles of clothing. If competition is to lead to optimal results there must be a reciprocal relationship between the industries in question. The borrowing industries must be highly adaptive and flexible, and industries engaged in overcoming limits must do so not as an end in itself, but as a means of making important contributions to the problems faced by the users: generators and users of technological advances must be stimulated and organized to help each other.

THE ESSENCE OF SUPPLYING IMPROVED TECHNOLOGICAL BUILDING BLOCKS: OVERCOMING LIMITS

To improve the efficiency of their machines (for example, on the basis of the same cost a new machine will produce a greater output than an older one), entrepreneurs must find ways to increase their thermodynamic efficiency. According to Sadi Carnot's theory of engines, which, in turn, paved the way for the second law of thermodynamics, the *thermodynamic efficiency* of an engine (the ratio of work out to heat in) is proportional to the temperature difference over which it can operate—and that is limited by the best available fuels and materials.[3]

Although Carnot's work is better known to engineers and physicists than to economists, there is no other discovery in science that has had a greater impact on economics. Carnot's theory says, in effect: Though I cannot tell you how to achieve a greater temperature difference, I can tell you, an engine developer, a way to measure your performance, if you are successful. Carnot established a way to award "Nobel Prizes" in the field of engines. For example, ask aircraft engine developers why the turbofan engine was so successful in reducing operating costs and you will be told that it provided a way to increase the propulsive efficiency. But, as of the time Carnot proposed his theory (about 1820) the only engines known were steam engines! In fact, the first impact of his theory was not on physics, but rather on raising questions about the desirability of discovering other types of engines to achieve higher limits than could be achieved with steam engines. For example, shortly after his discovery, the main question debated was whether the Sterling and the internal combustion engines seemed like promising bets to succeed the steam engine.[4]

Another example, in which physical limits are set by the laws of nature, is found in scaling. Though a few economists believe that a machine can be built twice as big without changing production functions, according to the laws of nature you can neither scale up nor down at will. To build a bigger plant than has been built to date you know beforehand that limits will have to be overcome by the discovery of stronger materials. This discovery was made by Galileo who, in his *Two Sciences*, showed why it was impossible to imagine one dog exactly twice as large as another without its having stronger bones.[5] As engineers frequently point out, Galileo discovered that their role is to build stronger bones.

It should not be assumed, however, that limits need to be overcome only to improve the thermodynamic efficiency of engines and to solve scaling problems. *All* significant advances in technology involve overcoming physical limits of one kind or another. The difference is that entrepreneurs are not aware beforehand of the limits; for example, the invention of specialized machine tools during the nineteenth century, and the more recent development of numerically controlled machine tools. During the nineteenth century, specialized machine tools were developed by armories with the objective of producing highly reliable rifles. Later, entrepreneurs, such as Pratt and Whitney, left the armories to set up specialized toolmaking companies for the sewing machine and watchmaking industries, in which the concept of interchangeable parts was employed to greatly reduce their costs. This process was repeated when Henry Leland left an armory to establish the Cadillac Company, where the concept of interchangeable parts was employed to make a high-grade automobile. Subsequently, other automobile firms exploited the process to lower the costs of their automobiles.

Commercial aircraft is another case in which the nature of the limits had to be discovered during the evolution of the technology. While it was known early that the costs of operating commercial airliners would depend on the efficiency of their engines, it was not generally appreciated by European aircraft firms that low drag (i.e., low wind resistance) would be equally important. Indeed, the essential reason the Americans succeeded before the European commercial airplane developers is that, as Miller and Sawers have shown, while the initial pioneering work on reducing drag was done in Europe in connection with gliders and racing planes, the Americans were first to recognize the advantage of low drag with respect to the economics of commercial airplanes. For many years finding inge-nious ways to reduce drag was the central objective in government research laboratories, university aerodynamics departments, and aircraft firms.[6]

Now, in my discussion of what is involved in overcoming limits, I do not mean to imply that individual discoveries can be predicted. Inasmuch as luck plays a major role, isolated discoveries cannot be predicted. The task of dynamic econom-ics is not to make microscopic predictions, but, rather, macroscopic predictions about the role of risk taking in bringing about a series of discoveries. In the following discussion I will be concerned merely with the process of making discoveries as viewed from the standpoint of the individual firm. From this discussion there will emerge an important conclusion that does, indeed, have bearing on how we go about constructing a predictive theory.

What, then, is involved in overcoming limits? Two quite distinct mental processes are entailed. The first, and classical, method for overcoming limits involves broadening the definition of the technology (as when new fuels and materials are found to increase the efficiency of an engine). Consequently, this can be described as an ideological outbreeding process. The second, and less under-stood, method of technological advance consists of combining fairly well known technological inputs in different ways to obtain distinct gains in performance. For example, Francis Clauser, of the California Institute of Technology, has found that, though the piston in an internal combustion engine performs some functions well, it works poorly during the mixing of air and fuel. Clauser is presently engaged in developing an engine to show that by performing the second function differently it will be possible to reduce emissions by an order of magnitude, while obtaining the same gasoline mileage as a diesel.

When entrepreneurs succeed in overcoming limits, whether by employing the first or the second mental process, they, in effect, substitute less restrictive for more restrictive constraints, which, from their point of view, provides a better theory of "what works." And a better theory it really is; because once the constraints have been softened they will know more about physical reality.

Whereas the first mental process can be looked upon as *discovery*, and the second, as *innovation*, there is no sharp demarcation between them. Since it is virtually impossible to borrow an idea from one application and use it in another without encountering new problems, nearly all so-called innovations involve an element of discovery. In the limiting case, when reasonably well known ideas are combined to obtain completely new insights, there is no real difference between an innovation and a discovery. On the other hand, inasmuch as each new advance is rooted in previously made discoveries, nearly all involve important elements of innovation.

The really important point to keep in mind is not the distinction between an innovation and a discovery but the distinction between an incremental and a discontinuous change—between gradually adding to one's knowledge (e.g., as in Bayesian probability theory) and having to unlearn something to overcome a limit.

When important limits are overcome, it usually turns out that the greater the improvement, whether measured in cost or performance, the more existing knowledge is made obsolete. In fact, the degree of replacement determines the amount of uncertainty and risk. As creative engineers are fond of making the point: "It is not what you do not know that prevents a significant advance, it is what you think that you know!" To illustrate: Suppose you want to lower your average golf score from 95 to 90. This can probably be accomplished by practicing more often. But, lowering your score to the 80s is an entirely different story, because to do so will involve unlearning many procedures that inhibit your progress. Unfortunately, while being involved in this "relearning" process you will be risking that your score might rise to 125!

Indeed, in *The Theory of Economic Development* (which was written before he made the ironclad distinction between a discovery and an innovation), Schumpeter took a position much like mine:

> It is not only objectively more difficult to do something new than what is familiar and tested by experience, but the individual feels reluctance to it and would so even if the objective difficulties did not exist. This is so in all fields. The history of science is one great confirmation of the fact that we find it exceedingly difficult to adopt a new scientific point of view or method. Thought turns again and again into the accustomed track even if it has become unsuitable....[7]

As the following quotation from the *Feynman Lectures on Physics* indicates, Schumpeter's position on the nature of scientific progress is no different from that taken by modern physicists:

> Each piece, or part, of the whole of nature is always merely an *approximation* to the complete truth, or the complete truth so far as we know it. In fact, everything we know is only some kind of approximation, because *we know that we do not know all the laws as yet. Therefore, things must be learned only to be unlearned again or, more likely, to be corrected.*[8]

It should not be assumed, however, that only scientists and engineers must overcome limits and in the process unlearn some beliefs to establish new "laws." Indeed, according to Piaget's writings, the entire process of child development can be so described. For example, whereas six- and seven-year-old boys play marbles according to such flexible rules that assure everyone can win, by the time the boys are ten or twelve, the more successful players manage to impose more definite rules on the game.[9] Consequently, if older boys want to continue to play marbles, they too must unlearn some things thought to be true to establish new "laws." Entrepreneurs who continue to overcome limits after the attainment of adulthood can be looked upon as people whose mental development was not prematurely arrested.

UNCERTAINTY AND RISK

Now that we have a general idea of what is involved in overcoming limits, what does this imply with respect to the definitions of risk and uncertainty? Knight distinguished between *true* uncertainty and *measurable* uncertainty, which he defined as *risk*.[10] Most modern economists have followed Knight, believing that the only risks with which real-life entrepreneurs can deal are those that can be measured in terms of probability distributions. My position is quite different. I do not believe that measurable uncertainties are genuine risks, but I do believe that there are better and poorer ways to deal with uncertainties when probabilities cannot be measured.

As an illustration of my point that measurable uncertainties are not genuine risks, consider the card game of blackjack. Assume that a player is trying to decide on the basis of the cards that already have been exposed, whether to draw another card when he has a score of fifteen. To be sure, the player has no way of calculating whether in this single instance drawing another card will result in a win or loss of a good deal of money. And because this calculation cannot be made, the uncertainties confronting the player are described as *strong*. But, if the laws of probability are understood, and the associated statistics are memorized, in repeated plays the player can count on winning a good deal of money from those less experienced. In fact, I know people who have done just this, which resulted in their winning so much money in Las Vegas and Reno that they were ultimately evicted from the gaming tables. Expert players will acknowledge that at times their memory fails them, but aside from this risk, there is no other risk for them when playing blackjack.

If members of firms could compute the probability that this or that effort to identify and overcome an important limit would lead to a successful conclusion, they could completely insure themselves against uncertainty by undertaking a sufficient number of projects to guarantee a successful outcome. Or they might decide that the reward was not worth the effort. True, on the basis of engineering science, engineers can often calculate the *payoff* likely to be involved in overcoming this or that limit. But a "cookbook" on how to do it is not provided. Consequently, strong uncertainties can be converted into weak uncertainties only by using one's imagination.

Nevertheless, when entrepreneurs cannot compute the probability of making a discovery, they are not powerless to reduce their risks. If attention is confined to a single discovery, the entrepreneur is actually in a better position than the blackjack player: that is, he has hints (i.e., feedback) from previous "experiments" made by his or other firms that, when coupled with imagination, can be used to discover the nature of the limits in question. Thus, while the blackjack player cannot influence the odds of the game, the entrepreneur can. In fact, most discoveries seem so obvious in retrospect that one wonders why they were not simultaneously made by a number of people. For example, according to John Pierce, Professor Emeritus, Caltech, and formerly an inventor at Bell Telephone Laboratories, one of the key hints for developing information theory was obtained from the entropy principle in physics.[11] Even with only a minimal understanding of the entropy principle and information theory, one must wonder why someone other than Shannon did not leap to develop information theory. Or to consider another case, an employee of the Ford Motor Company, Clarence Avery, is said to have obtained the idea for moving production lines from having visited a meat-packing plant. Afterwards, he asked himself why the process employed for disassembling carcasses could not be reversed for assembling automobiles. Again, one may wonder why such a seemingly obvious advance was not recognized by several companies. Indeed, in one sense there is good reason to wonder why most discoveries are not made simultaneously: the clues are invariably available long before the discoveries are actually made.

From another point of view, it is not altogether surprising that the relevance of important hints has not been generally appreciated. Chance plays a significant role in determining whether an important clue will be noticed, and its relevance appreciated. For this reason, real-world entrepreneurs often say that one lucky break can make a great difference. For example, in the case of moving production lines, it was not preordained that a Ford employee should visit a meat-packing plant. Nor was it preordained that Avery would be able to convince Henry Ford that the automobile industry could learn something from the meat-packing industry.

The role that luck plays obviously depends on how ambitious is the entrepreneur's target for reducing costs or improving quality. If the target is a five percent improvement to be made within the next year, the hints are likely to be so plentiful that not much good luck will be required. On the other hand, if the goal is a 50 percent improvement to be made within the next three years or so, then we are dealing with a discontinuity in which a significant fraction of the entrepreneur's current knowledge must be replaced. This, in turn, means that both good and bad luck will play a more central role, which is to say, the entrepreneur will be confronted with a higher degree of risk and uncertainty.

On the basis of previous experience, entrepreneurs have some rough ideas on the extent to which additional risk and uncertainty are involved in attaining their more ambitious objectives. It is said that, generally speaking, while something like three out of four efforts to bring about a minor advance will succeed, only one out of five attempts to bring about a major advance will succeed. However, there is no way to calculate which of the more risky projects is likely to succeed.

The question to be taken up next is this: If it is granted that luck plays an important role in making discoveries, what can entrepreneurs do to put good luck on their side while minimizing the consequences of bad luck?

SOME ENTREPRENEURIAL RULES

1. *Luck favors a questioning mind.* Pasteur's oft-quoted statement is that "Luck favors a prepared mind." But what did he mean by a "prepared mind"? It is obvious that he could not have meant a mind that thought it knew all the answers,

because such a mind could never be favored by chance. So, I assume that what he meant was a mind that had a fairly definite objective, but was also capable of raising sharp questions about how to get from here to there. Such questioning enables the entrepreneur to better understand (1) the nature of the constraints that must be modified to obtain very significant improvements in performance; and (2) the means for softening them. And the better that constraints are understood, the greater will be the likelihood of discovering the needed clues.

2. *An entrepreneur must always leap before he looks: he guesses about a hypothesis for taking technological risks before attaching a probability estimate to it.* Why? As when solving a murder mystery, more than one clue is generally needed. However, before the entrepreneur can put his imagination to work to discover additional relevant clues that would either support or deny the hypothesis, he must be willing to guess at a hypothesis on the basis of relatively few clues. Therefore, attaching a probability estimate to a hypothesis before he has put his imagination to work can seriously constrain his ability to be favored by luck. In other words, an entrepreneur must trust himself to test himself.

3. *Luck favors highly interactive organizations.* A highly interactive organization can be described as one in which the interactions are so diverse that the precise authorship of particular discoveries is always in dispute. How can a less interactive organization be distinguished from one that is more interactive? Suppose that a firm's data are collected on who telephones whom or who visits whom over a period of six months, and a prediction is then made about the pattern of communications for the next six months. If the pattern of communications, based upon either set of data, turns out to be highly predictable, you can be quite certain that the organization observed is unlikely to generate any significant advances. If it turns out to be highly random, the story will be entirely different. This is not to say that organizations can increase their discovery rates if they simply engage in a process of random communications. Rather, if the communications are determined by the necessity to resolve a real mystery, their patterns will invariably turn out to be highly diverse.

4. *Luck favors organizations that keep the costs of acquiring information to a minimum.* Before an important advance is made, it is generally necessary to become married to and divorced from a succession of hypotheses. This is not to suggest that, if some ideas for overcoming limits turn out to be disappointing, all of the ideas are wrong. Generally speaking, developing better hypotheses involves ascertaining which particular ideas were responsible for the disappointed expectations. Hence, it is imperative to minimize the costs of risk taking by undertaking critical experiments at the lowest cost and recognizing the sequential nature of the process. And in entrepreneural organizations no small amount of ingenuity is devoted to developing strategies for minimizing the cost of risk taking.

5. *When developing products or processes, flexible procedures can increase the likelihood of benefiting from good luck, while minimizing the consequences of bad luck.* In this context, *flexibility* means starting with a broad definition of the system

to be developed, testing its novel features in a very rudimentary version of the final system, and defining the detailed characteristics of the system only during the process of development. The reason for proceeding in much the same manner in which an artist paints a picture is that such a procedure imposes minimal constraints on the entrepreneur's ability to deal with uncertainty. The more constraints the entrepreneur initially imposes on his system, the smaller will be his ability to maneuver when faced with unexpected bad luck.

6. *Never attempt to dislodge a highly successful firm with a head-on attack.* According to classical economics, when the Ford Motor Company succeeded in making a 75 percent annual return on its invested capital after the development of the Model-T, and when the Douglas Company succeeded in making not quite as handsome returns after the development of the DC-3, firms should have flocked into these industries to make near copies which would have eliminated the monopoly gain.[12] Indeed, some classical economists seem to be obsessed by the worry that without adequate patent protection copying will be so swift that it will reduce the incentive for making discoveries.

However, in both of the cited cases, competitor firms did not act on the basis of the classical laws of economics for good reason: the products so quickly acquired a reputation for excellence that a Model-T called a name other than Ford or a DC-3 called by a name other than Douglas simply would not have been regarded as close substitutes. In the case of the Model-T, General Motors did try to develop a similar auto based upon a copper-cooled engine (i.e., an alternative much like the later-developed VW Bug), but finally gave up.[13] Consequently, when the successful challenges were made they neither took the form of imitations nor of close substitutes, but provided entirely new dimensions of performance. Although the 1925 enclosed Chevrolet cost more than the Model-T Ford (whose sales began to decline when challenged by secondhand enclosed cars), it was enclosed and a buyer had a choice of colors; and the Boeing 707 jetliner not only flew about twice as fast as the Douglas DC-7, but its seat-mile operating costs were actually lower.[14]

The moral: The development of close substitutes is an appropriate strategy with respect to a standardized commodity such as plastic pipe. But, when commodity space must be defined to include the reputation of the seller, it is not.

While such rules help insure that the elements of chance and necessity are not completely independent, they can never actually insure that the element of chance will be completely eliminated. The entrepreneur might be well poised to benefit from good luck—and it still might not come his way. Conversely, the possibility that an entrepreneur will be cursed by a siege of bad luck cannot be ignored. Thus, my conclusion is much the same as that reached by Machiavelli in *The Prince*: "....I think it may be true that fortune is the ruler of half of our actions, but that she allows the other half or thereabouts to be governed by us."[15] But it is important to add that the roles of fortune and necessity are by no means independent: if firms are not confronted with continuous competitive pressures, these rules will be ignored.

THE PROPENSITY TO ENGAGE IN RISK TAKING

What is the relevance of this discussion to the central issue before us: the relationship between risk taking at the level of the firm and macroperformance which measures the rate of progress in an industry? On the basis of the foregoing discussion, let us postulate wide differences in the average propensity to engage in risk taking. At the bottom of the scale, let us assume that firms are completely myopic in the manner they go about maximizing profits; that is, they will never develop a new product, and will only imitate after it has been successfully used. Next, consider firms that spend money on R&D but manage projects as if they were making investment decisions, insisting on a payoff in a time period no longer than a year. And, finally, consider firms which also invest R&D funds in projects that are both more promising and more uncertain—more uncertain, because if they do pay off it will be only in several years hence. Moreover, it should be apparent that the proportion of R&D resources devoted to high-risk projects can be varied (i.e., as in investment portfolio decisions), and when it is increased so will be the propensity to engage in risk taking. In short, we can postulate wide variations in the propensity to engage in risk taking.

Nevertheless, for reasons that will become clear, dynamic competition imposes a discipline on firms in particular industries to keep their *average propensity to engage in risk taking* (PERK) more or less the same. This is not to suggest, however, that firms can at will push up the rate of progress in any industry (e.g., the pinmaking industry). The equation of high-PERK industries to rapid performance gains is to be regarded as a dynamic equilibrium result; that is, if firms in an industry were not able to discover the ideas for significant advances, we would be unable to observe a high degree of risk taking. In other words, a high degree of risk taking when searching for gold assumes that there is gold to be found. A sustainable rate of progress is measured in terms of best or better-than-average practice achieved during a given time period; and it will become clear that, statistically speaking, an occasional long shot does not contribute to a prolonged rate of progress. On the other hand, when relatively high-PERK industries invest some of their R&D resources to bring about minor product improvements, this does not affect our conclusions, because such improvements do not determine the longer-run rate of progress.

The first key question to be considered is: How can a higher or lower PERK on the part of firms in an industry be translated into industry PERKs measurable in the same kinds of units? This is important, because to construct a testable theory we want a direct way to translate microbehavior into macroperformance. In terms of the general argument made in the previous section, it is assumed that the higher the value of PERK—the greater the amount of knowledge to be replaced in making advances—the wider will be the distribution of outcomes when new products are developed, with the proportion of project failures highest when PERK is highest, and lowest when PERK is close to zero. This assumption is illustrated by the first panel of figure 1.1. Anyone familiar with the history of technology will agree that the assumption is reasonable.

Next, let us assume that firms in an industry engage in approximately the same degree of risk taking over a five or ten year period. How will this be reflected in PERK as measured on an industry basis? It might seem that, as long as the same amount of knowledge is replaced annually, the width of the distributions, as shown in panel I, figure 1.1, will also remain the same. However, the second key assumption in my argument is that shown in the second panel of figure 1.1: either rapid linear or accelerating progress when PERK is relatively high. Once this assumption is made, it is relatively easy to show that, if the rate of progress is measured in terms of either best practice or better-than-average practice, the greater the average annual value of PERK, the more rapid the rate of progress (see chapter 6). But it should be kept in mind that the ultimate test of all theories is the ability to predict. And the chief role of the statistical model is to show how necessity, in the form of greater competitive pressures, can increase the role of good luck while minimizing the consequences of bad luck.

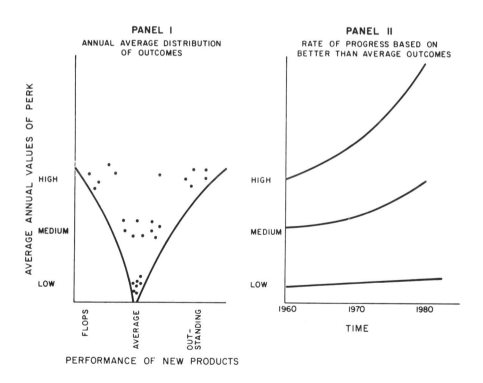

Figure 1.1 Microbehavior and Macroperformance.

How, then, is exponential progress to be explained? First, it may be noted that exponential progress in improving the performance of various technologies actually occurs in the real world. For example, according to Strassmann, American machine builders have accelerated the rate of progress associated with particular machine tools. Between the 1820s, when the efficiency of milling machines was only 33 percent greater than hand filing due to a slow rate of improvement, and the 1830s, when the efficiency of milling machines was increased by 400 percent, there was a very definite acceleration in the rate of progress.[16]

That this accelerating progress involved a variety of machines can be inferred from Strassmann's observation that Eli Whitney increased labor productivity by substituting capital for labor; later, an increase in the number of operations per machine permitted output per worker to increase more rapidly than capital per worker. Still later, machines that could substitute one tool for another automatically permitted a reduction of almost 50 percent in the amount of capital required per unit of output.[17] Other more recent examples are shown in figures 1.2 and 1.3. It will be noted that progress in reducing airline costs per-seat-mile is shown to be linear. However, if progress were to be measured in terms of flying times, it would be exponential.

Do productivity gains in entire economies come about at compound interest rates? On the basis of some straightforward calculations, it can be seen that at least in the manufacturing sections of economies they do. On the basis of productivity

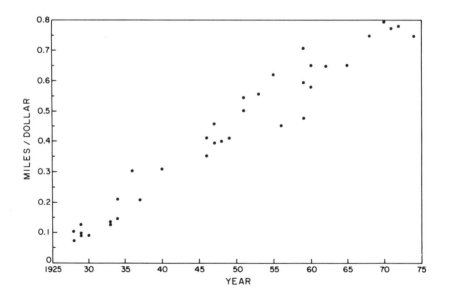

Figure 1.2 Progress in Reducing Seat-Mile Costs for Commercial Airliners.

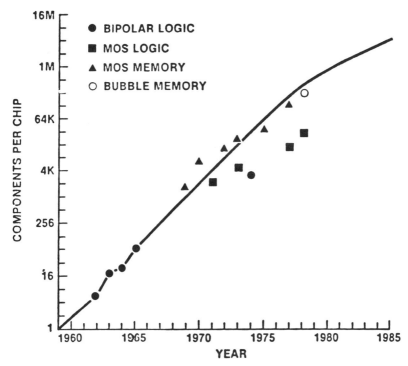

Source: Gordon E. Moore, Intel Corp., "Are We Ready for VLSI?"
Caltech Conference on VLSI, January 1979.
Figure 1.3 Semiconductor Performance.

data for seven countries (table 1.1), let us assume that the underlying process is exponential, and fit a least-squares-trend line to the productivity data for the period 1950 to 1979. The compound rate of productivity growth can be represented by the following equation: $\alpha = e^{\beta x}$, where x = the year and α and β are constants whose values are to be determined from the data. The values of the constants, the compound interest rate found by fitting a least-squares-trend line to the data points and the regression coefficients, are shown in table 1.1. The last column of the table indicates, with the possible exception of the United States, the correlation coefficient (r^2) is high.

Second, what is it that permits accelerations in the rate of progress? While the possibility of periods when there are marked increases of engaging in risk taking cannot be ignored, this is not my explanation. A more realistic view is that over reasonably long periods key inventions trigger dynamic processes in which earlier discoveries help pave the way for later discoveries, in the sense that the planor process in transistors paved the way for integrated circuits, the Boeing modern transport of the early 1930s paved the way for the DC-2 and the DC-3, organizing automobile plants according to the logic of a continuous process (rather than by

Table 1.1. Relative Rates of Exponential Progress 1950–1979.

COUNTRY	α	β	AVERAGE ANNUAL CHANGE IN PRODUCTIVITY	r^2
Japan	100.8	8.800	9.1	.99
Germany	100.2	5.537	5.7	.99
Denmark	95.4	5.536	5.7	.98
Sweden	109.9	5.276	5.4	.98
Canada	100.3	3.881	4.0	.99
United Kingdom	102.1	3.17	3.2	.98
United States	88.9	1.922	1.9	.83

Source: "International Comparisons of Trends in Productivity and Labor Costs" (Bureau of Labor Statistics, 1980).

type of machine) paved the way for automatic production lines, or that the concept of interchangeable parts paved the way for lowering costs in a number of industries. Moreover, discontinuous advances can also lead to a series of incremental advances. And when entrepreneurs learn just what has made some advances aimed at overcoming important limits quite unsuccessful, they will be able, at times, to turn misfortune into fortune in another application.

Now, it would be nice if real-world entrepreneurs had the almost unlimited ability to deal with uncertainty often credited to economic man; that is, whatever is obvious to everyone else in retrospect is obvious to the entrepreneur in prospect. But, while entrepreneurs commonly have a higher threshold for dealing with uncertainty than managers, no one's ability to deal with uncertainty is unlimited.

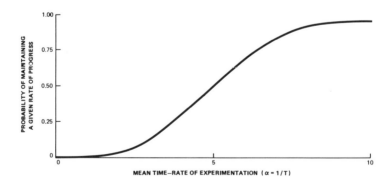

Figure 1.4. The Numerical Requirements for Steady-State Progress.

And, because it is not, earlier advances can help make possible the recognition of possibilities that otherwise would be ignored, thereby permitting compound-interest-rate progress, which always has some upper limit, because the larger the advances, the more imagination will be required to recognize relevant clues.

In short, whether PERK is high or low, present advances may help pave the way for future advances. Obviously, the larger the advance, the greater will be the yield of information, which, in turn, will illuminate the way for further large and/or a series of minor advances.

It is important to remember, however, that the rate of progress depends not only on PERK, but also on the *number of products developed* during a time period (figure 1.4). The particular period will, of course, differ from industry to industry, depending on the time required to develop various products. But quite irrespective of whether the period of gestation is one year or four, if the number were only two or three, all might be unfavorable. Conversely, when the number of experiments per time period is over ten, then additional experiments only have a marginal impact on increasing the probability of steady-state progress.

In principle it might seem that the greater the value of PERK, the greater will be the requirement for numerous experiments. Nevertheless, how large a particular discontinuity seems to the members of an industry depends on the size of the advances they have been bringing about.

In summary: One major aspect of technological progress concerns competition to develop technological inputs which will provide better and better substitutes. This activity involves overcoming limits that will open up opportunities for lowering costs and/or providing higher performance alternatives. The individual firm must operate under conditions of strong uncertainties, trying the best it can to put good luck on its side. But, when entrepreneurs in something like ten independent profit centers ask sharp questions, the result will be to convert strong into weak uncertainties for a series of discoveries; that is, individual discoveries which are unpredictable as isolated events become quite predictable as a series of such events. Relating risk taking and numbers of "experiments" at the microlevel to the rate of improvement in the performance of a technology allows us to construct a testable theory.

To be sure, predictions cannot be made on the basis of relatively small changes in the value of PERK, but on only those changes that are likely to result in quite significant changes in the rate of progress. Only as the period of observation becomes longer and longer should the effect of relatively small changes become discernible. Likewise, we can reason from various rates of progress to various values in PERK only when the rates are substantially different; for example, when the rate of technological advance in a particular industry increases or declines by 25 percent.

Chapter 2
UTILIZING TECHNOLOGICAL BUILDING BLOCKS TO GENERATE PRODUCTIVITY GAINS

The concept of relating PERK to the rate of progress, as discussed in the last chapter, is actually more applicable to predicting the rate a technology will evolve than it is to predicting the rate of productivity gain, and for a fairly obvious reason: technological inputs for productivity gains can come from a wider diversity of sources. Indeed, the primary argument to be made in this book concerns productivity gains and not technological advances per se, except to show their relationship.[1]

This is not to say, however, that all productivity advances necessarily involve risk taking. In particular, productivity increases can occur as a result of changes in the product mix, whether this takes place within a single firm or an entire economy. For example, during the period from 1948 to 1965, the average length of American cars was increased by two-and-a-half feet, and their horsepower more than doubled. Because manufacturing costs did not increase nearly as much as prices, this was a change in the product mix that resulted in productivity gains.[2] Some difficulties were encountered in building larger engines, but this always happens when the product mix is changed. Such changes also can take place within an entire economy: when manufacturing expands at the expense of farming, this shift in itself brings about gains in total factor productivity (i.e., productivity gains measured with respect to both labor and capital inputs). Or the opposite can occur when there is a shift from manufacturing to services. However, because it is next to impossible to measure productivity in the service industries, it is by no means apparent to what extent the latter shift involves a genuine decline in productivity gains. To consider a somewhat different kind of shift, productivity gains can sometimes appear to be quite handsome when measured in terms of labor inputs; but, when capital is substituted for labor, the gains can turn out to be very meager when both capital and labor inputs are taken into account. (American agriculture during the period 1890 to 1925 is the classic example.) As it happens, the relevance of the distinction between pure productivity increases and increases resulting from a reallocation of resources was appreciated first by Swedish economists. (In a recent article, Bo Carlsson calculated the share of Swedish productivity gains that can be described as pure productivity increases.)[3]

The following will concern only pure changes in productivity, as distinct from changes that result from a reallocation of resources. Pure changes can occur as a consequence of risk taking in either developing or introducing new technologies.

PROPOSITIONS

1. *Productivity gains in manufacturing are ultimately limited by rates of progress in technological inputs.* It should be apparent that the users of new technology also face risks. They can neither be sure that the performance of new machines or semiconductors will be as high as their manufacturers claim nor what problems will be involved when adapting their own organizations to make best use of them. For example, you may be considering buying a word processor machine to use in your home. But how can you be sure that the investment will be wise before actually using one?

So, to be realistic, let us assume that the using industries do not always choose the very best alternatives (e.g., as shown in the distributions in figure 1.1); to be more specific, assume that they choose only among the better-than-average, and that not all borrowers initially adopt the new technology. Furthermore, assume that initially only a few make the adoption, with the proportion of adopters increasing only gradually.

Now, if we make these assumptions, it should be obvious that the rate of productivity gain in the using industries is limited by the propensity to engage in risk taking in the various industries engaged in developing new technological inputs. Those firms engaged in utilizing technological gains to bring about productivity advances are, so to speak, engaged in the business of making rabbit stew. But it should be apparent that the ability to cook a delectable rabbit stew is limited by the availability of rabbits.

It also should be apparent that the rate of productivity gain in the using industries will depend on the rate of adoption of new machines: the more rapid the adoption rate, the more rapid will be the rate of productivity gain. The determinant of the adoption rate is the next subject to be discussed.

2. *The all-important factor in determining the adoption rate is the degree of risk firms impose on each other.* Because Edwin Mansfield is generally regarded as a leading expert on the diffusion of new technologies, I shall start with a brief discussion of his and his associates' work to indicate that our views on the role of competition are in substantial agreement.[4]

From a statistical point of view, the diffusion process can be described as a "bandwagon effect" that can be represented in the form of a logistics curve: A few boys jump into a river; and, after they do so, more and more boys decide to take the risk and jump in too. So we get a curve that, though starting out slowly, rapidly rises; it finally flattens when only a few timid boys are left on the riverbank while the others are joyfully swimming in the river.

On what does the speed of the process depend? One factor, it can be agreed, is the investment cost involved in adopting the new technology. As far as the developers of new technology are concerned, its counterpart is to be found in the cost of experimentation. For example, no one will question that exceptionally rapid progress in the semiconductor field has been accelerated by the low cost of experimentation. One semiconductor firm encourages engineers to take equipment home for experimentation in their garages, which certainly would not be a practical procedure for most other technologies.

The rate at which new technology is adopted will depend on its expected profitability; and subjective estimates of profitability will tend to become more and more firm as the boys who jump into the river find for themselves that swimming is fun. The same phenomenon is involved with development of new technology. To be sure, when a firm develops an entirely original product for a new market—when it acts as a marriage broker between the economically advantageous and the technologically possible—its notions on expected profits will be more hazy. But, if a firm is successful, the same will occur when the rivals step in.

Another important determinant, Mansfield found, is the physical age of the managers when the adoption is made, that is, younger managers adopted numerically controlled machine tools earlier than older managers.[5] However, this does not necessarily mean that older managers are psychologically less able to take risks. The reason may simply be that inasmuch as younger managers are likely to remain with the firm longer than older managers, they tend to have a longer time horizon. Why go through the struggles involved in introducing computerized machine tools if you are going to retire in a year or two?

It also has been found that introductions correlate with the number of echelons in the decision-making process: other things being equal, the more echelons of decision makers the slower will be the rate of introduction; the fewer, the more rapid.[6] The counterpart in organizations that are quick to develop new ideas is simply this: either organizations are composed of relatively few echelons of decision makers or the detailed organizational chart is seldom observed. Even more likely, they are in such a constant state of flux that an organizational chart has meaning at only an instant of time.

Nonetheless, while such findings are undoubtedly correct as far as they go, they are highly related to competitive pressures—pressures within the machine tool industry and in industries using machine tools. Why? Glance at the data shown in tables 2.1 and 2.2. The first contains information on the length of time before initial use of numerically controlled machine tools and the second, on the length of time elapsing between firms' commitments to spend 10 to 40 percent of their machine tool purchases on numerically controlled machine tools. Considering the fact that the payoff period for numerically controlled machine tools (NC) is said to average something like three years, both the time until first adoption and that of expanding their use seems to be very long. The reason, as table 2.3 indicates, is that there has been a large decline in the competitiveness of American products—a decline that

Table 2.1. Average and Standard Deviation of Number of Years That Firms Waited Before Beginning to Use NC (as Measured from the Date When NC Was First Used in the Industry).*

INDUSTRY	AVERAGE	STANDARD DEVIATION
Aircraft engines	4.00	2.71
Airframes	7.89	4.64
Printing presses	7.29	4.54
Coal-mining machinery	5.00	3.46
Digital computers	6.73	3.84
Large steam turbines	0.50	0.50
Machine tools	3.79	2.23
Farm machinery	3.71	3.09
Tools and dies	4.58	2.61
Industrial instruments	1.17	1.64

Source: Edwin Mansfield et al., *The Production and Application of New Industrial Technology* (New York: Norton, 1977).
* Based on a sample of firms using NC as of 1970, four in aircraft engines, nineteen in airframes, seven in printing presses, four in coal-mining machinery, fifteen in digital computers, two in large steam turbines, nineteen in machine tools, seven in farm machinery, twelve in tools and dies, and twelve in industrial instruments.

has had a very serious impact on machinery-related industries. The automobile industry is the single largest user of machine tools. The absence of dynamic competition in that industry from the end of World War II until the mid-1960s meant that it put relatively little pressure on the machine tool industry to quicken its rate of adoption.

Conversely, it does not seem to be an accident that Japan now leads the world in the production and exportation of numerically controlled machine tools. This is a reflection of not only a high degree of competition in the machine tool industry but also in the user industries as well. True, numerically controlled machine tools were not adopted as early in other countries as they were in the United States; but once diffusion started it proceeded rapidly. For example, in 1975, numerically controlled machines accounted for 21 percent of U.S. machine tool shipments, 24 percent of Swedish shipments, and only 12 percent of Japanese shipments. But, by 1980, the corresponding figures were 26 percent for the United States, about 30 percent for Sweden, and 39 percent for Japan.[7]

However, while Mansfield's work does not stress the importance of competition in the user industries, he is fully aware of the importance of competition within the supplying industries. He recognizes that: "The larger the proportion of firms already using the innovation, the less risky it is for a nonuser to begin using it, and the more competitive pressure there may be on the nonuser to begin using it."[8]

Table 2.2.   Average and Standard Deviation of Estimated Number of
Years From the Time When 10% of a Firm's New Machine Tool Purchases
Were NC Machines to the Time When 40% Were NC by Industry.*

INDUSTRY	AVERAGE	STANDARD DEVIATION
Aircraft engines	6.1	1.1
Airframes	4.3	0.8
Printing presses	3.1	1.9
Coal-mining machinery	2.8	1.2
Digital computers	3.9	2.5
Large steam turbines	4.8	0.4
Machine tools	3.6	1.4
Farm machinery	6.5	2.5
Tools and dies	3.5	1.0

Source: Edwin Mansfield et al., *The Production and Application of New
Industrial Technology* (New York: Norton, 1977).
* Based on a total of fifty-nine observations, three in aircraft engines, twelve
in airframes, three in printing presses, three in coal-mining machinery, nine
in digital computers, two in large steam turbines, seventeen in machine tools,
three in farm machinery, two in tools and dies, and five in industrial instruments.

Mansfield and colleagues also appreciate that, if such competitive pressure can
influence the rate of adoption, once a chain reaction has started it can also influence
the length of time before adoption.[9] It seems reasonable to assume that the greater
the competitive risks, as measured in terms of changes in market shares, the
shorter will be the time before adoption, and the more rapid will be the rate of
diffusion.

Consequently, the argument is relatively simple. As already noted, the availability of better technological inputs will greatly depend on the degree of competition in industries producing them. But, given the availability of technological
inputs, the rate of diffusion (and, hence, the rate of productivity gain in the user
industries) will depend on the prior degree of competition in those industries.
Quite obviously, the adopter of new technologies also must consider two risks: the
risk involved in making the adoption, and that involved in failing to make it.
Therefore, as figure 2.1 indicates, the greater the value of PERK, the sooner
adoption of a new innovation will begin, and the more rapid will be the rate of
diffusion.

It must be emphasized, however, though precise predictions cannot be made about
the rate of adoption, we do know that the prior degree of competition will be a
major determinant. Assuming more or less equal profit opportunities, and more or
less equal investment costs, a greater adoption rate presupposes a higher *revealed*
propensity to engage in risk taking. But, before the fact, we can only reason that
the greater the prior degree of risk taking, the greater will be the ex post rate of
diffusion.

3. *In the long run the rate of discovery will be limited by the degree of competitive pressure in the user industries.* If we are considering a period such as five or ten years, then it is safe to assume that the rate of productivity gain in the using industries will be limited by increases in the performance of technological inputs. On the other hand, in the longer run the rate of discovery is likely to be limited by a lack of pressure from the demand side. This is not to say that a lack of demand will immediately be reflected in a slowdown in technological progress in the supplying industries. As long as competition exists in the generation of new ideas, and the risks are borne primarily by the firms engaged in providing the new technology, an abundance of competition on the demand side is not necessary. For example, banks can use computers to improve their productivity without taking undue risks. To take a more spectacular example, roughly half of the total costs of airline companies are represented by the costs of airliners. During the period from the end of World War II until about 1965, very large increases in airline productivity (about 15 percent annually) occurred primarily because of the replacement of less efficient airliners.[10]

Though large productivity gains in industries that feature little or no competition can continue for five or possibly ten years, in the longer run it can be predicted that a dampening in demand will be reflected in a drying up of the generation of new ideas and suppliers becoming locked into a particular technology. Thus, as with Marshall's famous scissors, both blades are needed to do the cutting. But in the longer run it is the demand for new ideas that is most binding. The underlying reason is that when competition slows down in industries mainly engaged in

Table 2.3. Sales by U.S. Firms as a Percentage of Total U.S. Sales.

INDUSTRY	1960	1970	1979
Autos	95.9	82.8	70.0
Steel	95.0	85.7	86.0
Apparel	98.2	94.8	90.0
Electrical components	99.5	94.4	79.9
Farm machinery	92.8	92.2	84.7
Industrial inorganic chemicals	98.0	91.5	81.0
Consumer electronics	94.4	68.4	49.4
Footwear	97.7	85.4	82.7
Metal-cutting machine tools	96.7	89.4	73.6
Food processing machinery	97.0	91.9	81.3
Metal-forming machine tools	96.8	93.2	75.4
Textile machinery	93.4	67.1	54.5
Calculating and adding machines	95.0	63.8	56.9

Source: Business Week, June 30, 1980, p. 60. Department of Commerce.

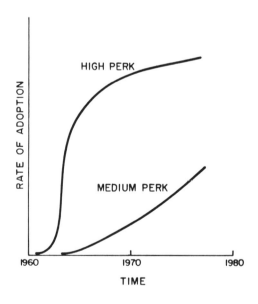

Figure 2.1. Annual Average Values of PERK Versus the Rate of Adoption.

borrowing new technology, they ultimately lose their ability to assimilate new ideas. As Simon Kuznets stated in his Nobel Prize lecture:

> If technology is to be employed efficiently and widely, and, indeed if its own progress is to be stimulated by such use, institutional and ideological adjustments must be made to effect the proper use of innovations generated by the advancing stock of human knowledge.[11]

TWO FURTHER PROPOSITIONS

1. *If the rate of productivity increase should decline in an entire country, and if the decline cannot be attributed to a reallocation of resources in favor of the lower productivity industries, then it must be attributed to a decline in risk taking.*

One can argue, of course, that if the distributions shrink this need not imply a genuine decline in risk taking, but only that there is a shortage of opportunities. However, there is good reason to suppose that the generation of new ideas is not subject to the law of diminishing returns. All technological discoveries can be looked upon as ideological mutations of one kind or another; and the more mutations that have been made, the more hints there will be for creating new ones. To be sure, in particular fields it may become more and more difficult to generate new ideas. But there is no reason to suppose that the industrialized countries are facing a genuine shortage of ideas.

What we cannot answer is whether a pure productivity decline is the result of a decreasing propensity to take risks on the part of the generators or the users—or, more likely, both. For reasons already indicated, their propensities to engage in risk taking are so highly related that it is impossible to know which was mainly responsible.

2. *If a country has a lead over others in the rate of productivity advance in particular industries, and if this advantage is not offset by higher factor costs, the country will have an export advantage in the same commodities for which it has a productivity advantage.* For example, it seems to be no accident that, during the period 1900 to 1925, the United States was not only the leader of the world in productivity gains in the automobile industry, but it had a substantial export surplus in both automobiles and machinery used in their manufacture. Despite the fact that the Ford Motor Company was the first to pay the almost unheard of salary of five dollars a day, its productivity advantage outweighed any disadvantage the United States may have had in factor costs. Thus, a relatively high propensity to engage in risk taking leads not only to rapid productivity gains, but to a relative advantage in "competitiveness" in international trade. Conversely, when a country's rate of productivity gain decreases relative to that of others, a declining ability to compete in international markets is almost inevitable.

Countries trade partly in terms of dynamic advantages stemming from risk taking and partly in terms of factor cost differences. When a country has a significant dynamic advantage in particular products, it can enjoy an export advantage even though its wage rates are well above those of other countries. However, when it does not have a dynamic advantage, differences in factor costs are likely to be decisive.

Chapter 3
IMPLICATIONS FOR MACROMODELS TIED TO STATIC EQUILIBRIUM ASSUMPTIONS

SOCIAL ACCOUNTING

Almost all macromodels, be they social accounting or others, have either a weak artificial connection or no connection whatsoever with underlying micro-behavior. For example, according to Keynesian models, firms play an entirely passive role; and the distinction between more and less prosperous times is determined by whether or not particular aggregate relationships add up to a full employment level of GNP. According to the monetarists, the economic universe is either in or going toward a static equilibrium. Hence, only monetary variables determine the economic stability of the country. Consequently, while these models can make good predictions as long as there is no change in technological risk taking or the manner in which price decisions are made, the story is entirely different when the underlying microbehavior changes. (The question of how changes in microbehavior can and do increase the amplitude of business cycles will be discussed in chapter 9.)

My present concern is with the various attempts to explain the productivity decline in the United States, which can be described as a macroapproach that is performed under the label of *social accounting*. It must be emphasized, however, that I am *not* implying any criticism of the people involved; rather, my skepticism is toward the barren approach they chose to follow. For example, although the approaches taken by Edward Dennison and Zvi Griliches are quite different, I have no doubt that they have done as good a job with social accounting as anyone in the economics profession could do.

Consider, for example, private accountants who might be involved in explaining declines of productivity performance in their own firms. Suppose that they were thoroughly trained in classical economics and well grounded in econometrics, have IQs over 150, and hold regular meetings to discuss their findings. But they never talk to anyone in their R&D organizations to discover whether the technological inputs being developed either inside or outside their firms are continuing to improve. Nor do they talk to anyone on the shop floor to learn if operations there are becoming more and more routinized. Nor do they seem to be particularly concerned that, while tight cost constraints are the driving force in productivity gains, once they are relaxed these gains can rapidly evaporate.

Suppose that one of these accountants notices the rate of productivity advance in his firm has been steadily declining relative to that of other firms, a puzzling trend for which he is clever enough to come up with a "let's not be too disturbed" explanation. However, in the 1970s, when he observed a very sharp decline in productivity gains, what would you expect him to say? This is what Dennison said: "What happened is, to be blunt, a mystery."[1]

Now it is true that, if productivity gains are seen as arising from some fairly immutable forces (like continuing exogenous advances in the stock of knowledge, coupled with the continuous introduction of new technology and a highly automatic process for catching up with best practice), a seemingly sudden decline must be recognized as very surprising. It is as if productivity gains were generated in a static equilibrium economy which suddenly collapses. On its *suddenness,* my answer to Dennison is simply that the forces which brought about the U.S. productivity decline did not occur suddenly. In the late 1960s, a number of industries found that they could, with impunity, raise their prices three times as rapidly as prices rose in manufacturing as a whole. When they did, their incentives to generate productivity gains declined. What happened is no mystery whatsoever.

Zvi Griliches's work provides a better illustration of the pitfalls of macromodels, because it is concerned with explaining macroevents by relating them to each other. In particular, he has been interested in explaining productivity advances by showing that the rate of productivity increase is highly associated with investment in R&D. It can be agreed that as long as the fundamental parameters of an economic system do not change—PERK, in particular—its rate of productivity advance is likely to be highly associated with the rate of R&D spending. As long as PERK remains constant in manufacturing as a whole, the proportion of R&D resources devoted to more and less risky projects will remain approximately the same, and the rate of technological progress, whether reflected in new products or new technological processes, will remain the same. However, a high correlation coefficient between R&D spending and productivity advances does not imply a causal relationship.

Nevertheless, the logic of social accountants is somewhat different. Not only is the pursuit of productivity advances regarded as an end in itself, but investment in R&D is regarded in the same way as any other investment decision.[2] However, if this point of view is taken, it is not easy to explain why productivity expenditures declined, nor why, as Griliches found, a decline in the rate of productivity advance *per dollar of R&D expenditure* was the major factor in explaining the productivity decline. Indeed, the underlying macrorelationships are supposed to be so stable as to preclude such events from occurring. It is as if someone had propounded a theory about the color of ducks on the basis of observing only white ducks. Therefore, when a black duck is seen, the duck theorist simply refuses to believe that the bird is a duck. And this is in some degree the reaction of Zvi Griliches:

Thus I interpret my lack of findings as reflecting the turmoil of the times rather than a true underlying trend shift. In any case, it is unlikely that the recent productivity slowdown can be blamed primarily on the R&D slowdown. If anything, causality may lie in the other direction.[3]

Why has the amount of productivity advance per dollar of R&D expenditure declined? The reason, quite simply, is that PERK has declined; otherwise, investment in R&D would be buying the same increases in productivity it once did. Conversely, when we learn that the value of PERK and the rate of productivity advance are directly related, then, unless it is assumed that a greater proportion of R&D resources are being devoted to better products, we can be quite certain that PERK has declined.

STATIC EQUILIBRIUM THEORY CANNOT EXPLAIN EVERYTHING

Why are at least two distinctly different theories needed to explain economic reality? In this section I will argue that, while static equilibrium theory can play a very useful role in understanding economic reality, by trying to comprehend everything from the point of view of macromodels tied to static equilibrium assumptions, we, in effect, rule out explaining economic change. Because the macromodels implicitly assume a microworld either in or going toward a static equilibrium, all sorts of rationalizations must be invented to explain departures from the norm. The more basic question is whether there is more than one kind of economic process. No one will deny that, when explaining price changes associated with a short-run interruption of supplies, equilibrium analysis can be very useful. On the other hand, the shifting of production functions can be better described as movements *away from an equilibrium.* For example, assume that PERK remains constant in successive time periods, and a number of limits are overcome; consequently, as they are overcome, new constraints are identified. Such activity must be described as movements away from an equilibrium, because by overcoming the limits entrepreneurs are, in effect, changing the production functions of the world: they are engaged in making history.

This point is not new in economics. It was made in 1921 by Frank Knight when he wrote:

I must regard it as one of the major errors of classical tradition that it failed, and still largely fails to make a sharp and correct theoretical distinction between the workings of a system under given conditions, including movements towards equilibrium, and changes in the given conditions or the content of the system itself.[4]

My answer to Knight's challenge is the following: If you assume given initial conditions with respect to demand and cost functions, then, whether considering movements toward or away from an equilibrium (e.g., as in cobweb problems), you are dealing with a static system. However, while lags in either supply or demand adjustments may prevent movements toward an equilibrium under given initial conditions, when goods or services become more and more similar in price and other dimensions, such movements can be described as going toward an equilibrium—not necessarily a stable, enduring equilibrium in the longer run, but, nonetheless, a short-run equilibrium. On the other hand, continuing changes involved in reducing costs and prices and/or improving performance on the basis of more or less the same prices must be described as movements away from an equilibrium—*as dynamic movements that involve the changing of initial conditions*.

Though many economists regard all changes as representing movements toward an equilibrium, it should be clear from this discussion that they are not: if costs and prices become more and more similar the movement is toward an equilibrium; if not, the movement is away from an equilibrium. It should be apparent that not only entirely different phenomena are involved in movements toward and away from an equilibrium, but different theories are also required to explain them.

In science, physicists do not attempt to explain everything in terms of one theory. Consider, for example, the difference between the first and second laws of thermodynamics. As it happens, the first law (the conservation of energy) has the same flavor as classical economics: whatever the form of energy, at each instant of time the accounts are always in perfect balance—or, as my students say, "Under the first law you never can do better than break even." Although the first law of thermodynamics is not an equilibrium law (if it were it would be inconsistent with the second law), its spirit implies an unchanging world; that is, the total energy in the world always remains constant. Thus, the first law can be likened to microeconomics: the manager who carefully balances marginal utility with marginal cost is engaged in first law reasoning. The social accountant who sees productivity gains driven by some mysterious unchanging force is also engaged in first law reasoning.

The second law of thermodynamics has a decidedly different flavor: in effect, it says that, while the total energy of the world is unchanging, the *useful* energy is always declining. Or, as is often said, though the first law implies that you may think you can break even, the second law tells you that you really cannot! Why? When coal and oil are taken from the ground (in which form the molecules are reasonably well mannered) and burned, the consequence is an increase in the randomness of the molecules that is quite irreversible. Consequently, while the accounts are always in perfect balance, the physical world is moving from order to disorder (i.e., entropy, which is a measure of randomness, is increasing). For those who prefer to believe that they live in a completely ordered and unchanging world, the second law is not a pleasant fact. But, if science is to provide a better and better understanding of physical reality, one has to live with it.

The difference between physics and economics is simply this: in physics, a system going toward more unpredictability (increasing entropy) is unfortunate in that it consumes useful energy. In economics, taking smaller and smaller risks means going toward more and more predictability—which is unfortunate from the point of view of making good use of unexploited potentialities. While from the standpoint of physics a high degree of entropy or randomness is a bad thing, this is not the case in other disciplines. For example, from the point of view of information theory, randomness is a good thing: as we already have seen, risk taking provides information about alternatives that otherwise would not be available, and, by so doing, increases the opportunity for favorable longer-run outcomes. Moreover, from the point of view of a modern biologist, a vast amount of diversity in the gene pool is good, because it provides a greater degree of adaptation in the face of a changing environment.[5] As animal breeders have known for many years, inbreeding to emphasize particular traits serves to produce very docile and nervous animals highly incapable of dealing with a changing environment.

In further developing the argument, I am taking my cue not so much from modern physics, biology, or Prigogine's nonequilibrium processes in chemistry (all of which have the same general flavor) as from the following statement written by Adam Smith in his *Wealth of Nations*: "The progressive state is in reality the cheerful and the hearty state to all the different orders of the society. The stationary, dull; the declining, melancholy."[6] If Adam Smith had really approved of an economy in which risk taking had no role, he would have preferred a dull stationary state to a hearty progressive state. In fact, from a macro point of view, Adam Smith can be described as a Schumpeterian long before Schumpeter (although, from a micro point of view, it must be acknowledged that Adam Smith's description of the activities of the chief clerk in a pin mill did not accord with Schumpeter's concept of entrepreneurship).

Economics got off to a bad start by trying to perfect the "science" of the stationary, dull, and completely predictable economic state before turning to dynamic questions. As the above quotation plainly shows, Adam Smith's vision of the hearty state was not one of an economic system involved in a zero-sum game; rather, it is the vision of a positive-sum game. And, although a few economists continue to believe that the hearty, positive-sum state is a special case of the dull state, the truth is precisely the opposite; that is, while the dynamic laws assume changing production functions, the static laws assume unchanging production functions and an economy at rest.

Chapter 4
DYNAMIC COMPETITION

Dynamic competition occurs when firms bring either continuous or intermittent pressure on each other to reduce costs or provide better-quality products at about the same cost. When a firm takes a risk, and is successful in bringing about an impressive advance, it almost automatically imposes risks upon other firms (i.e., the hidden foot). The essence of dynamic competition involves balancing the risks encountered when making discoveries or introducing innovations against the penalties incurred from having a market stolen away by a competitor. Generally speaking, the greater the degree of risk taking by a firm's rivals, the greater will be its penalties for failure to take risks.

Dynamic competition imposes a discipline on firms irrespective of whether they are too myopic or too farsighted. For example, suppose that five years ago a firm's top leadership had entered the semiconductor business on the basis of taking only trivial risks. Such a myopic strategy actually resulted in the collapse of several firms. Conversely, one farsighted firm, Shockley Laboratories, failed in part because it concentrated its R&D on possibilities that might be realized in only a decade. To be sure, highly specialized firms often can find niches in a dynamic industry; but they cannot hope to become major factors. Firms that obey the discipline forced on them by their rivals can hardly be described as demonstrating the heroic entrepreneurship praised by Schumpeter. Awareness of the penalties involved for failure to take the appropriate-sized risks is the best insurance against failure. Moreover, the greater the amount of risk a firm expects from its rivals, the greater will be its incentive to adopt an internal reward system favoring a high degree of individual risk taking.

When firms engage in similar policies (R&D portfolio choices) to encourage risk taking, and when one firm has no incentive to change its *policies* as long as others do not change theirs, this behavior can be described as a *dynamic* Nash equilibrium. To be sure, a Nash equilibrium is usually defined in quite static terms; that is, it is assumed that one firm will not change a particular *decision* unless another does so. However, it may be noted that there are a number of game theorists who have used the concept of a Nash equilibrium to define a strategy as a *policy*, and not as a decision.[1]

Dynamic competition provides the driving force for the maintenance of a steady-state dynamic equilibrium by stimulating the questions that lead to hundreds of discoveries and innovations. These, in turn, add up to either linear or accelerating progress when measured on a macroscale. Mathematically speaking, all that is required for steady-state progress, as we already have seen, is that PERK remain constant over reasonably long periods of time. But to explain why PERK remains constant, we need to understand the forces behind the maintenance of a dynamic equilibrium.

One of these forces can be described as the *push* of the hidden foot, that is, the uninsurable risk a firm incurs from its competitors for failure to venture into activities that would result in either making discoveries or bringing about innovations. Entry of new firms, newly established subsidiaries of older firms, and foreign competition are the principal factors in determining whether there will be an adequate supply of hidden-foot feedback (i.e., an adequate supply of challenges). If individual discoveries are to add up to steady-state progress, existing firms must be constantly prodded; which is to say, the "wolf" needs to show up quite regularly! In short, there is no automatic force to maintain dynamic equilibria. Yet, dynamic competition does not involve the indeterminacies associated with oligopoly theory.

Another equally important force is the *pull* exercised by strong positive incentives. More specifically, if dynamic competition is to endure, it must increase the market for a group of imperfect substitutes. It seems to be no accident that whenever dynamic competition flourishes—whether in the steel, meat packing, or machine tool industries during the nineteenth century, or in the automobile, radio, commercial aircraft, computer, semiconductor, or petrochemical industries during this century—the total output of the industries in question expands at the very time individual firms experience both local prosperities and recessions. In a search for new gold nuggets, it must be believed that though one clue might end in disappointment, another could end in success.

When an individual firm decides to take a technological risk, just how successful it will be in capturing a larger share of the market cannot be known. However, for the market to grow, all that is needed is a system of strong *local incentives*. As already noted, when firms take technological risks, externalities are generated that will facilitate the advent of further major advances or a series of minor advances. The combined effect of such risk taking will be to generate a growth in markets that no individual firm could possibly bring about. Dynamic competition should be thought of as a *cooperative game* in which the elements of necessity and luck are not independent.

In the first section of this chapter I will discuss in further detail the nature of dynamic competition. Then, after explaining why dynamic competition was left out of Adam Smith's economics, I will take up the following topics: the crucial importance of entry; why the static theory of the elasticity of demand is to be regarded as a special case of dynamic competition; and the importance of knowledgeable consumers for the maintenance of high-demand elasticities.

NATURE OF DYNAMIC COMPETITION

Dynamic competition generates better or less expensive alternatives. It can be defined as an effort on the part of several firms to increase the competitiveness of their products as measured in several dimensions. This, of course, is a far cry from the conventional definition of competition in which the goodness of competition simply depends on the number of sellers. To understand how competition works in the real world it is necessary to take a point of view similar to that of the participants. Entrepreneurs in the American chemical industry, the Swedish machine tool industry, or the Japanese automobile industry believe that competition is an effort to do better than your competitor.

That one need not be involved in industrial competition to understand its basic nature is illustrated by the following definition: "Competition consists of trying to do things better than someone else; that is, making or selling a better article or the same article at a lesser cost, or otherwise giving better service."[2] This was written by Louis D. Brandeis, who, though receiving his undergraduate degree in mathematics at Harvard, by no stretch of the imagination can be described as a business entrepreneur. Since Brandeis was a lawyer, and inasmuch as lawyers are not especially noted for qualifying as dynamic thinkers, this raises a further interesting question: Why did Brandeis choose a dynamic definition of competition? Anyone familiar with Brandeis's writings will agree that he was a great admirer of Thomas Jefferson. In fact, in his *Curse of Bigness*, Brandeis said that competition was not an end in itself, but merely a measure to promote in the business sphere Jefferson's concept of democracy.[3] What is meant by Jeffersonian democracy? One interpretation, emphasized by Kaysen and Turner in their pathfinding book, *Antitrust Policy*, is that Jeffersonian democracy means dividing large firms into small firms to limit the concentration of political and economic power.[4] It cannot be denied that this motivation played a very important role in the establishment of the antitrust laws.

While there is no denying that Brandeis was strongly influenced by the writings of Thomas Jefferson, my interpretation is somewhat different. In the first place, Jefferson was a great believer in dynamic competition. In the letters he wrote to Madison at the time he was U.S. Ambassador to France, Jefferson claimed there was no reason why the United States should not overtake Europe in all types of inventiveness. Moreover, inasmuch as he did not believe in absolute truth, Jefferson's philosophy was much like that of most successful business entrepreneurs. Consider, for example, the following passage from one of his letters:

I join you ... in branding as cowardly the idea that the human mind is incapable of further advances. This is precisely the doctrine which the present despots of the earth are inculcating, and their friends here re-echoing; and applying especially to religion and politics; that it is not possible that anything better will be discovered than what was known by our forefathers.... To preserve the freedom of the human mind and freedom of the press, every spirit should be ready to devote itself to martyrdom; for as long as we may think as we will, and speak as we think, the condition of man will continue in improvement.[5]

Was Brandeis right in believing that promoting competition, as he understood it, was the same as promoting Jefferson's concept of democracy? It should be apparent that by promoting an invigorating environment in which entrepreneurs continually ask themselves penetrating questions, dynamic competition assures that the human mind will continue to develop. Conversely, industries wherein there is little or no dynamic competition, and that operate on the issuance of commands, are best described as *feudalistic capitalism*.

At the time Jefferson wrote, the Age of the so-called Enlightenment, it was fashionable to believe that the world was enlightened for all time to come. Insofar as it assumes a world of perfect information, or a world in which entrepreneurs can buy information just as they can any other commodity, classical economics can be described as a direct descendant of that age. But dynamic economists are followers of Jefferson in that they believe that the assumption of a fully enlightened world is directly contrary to human experience and, as such, it is a very unscientific point of view. Entrepreneurs who pretend they know everything, and maximize their profits by assuming that their information is perfect, are doomed to failure unless in one way or another they are protected by the government. If you can find unprotected firms that maximize their profits in the classical manner you should rush to your stockbroker to tell him to sell their stocks short!

Implicit in Brandeis's definition of competition are four important points. *First*, the concept of the hidden foot is implied— success of one firm creates a risk for others.

Second, it is a *dynamic* concept of competition. Whether an improved mousetrap increases the probability of catching mice or a new automobile reduces the probability of costly repairs, doing something better changes initial conditions. Conversely, if Brandeis had chosen the words *best* and *least*, instead of *better* and *lesser*, this would have implied a static definition of competition in which initial conditions must be taken as given.

Third, it should be apparent that if one firm succeeds in making an innovation or a discovery it will provide a better substitute; therefore, it will have increased the elasticity of demand, which is tantamount to increasing the degree of competition as defined by many static economists.

Fourth, it should also be apparent that dynamic competition directly influences the rate of productivity gain. Either price or quality competition with tight price constraints provides a necessity to reduce costs: if firms take their production functions as a given, they may have no way to avoid large losses. The degree of pressure firms impose on each other during the course of dynamic competition determines the industry rate of productivity advance. When firms from a particular industry generate higher productivity gains in one country than in another, we can infer a higher degree of pressure, and, therefore, a greater value of PERK.

Consider the difference in productivity performance of the United States and Japanese automobile industries. True, if Japan had merely caught up with the United States by copying its automotive manufacturing technology the values of PERK would have been small, which is to say, for both the United States and Japan the dots would have been at the bottom of the diagram (see figure 4.1). According to the evidence (to be supplied in the next chapter), Japanese automakers have not only surpassed those of the United States in productivity, but have demonstrated a willingness to take far greater risks in the almost continuous development and introduction of new process technology. By way of contrast, American firms have not imposed nearly the same degree of challenge on tooling firms. This is the primary reason for the large differences in the relative values of PERK. Figure 4.1 shows the actual rate of productivity advance in the Japanese and United States automobile industries and the inferred values of PERK.

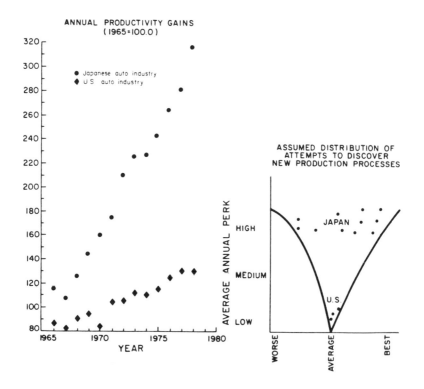

Sources: Japanese Dept. of Labor Statistics, 1982; U.S. Dept. of Labor Statistics, 1982.
Figure 4.1. Reasoning From Rate of Productivity Gain to PERK.
Note: Japanese productivity data based on labor hours per compact car.

Does this picture accord with what we know today? As Lawrence White pointed out in his careful study of the U.S. automobile industry, until 1965, at least, competition occurred in terms of style rather than price.[6] His research concluded that a kind of price leadership existed in which General Motors prevailed. Ford and Chrysler would announce their prices first. Then, within a few weeks after General Motors announced its prices, they would revise theirs, usually upward. However, General Motors did enjoy a marked advantage over other companies in terms of profitability. It may be true that, because of the fear of an antitrust suit, General Motors was loath to bring pressure against Ford and Chrysler, which could have resulted in their being driven out of business. Nevertheless, as I pointed out in my book *Dynamic Economics*, measured in terms of changing company fortunes, there was much less rivalry in the U.S. automobile industry after World War II than during the 1920s and 1930s. Chrysler, founded in the mid-1920s, rose to second place in the industry during the 1930s, and Ford, after being the dominant firm in the industry in the early 1920s, dropped to third place during the 1930s.[7]

As far as Japan is concerned this much can be said. First, Japanese automobile firms possess the internal flexibility—the ability to respond quickly to opportunities and challenges—that goes hand in hand with dynamic competition. Second, since 1945 there have been several new entrants into the Japanese automobile industry, and these could not have grown without putting older firms under pressure. Third, a greater willingness to take risks is indicated by the development of two novel automobile engines (the Wankel and the stratified charge), the adoption of *quality circles of workers*, and an entirely new concept for competing on a basis other than scale economies.[8] Finally, according to every description I have been able to obtain, the Japanese automobile industry is, indeed, characterized by robust internal competition. According to Hiroto Ohyama, a well-known Japanese engineer, the picture is as follows:

> It would be quite true that Japan has attained high productivity in auto manufacturing. However, it is a serious misunderstanding that MITI (the Ministry of Trade and Industry) solely helped the industry to have attained such a high productivity. MITI, in fact, functioned to impede the incoming investment from overseas, and to foster parts makers at the early stage, say, the 1950s and 1960s. But, there is no evidence of MITI taking an active role to foster the auto industry's high productivity. In my view, the determinants of the Japanese high productivity in the auto industry stem from the highly competitive nature of the industry itself. To compare with the U.S. counterpart, the Japanese auto industry is not oligopolistic, we have two big companies, Toyota and Nissan, but the industry can be said to be composed of eleven companies. Among those manufacturers, five or six companies compete against each other on a full assembly line basis. We can say this, that the competition among the eleven Japanese companies in the domestic market are more intensive than competition in the U.S. and European sense.[9]

The main point to be emphasized is that, by making international comparisons of productivity performance, the United States now has a yardstick for determining how well dynamic competition is working. Even though Brandeis did not formulate his concept in mathematical terms, it certainly can be done. Moreover, only because it applies to the real dynamic world do we have a means of testing it.

RELATIONSHIP TO ADAM SMITH ECONOMICS

Why do I, as a dynamic economist, include a hidden foot as well as a hidden hand in my description of economic reality? The reason is that I, no less than Adam Smith, want to describe economic reality as accurately as possible. To have observed organized dynamic competition in the form it takes today, Adam Smith would have had to have written *The Wealth of Nations* something like seventy-five years later than he actually did. Then he could have seen for himself the rivalry flourishing in the English and Scottish iron and steel industries and the impact on the burgeoning of ideas associated with accelerating progress. So, by relating competition in ideas to the progressive economy for which Adam Smith preached, dynamic economists are merely returning to the task he left undone.

The English and Scottish firms involved in such competition were obviously acting in their joint interests. By engaging in price competition that resulted in the discovery of ways to reduce costs of iron and steel, and in quality competition that made their products better substitutes, they were able to sell far more iron and steel at home and abroad than otherwise would have been possible. This is not to say, however, that the entrepreneurs concerned were aware of the longer-term benefits or that they could appreciate beforehand how one idea would help pave the way for others. It seems more reasonable to assume that the attraction was more like that involved in many, but not all, professional sports today: some combination of adventure, fame, and making money. Though there are many people who think of competition as being the antithesis of cooperation, the fact is that, like sports, dynamic competition is a game that can be described in both competitive and cooperative terms.

To be sure, Adam Smith understood the role of risk taking in bringing about progress. Indeed, he was concerned that the hazardous trades would entice so many adventurers that profits would be reduced "below what is sufficient to compensate for risks."[10] But what he did not understand, and could not be expected to understand, because he wrote during a period in which highly organized forms of competition were only beginning, is that dynamic competition provides an important, if not the most important way to increase the wealth of nations. In particular, while in the short run the wealth of nations can become greater by increasing the degree of specialization, in the longer run it is the sport of pushing out the frontier of technology and the creation of entirely new ideological mutations that have the principal impact.

THE ROLE OF ENTRY

To state that all newly founded firms are risk takers would be a gross exaggeration. Some enter merely to become suppliers of well-defined products to larger firms. Nevertheless, while they certainly are not alike, it is my conviction that newly founded firms provide the best illustrations of Schumpeter's hero entrepreneur. Indeed, I suspect that it would be very difficult to find more than a handful of large and successful firms that had not been founded by the revolters he so much admired. It also should be kept in mind that the incentives of newly founded firms are different from those already established: to become established they must be prepared to take greater risks; and many fail.

A variety of studies on the automobile, radio, aircraft engine, computer, and semiconductor industries have shown that new entrants have contributed far more than their share of successful discoveries.[11] From where do revolters come? On the basis of various accounts that have been written, there can be little doubt that a majority come from the longer-established firms where they have been unsuccessful in selling their ideas. Thus, before Pratt and Whitney entered the machine tool business they had worked for a military arsenal that, understandably, did not want to diversify into the commercial machine tool business. And, when Pratt and Whitney ventured into the air-cooled aircraft engine business during the 1920s, it was with dissidents from firms engaged in making a water-cooled engine. In the automobile industry there are numerous examples of people like Walter Chrysler, who left Buick to start his own firm. The principal difference between these and more modern industries, such as computers and semiconductors, is the number of times entrepreneurs have left established firms to start new ones. In the fields of semiconductors and computers examples can be found of entrepreneurs who left existing firms as many as three times in order to establish new companies.

Static economists believe that existing firms never lose a moment to snatch a profit possibility, and new enterprises enter an industry only when existing firms are reaping monopoly profits. But according to W. Paul Strassmann, during the nineteenth century, too, entrepreneurs left existing firms because it was easier to promote a somewhat unconventional idea by starting a new firm. In a discussion of the U.S. steel industry, he points out:

> Even successful engineers, in spite of all their caution and prestige, had difficulty in persuading employers to finance innovations. Fritz, Holley, Taylor, and others, time and time again insisted that the problem of convincing employers was the "greatest difficulty," "the principal hindrance," or required the "fight of my life."[12]

Nor does the situation appear to be different in countries other than the United States. This is indicated by an MIT study of new firms founded in Sweden during the 1970s:

The motives of the founders for starting their enterprises are complex, but in the main they have mentioned market opportunities which they perceived in their earlier work and which were not valued or pursued by previous employers. In many instances, they have tried to get management or sponsors within their prior firm to pursue the business, but found it necessary to carry forward on their own in order to have it come to fruition. A striking feature of the sample is the degree to which founders' fathers were self-employed, which is true of nearly half of the founders.[13]

Although the profitability of these new firms differed widely, the median return—about 30 percent annually—was a good deal above that for Swedish firms in general. Moreover, their products were highly competitive in international markets: almost half of the firms exported more than 80 percent of their output.

There does seem to be a major difference between the experience of new firms in the United States and those not only in Sweden but other industrial countries as well. Whereas in the United States there are numerous examples of firms, such as Texas Instruments or Hewlett-Packard, which rose to be giants in a relatively few years, in Sweden such happenings have been very rare since the 1920s.

Erik Dahmén's excellent book on the economic development of Sweden during the 1920s and 1930s contains a wealth of information on the entry of new Swedish firms during that period.[14] The general conclusion is that, while there were many entries during that period, only a handful of firms rose to take their place with the giants established during an earlier period of rugged individualism. The successful new entrants were either bought out by existing large firms, or, as suppliers to new firms, they became parts of "development blocks." From where, then, did the dynamism of the Swedish economy come? According to Dahmén, the dynamism came from consumers emulating the consumption habits of their relatives in America, as well as from Swedish suppliers, who, during the 1920s, brought a virtual revolution in Swedish industry by shifting their attention from German to American technology. It also may well be true that inasmuch as Swedish firms are engaged in international competition to a much greater extent than U.S. firms, they have remained extremely flexible.

Thus, while the Swedish experience with the growth of small firms is entirely different from that of the United States, it is clear that the dynamism of the Swedish economy was not nearly as dependent on the establishment of new firms as was that of the American economy. Only in the chemical industry have U.S. firms had a long history of being export-minded. Therefore, the lack of challenges by new entrants may have been compensated for by the increased degree of involvement in international competition.

The United States's relative advantage in the establishment of firms that could become large probably stemmed from the willingness of these firms to take risks, and from a greater availability of risk capital that was provided mainly through private sources other than banks. The willingness to engage in risk taking no doubt stems from a fact recognized by Simon Kuznets many years ago: with millions of immigrants during the nineteenth century, the United States acquired a dispropor-tionate share of risk takers.[15] The greater availability of risk capital might have been the result of people not knowing each other very well. When the potential suppliers of risk capital have an intimate knowledge of a firm's trials and tribulations in bringing a new product into the market, this breeds distrust rather than trust.

Not all significant advances are brought about by new entrants. As is generally known, well-established firms do bring about significant advances. In fact, very startling changes in older technologies are commonly made at the very time they are being challenged. As James Utterback has noted, important changes in ice-making technology were made at the time it was being challenged by refrigeration; and an order-of-magnitude improvement in gas mantles was made after this technology was challenged by electric lights.[16] More recently, there has been such great improvement in the design of safety razors that many people are abandoning their old electric razors in favor of new safety razors. In response to a challenge by the synthetic fibers industry, a dramatic improvement was made in reducing costs and improving the quality of cotton textiles. In this case, it may be noted, the machinery employed for making these productivity advances came mainly from Japan and Germany. Indeed, U.S. cotton textile firms have become so ingenious in combining the best of German and Japanese textile machinery technology that their costs have declined enough to enable them to become exporters. Or to take another example, Ann Friedlander has shown that, after World War II, rivalry between railroads and trucking resulted in a decline of tonnage hauled by railroads—from about 65 to less than 50 percent. This challenge was followed by an annual increase in productivity in the railroad industry from 3.8 to 5.8 percent that was associated partly with closing inefficient lines and partly with the introduction of innovations such as piggyback and unit trains, the ideas for which had been known thirty years earlier.[17]

However, it should not be assumed that firms engaged in producing older technologies respond only when their very existence is threatened. As Schumpeter recognized in his book, *Business Cycles*, short of a fight for existence, such challenges play an important role.[18] Before Boeing developed the 707 commercial airliner, it had lost fifty million dollars selling some fifty stratocruisers (a plane with much higher operating costs than the other alternatives then available).[19] Before RCA developed television, Philco and Emerson had substantially reduced RCA's share of the market by featuring relatively inexpensive radios.[20] As of the time Henry Ford developed a durable and inexpensive car, the market for relatively inexpensive flimsy runabouts was crowded, with even Sears & Roebuck in that race.[21] Consequently, what alternative other than to develop a relatively inexpensive durable car did Henry Ford really have? Or to consider more recent history in the automobile industry, both the VW Rabbit and the Honda lines of front-wheel drive automobiles were preceded by periods of sharp business reverses. What these firms did was to turn adversity into good fortune.

In some instances it might be argued that the firm in question was playing the role of a new entrant. By developing television as a much-improved substitute for the radio, RCA challenged all firms in the radio business. In the case of Boeing, not only was its post-World War II stratocruiser a flop, but, as it happened, all but one of its previous attempts to enter the commercial airplane business via producing derivatives of military airplanes turned out to be disappointing—and if the company had to depend at that time on profits from sales of commercial airliners it would have gone out of business. What was new about Boeing's effort to develop the prototype of the 707 was the attention devoted to making it an economical airliner, whose seat-mile costs were guaranteed to be no greater than those of piston-driven airplanes.[22] Certainly, a good deal was learned as a consequence of designing and building jet bombers, but it would have been impossible to provide such a guarantee by developing derivatives of either the B-47 or B-52. Success hinged upon the development of an entirely new strategy; and it was this that stimulated a faltering industry.

For another illustration consider the case of AT&T. Although none resulted in a serious loss of business, AT&T has experienced almost continuous threats to its monopoly position brought about mainly by new entrants and, more recently, by larger firms such as RCA.[23] These threats began when some private firms installed their own microwave systems and others entered the telephone business by connecting the telephone systems of several companies—a process that was remarkably similar to that which occurred soon after the telephone was originally invented—and, since the 1950s, the diversity and number of threats have continually increased.

The impact of these challenges, according to insiders, has resulted in a change in the character of Bell Telephone Laboratories (BTL) and an increase in the number of important discoveries introduced into the telephone system. Actually, the change in BTL's character began during World War II when new experimental radars were operationally developed while being tested in combat operations! However, without a continuing series of new challenges after World War II, there is little doubt that BTL would have quickly reverted to its prewar staid personality.

Not only did the character of BTL change in the face of competitive challenges, but also its dynamic efficiency. Insiders say that, measured in terms of the number of profitable inventions put into practice per unit of time—inventions such as that which doubled the capacity of the undersea telephone cables at a cost of but a small fraction of the initial investment—BTL's creative output was, in relation to its R&D budget, several times larger after World War II. And AT&T was understandably fearful of losing Bell Telephone Laboratories or Western Electric as a result of the U.S. government's antitrust suit. Without both of these organizations AT&T would be hampered from taking action in the face of additional competitive threats.

Further research is needed to document the increase of creative output that resulted from continuous competitive threats. The more interesting question, I submit, is why has AT&T done so well in dealing with competitive threats and General Motors so poorly? Both have very large research laboratories. It must be remembered that, while the giant AT&T had to deal with new challenges during the entire postwar era, GM was allowed to bask in its glory for a period of about fifteen years because, while U.S. automobile firms were at war with each other during the 1930s, shortly after World War II they declared peace on all but stylistic war fronts.

Nevertheless, the degree of AT&T's success in keeping the wolves away from the monopolists' doorstep should not be exaggerated. In the first place, as was the case with communications satellites, not all the technological efforts were as successful as its rivals. Second, to limit encroachment on its territory, AT&T has been able to use the regulatory machinery to its own advantage (for example, by adoption of regulations that had the effect of preventing communications satellites from putting underseas cables out of business).

The main requirement for the continuance of a dynamic equilibrium is more or less continuous entry. And entry is finally slowed by the one, two, or three order-of-magnitude increases in entry costs occurring as a result of the increasing importance of scale economies and the various types of vertical integration that invariably occur during the evolution of a technology. Thus, according to Ralph Epstein's book, *The Automobile Industry*, when Essex entered the automobile business, it cost at least three orders-of-magnitude of what it cost Henry Ford.[24] When Henry Ford entered the automobile business only very rudimentary production lines were employed; and the Dodge Brothers Company not only furnished the engines, but also financial backing for Ford. However, when Essex entered the business some twenty years later, the situation was entirely different. In the semiconductor industry during a twenty-year period there was for similar reasons a two or three order-of-magnitude increase in entry costs.[25] Leaders in the semiconductor industry are of the opinion that today their industry is at a competitive disadvantage with their Japanese counterparts, because the latter have received government support for building highly automatic capital-intensive plants which would be impossible for U.S. semiconductor firms to finance. Hence, it is not very difficult to explain why during the evolution of a technology there is typically a very large decline not only in the number of firms involved, but in new entries and risk taking as well.

Finally, it should be emphasized that both entry and lack of entry (and not concentration ratios) determine an industry's dynamic performance. Because of new entries, a relatively concentrated industry—or even a so-called monopolist such as AT&T—can remain highly dynamic. But, when entry is absent for some years, and expectations are premised on the future absence of entry, a relatively concentrated industry is likely to evolve into a tight oligopoly. In particular, when entry is long absent, managers are likely to be more and more narrowly selected; and they will probably engage in such parallel behavior with respect to products and prices that it might seem that the entire industry is commanded by a single general! In short, with the absence of challenges from new entrants or foreign competition, it can be predicted that the rate of productivity advance will decline;

and, if such declines are to be offset, new challenges must emerge. Only in this way can a dynamic equilibrium embracing an entire economy remain stable.

RIVALRY INCREASES THE ELASTICITY OF DEMAND

A zero-sum game can be defined as one in which gains exactly offset losses, and a positive-sum game as one in which the sum of the gains is greater than the sum of the losses. To better understand what is involved in such a game, consider the following example. Surgical teams are observed competing to reduce fatalities associated with various heart operations. When inquiring into the immediate reason for such competition, you think that what you are observing is a zero-sum game. Diagnosticians refer patients to various heart surgeons on the basis of their track records in performing successful operations. So, if you think of the game in terms of one surgical team building its practice at the expense of another, then the game may seem to be a zero-sum game. In fact it is not a zero-sum game, because the competing teams of surgeons hold regular meetings not to discuss discoveries they are in the process of making, but those they have already made. When you ask them why they do this, the common reply is, "We are also interested in increasing the *total* number of *successful* heart operations." From their point of view, dynamic competition is considered as a *self-organizing cooperative game* in which necessity increases the role of luck. When asking surgeons where they get ideas for such a game, you will be given a variety of answers; but most compare their game to professional golf, which draws ever-larger crowds of observers.

Dynamic competition, therefore, is the driving force in increasing the total demand for heart operations. But the ex post result will be to increase the elasticity of demand as it is usually defined—that is, substitutes are available in the form of various medicines which have the effect of restricting the power of the surgeons to perform unnecessary heart operations. Thanks in good part to the insistence of the diagnosticians, various tests have been developed which, while not infallible, make possible a better decision as to whether or not a heart operation is needed. In short, a greater availability of substitutes simultaneously curbs the power of the sellers and provides the buyers with greater control over their destinies.

Thus, when thinking of competition in a static sense, I am in agreement with those economists who believe that the elasticity of demand is a better concept than concentration ratios. If it is assumed that the static role of competition is to minimize the infliction of high prices or poor quality on consumers, then it is the availability of substitutes, and not the number of sellers per se, that restricts their ability. Unlike some static economists, I do not believe that the economic universe was endowed with so many substitutes as of the time of its creation that one is lurking in every bush. It is the presence or absence of dynamic competition that determines the elasticity of demand. With new challenges from domestic or foreign firms the elasticity of substitution will increase; without new challenges alternatives will become more and more alike in all dimensions, and the elasticity of demand will decline. It can be agreed that Keynes was correct in describing the concept of the elasticity of demand as Marshall's most important contribution to economics. His own famous statement, "When you owe the bank one hundred pounds, the bank owns you; but when you owe the bank one thousand pounds, you own the bank," basically refers to the expectations associated with high-and low-demand elasticities: in demand-elastic industries firms act as if the "bank" (i.e., consumers) owns them; but in demand-inelastic industries firms act as if they own the consumer. Using this concept, we can directly build a bridge between static and dynamic economics. In particular, the static case holds only in the short run when the value of PERK is close to zero.

HOW TO DISCOVER IF DEMAND IS ELASTIC

Can the entrepreneur compute beforehand the elasticity of demand for a new substitute, which, if successful, will result in an increase of the observed elasticity of demand? Absolutely not. Assuming that the elasticity of demand is known is the wrong way to proceed. The right way is to introduce a new product into the market in limited quantities to discover what the consumer response will be. As in science, experiment is the final judge of truth. An example may help to clarify what is meant by "testing" the market. Shortly after World War II, there was a great debate within the firms making sulfa drugs as to whether the demand for these drugs would be inelastic or elastic with respect to price. According to the conventional point of view, physicians would prescribe the drugs for only quite specific illnesses, which is to say, the demand was believed to be quite inelastic. On the other hand, according to the unconventional point of view (primarily advocated by Richard V. Gilbert, a former economics faculty member at Harvard and a vice-president of Schenley—a new entrant in the drug business), the list of illnesses for which the drug would be prescribed would depend on the price. He argued that across the line of many illnesses the new drug would provide a better substitute for older known drugs.

It was very important for the management of the Schenley Liquor Company to verify that the demand was elastic, because to get a jump on its competitors it had to determine what kind and size of production facility to build. Before making that determination, the drug was introduced in limited quantities into similar communities at quite unlike prices to ascertain whether Gilbert was right. When firms have leaders who are smart enough to know they do not know everything, that is the way they proceed. On the other hand, if they are not so smart, what they do is build an Edsel! In general, *each time* a firm introduces a significantly better substitute, be it a new drug or the VW Rabbit, the market must be tested before the actual response to that particular product can be known.

KNOWLEDGEABLE BUYERS

For high demand elasticities to develop, buyers of either intermediate or final goods must have a discriminating sense of taste. It seems to be no accident that dynamic competition flourishes most when there are expert buyers, a condition which is best met when firms in competitive industries buy intermediate products from other industries. Those who buy semiconductors for use in various products are undoubtedly highly expert comparison shoppers. It would be wrong, however, to assume that buyers from uncompetitive industries necessarily engage in the same degree of comparison shopping as do buyers of intermediate products in more competitive industries. Weakness of competitive pressures will be reflected not only in lower productivity gains, but in higher input costs as well.

Competition in final goods products also presupposes consumers who insist on engaging in comparison shopping. I suspect that for this reason there is more competition in the manufacturing of women's clothing than in men's. Another example concerns the early Japanese cars that were unreliable and shoddy. These automobiles contrasted so much with other features of Japanese life that Japanese consumers loudly demanded that the discrepancies be removed. While consumer risk takers played an important role in making it possible to sell Japanese cars in Japan, consumers who were not risk takers played a key role in later improvements in reliability.

Before foreign cars were introduced into the United States, the ability of the consumer to make quality comparisons was very limited. But, when consumers were provided with a wider menu of substitutes, the shift to foreign cars occurred in a highly predictable way. Market surveys made by General Motors during the mid-1960s showed that the majority of consumers who had shifted allegiances to foreign cars were better educated or from college communities. Even the General Motors executives living in Ann Arbor, Michigan, drove a higher percentage of foreign cars than those living in Detroit!

CONCLUSIONS

Both David Ricardo's and Karl Marx's economics assumed a zero-sum world, that is, a world in which the size of the pie is strictly fixed. Because of their interpretation, they had no use for the dynamic competition discussed in this chapter. Marx saw the entire economic problem as a struggle between the capitalists and workers over fixed resources. It must be acknowledged that even today there are one or two economists who are throwbacks to that age. In his book, *The Zero-Sum Society*, and in his later condemnation of the antitrust laws, Lester Thurow, of MIT, has demonstrated a complete misunderstanding of what young game theorists regard as obvious: dynamic competition is a form of cooperation to increase the size of the pie![26]

When the game is played with reasonably knowledgeable consumers and rules that do not allow everyone to win, the result can be an economic miracle. When the game is played as a simple struggle for survival, those firms that prosper are not necessarily the fittest from the point of view of their contributions to economic well-being. Firms can survive by investing in huge advertising expenditures that can, in turn, limit entry. They can survive as tight oligopolies aimed at creating for their members an environment of minimal risk and uncertainty. Firms can survive by seeking protection from foreign competition. There are many ways firms can survive by making the demand for their products artificially inelastic. To proclaim that only the fittest survive, therefore, is tantamount to proclaiming the fittest is the fittest.

Chapter 5
DYNAMIC EFFICIENCY AS A PROCESS

The goal of static efficiency (combining given inputs in an optimal manner) differs conceptually from that of dynamic efficiency (changing production functions in profitable directions). To some degree both objectives must be pursued simultaneously. Although the main preoccupation of dynamically efficient firms is the continuance of improvements in products and production processes, at some point in the development of every product attention must be paid to static efficiency. At the other end of the spectrum, it can be observed that no firm is completely static. No industry for which I have data has ever exhibited a zero rate of productivity gain (i.e., unchanged production functions for a period as long as ten years). Change was ever so slow during the Middle Ages, but it never stopped. If the rate of progress in a particular industry falls below some minimum threshold figure, a highly discontinuous change in its firms' behavioral characteristics will be observed. The key internal cultural differences between more and less dynamic firms are as follows:

First, the leader of a progressive firm is not a stern general who directs his forces from a position far removed from the scene of the battle. Rather, the entrepreneur's entrepreneur is the key figure in the question-raising process, who must be very familiar with the nature of the operations involved. Because new questions are continuously raised, and the nature of the operations changed in response to new knowledge, the strategy of progressive firms can be pinned down only at a moment in time.

Second, dynamic efficiency must be understood as a process, and not as a method, for making individual decisions. It is a process because, in response to feedback suggesting opportunities, new methods must be found for resolving problems. Alert observers at all levels of the organization can influence corporate strategy. Oftentimes, feedback that would be completely ignored in other less dynamic firms turns out to be of decisive importance. Because new opportunities do not turn up regularly, highly flexible organizations are required to take advantage of them. The role of flexibility is not only to quickly and efficiently go from the idea stage to the implementation stage. The flow of ideas resulting in significant innovations is encouraged not only by a powerful reward system, but also by entrepreneurs who know that it will not take ten to twenty years to implement their ideas. Thus, there is a reciprocal relationship between flexibility and the generation of ideas.

Third, in the past, time-and-motion studies, which tended to regard workers as mere cogs in a machine, played a key role in the administration of American firms that were designed for large-scale operations in mass markets wherein there was little or no foreign competition. In flexible firms it is essential to encourage workers to become creative and adaptive. If the U.S. is to become a more successful participant in international competition, the highly adversarial relationship between management and workers, resulting from the feudalistic practice of capitalism, will have to be changed.

In this chapter three related aspects of dynamic efficiency will be discussed. The first is the relationship between firms' internal and external incentives. The general argument to be advanced is that, in a dynamic equilibrium, firms, if they hope to survive, must match their internal rewards for risk taking with the degree of risk imposed on them by other firms. The second is the trade-off between static and dynamic efficiency. The fundamental argument to be advanced here is that, inasmuch as all people and organizations have a finite ability to deal with uncertainty, it is impossible in a single organization (as distinct from a firm composed of several quite different organizations) to insist on making simultaneously quite predictable and highly significant advances. It is impossible, because the pursuit of dynamic efficiency requires people of different personality characteristics, who are organized and rewarded differently.

The third part of the discussion is mainly concerned with two types of flexibility. "Type I" flexibility is built into production processes so they can produce quite dissimilar existing products on one production line—whether dissimilar styles of shoes or models of automobiles. It is aimed at a rapid short-term response to changes in market conditions by permitting very significant shifts in the composition of output without the usual penalties involved in closing down entire production lines. If the demand for commodity A turns out to be greater than expected, and if sales of commodity B turn out to be disappointing, the firm can shift emphasis from the second to the first, with relatively minor penalties.

"Type II" flexibility, on the other hand, is concerned with the ability to make good use of newly disclosed opportunities, be they opportunities for improving the production process or developing and producing new products. While Keynes was no doubt correct in believing that in the longer run we will all be dead, type II flexibility is designed to insure that in three or four years from now firms still will be prospering. To rapidly respond to uninsurable changes in market conditions and unprogrammable advances in technology, firms obviously must be alert to feedback that suggests opportunities for new products and production processes. Rapid response not only requires that feedback be heeded, but also that it be acted upon. This requires highly flexible organizations, from R&D to tooling to production, in which people take broad views of their responsibilities. A firm designed for static efficiency is composed of specialists, all with well-defined tasks. By contrast, type II flexibility requires highly adaptive people, from workers to top executives, who have had a diversity of experiences and are more concerned with getting the job done than with who does what. With type II flexibility a plant is not composed of equipment optimized to produce only one particular design; rather, it is a production process that more or less continuously evolves to represent the best current thinking, and not the ideas of twenty years past. To be sure, many mistakes are made along the way. It is the early recognition of mistakes that adds up to a compound-interest process. However, firms cannot hope to enjoy the benefits of specialization and flexibility simultaneously. The specialization argument results in relatively large and inflexible plants, whereas flexible operations require both general-purpose workers and relatively small plants.

To better understand types I and II flexibility, I was greatly assisted by discussions with members of Japanese and Swedish automobile firms, as well as by knowledgeable people from a number of American firms in highly competitive industries. What surprised me was the similarity in their behavior: the degree to which they were playing the same game.

INTERNAL VERSUS EXTERNAL INCENTIVES

Let us say that you head a large chemical company that must face genuine risks imposed by worldwide chemical companies (e.g., the loss of a valuable market), and that you, personally, are not going to make the needed discoveries, because your job is not that of an entrepreneur, but rather of an entrepreneur's entrepreneur. One positive action on your part might be to tell your chemists to go forth into society to discover the real problems so they can perform the role of matchmaker between what seems to be economically desirable and the technologically possible. Furthermore, you can advise them that it is important to interact not only with people inside firms, but with potential customers; and they should behave in much the same manner as did Charles Kettering when he invented the self-starter for automobiles and the diesel locomotive.

You are likely to find that, while a few chemists will understand this kind of sermon, chemists are no less responsive to doing what is required to get ahead in a chemical firm than are people in general; that is, their behavior is strongly influenced by pecuniary and nonpecuniary rewards. In the late 1950s I consulted for the chairman of the board of a chemical company (whose career began as a research assistant to Charles Kettering) who instituted a system of rewards that resulted in twelve chemists earning more money than he, the chairman of the board! He felt that the improvement in the competitive position of his firm fully justified such rewards. Few firms go that far, but all the dynamic firms with which I am familiar take special pains to evaluate the accomplishments of creative engineers and scientists, and reward them accordingly. Inasmuch as the authorship of particular discoveries is very difficult to pin down, such reward systems must be arbitrary. However, when this is pointed out to people in such firms, the common reply is, "Yes, but it is quite as arbitrary to assume that all people are alike in their creativeness!"

To carry the discussion one step further, I assume that, whether or not they are conscious of it, the leaders of dynamic firms are engaged in creating an internal system of incentives that is the *mirror image of their external incentives*. For example, many highly creative firms insist that they refuse to promote anyone who has not made a mistake. Why? They say that if the firm must make mistakes to get ahead, so must the individual. The reason for the strong resemblance between their internal and external incentives should be apparent. A firm that insufficiently rewards entrepreneurs for taking risks that might pay off in only three or four years, while its rivals take such risks, could be seriously penalized. Conversely, if it encouraged scientists and engineers to dream about technological possibilities ten years in the future, it also could be penalized. Thus, dynamic competition disciplines not only highly dynamic firms but also their members.

It should not be assumed, however, that nonpecuniary rewards are unimportant. In fact, a nonpecuniary reward that results in general recognition of an important achievement is probably more important than a bonus given secretly. One important difference between industry in Japan and the United States is that in Japan nonpecuniary rewards play a much larger role. For example, in Japan, an executive who is thirty-five years of age can expect to earn much less than one who is fifty years old, but the younger executive can nonetheless be rewarded by being given a broader responsibility. Furthermore, in some Japanese companies ten gold-star awards are presented annually to workers who come up with the most valuable suggestions for making changes on the production lines—a procedure that not only sharpens the thinking of the workers, but also those involved in making the evaluations. These awards do not result in large pay raises, but the recipient does receive an all-expense-paid trip abroad—which makes them highly coveted.

On the other side of the coin, industries having to deal with relatively little hidden-foot feedback put their main emphasis on protecting a way of life, and their managers are rewarded in terms of higher positions in the administrative hierarchy. Other internal incentives can also play an important role in fostering such behavior, for example, providing retirement benefits in a form that assures that the longer a person stays with a firm, the more expensive it becomes to leave. Such firms are merely responding to a situation in which their capacity for dealing with risk and uncertainty is so low they do not dare impose significant risks on others.

Finally, assume that a firm has not had to contend with much risk and uncertainty during the past ten years, but now finds itself confronted with new challenges. Can the top leadership change the internal reward system so it more closely corresponds with the external signals? Over a period of ten years small steps might be taken for rewarding on the basis of accomplishment; however, because incentives that reward on the basis of performance threaten the established bureaucracy, this would not be easy. Though the president of the company in question might favor moving in this direction, he is constrained by the fact that organizational morale cannot be allowed to slip very far during the transition.

In short, rewarding on the basis of accomplishment presupposes highly fluid organizations. Once organizations are no longer fluid, trying to change their reward systems is tantamount to changing the culture of the firms.

THE TRADE-OFF BETWEEN STATIC AND DYNAMIC EFFICIENCY

The pursuit of static efficiency can be described as a fine-tuning operation whose objective is to make best use of existing information. To be sure, this is a limiting case in which the degree of motion in shifting the production possibilities curve has come to a standstill. But, even so, it is quite reasonable to assume that the

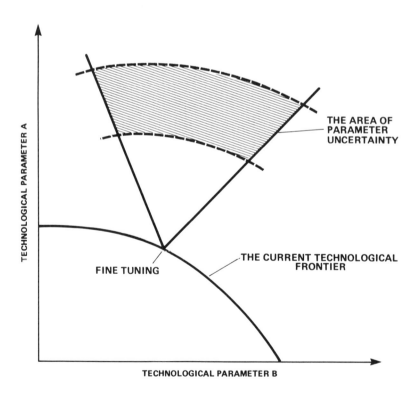

Figure 5.1. The Trade-off Between Static and Dynamic Efficiency.

further we go toward this limiting case, the more firms will behave on the basis of making many tiny optimizations their main goal.

However, inasmuch as firms cannot be simultaneously optimized for high and low degrees of uncertainty (anymore than a small law firm can be optimized to deal with both criminal and probate law cases), there is a trade-off between static and dynamic efficiency. This is shown in figure 5.1, which indicates that members of any reasonably cohesive organization cannot simultaneously aim for highly significant advances and engage in the detailed optimization problems inevitably involved in producing an operational piece of equipment.

Assume that a firm is operating at the current technological frontier, and parameter A represents the thrust of an aircraft engine in relation to its weight, parameter B, the thrust in relation to its fuel consumption. Then, choosing an ideal aircraft engine combination (i.e., the goal of static efficiency) is a fine-tuning operation along a familiar trade-off line. For commercial aircraft the trade-off would feature engines designed to emphasize minimum fuel consumption, and for a fighter-interceptor the choice would be in terms of a minimal weight engine. By contrast, extending the frontier might involve activities like discovering better materials, ways to achieve greater propulsive or thermodynamic efficiency, or the development of high-speed propellers as a substitute for the turbofan engine. In this case, a dynamically efficient organization would aim to maximize the improvement of the efficiency of a new engine, which later might be tailored for a variety of specific airplanes. However, no single organization can hope to achieve static and dynamic efficiency goals concurrently unless, of course, R&D budgets are unlimited. Generally speaking, diverse personalities are involved because, whereas static efficiency requires meticulous attention to detail, dynamic efficiency requires a sense of imagination and adventure, as well as attention to detail.

Single firms can have within them organizations of quite different personalities; consider the difference between Bell Telephone Laboratories, which is optimized for pushing out the frontiers, and Western Electric, which is optimized for fine tuning. If both activities were combined in the same organization, telephone technology would not have advanced so rapidly, nor would the telephone system be nearly so reliable.

It can be seen, therefore, that, as a process, dynamic efficiency can thrive only in a multipersonality company—one that does not attempt a happy compromise between imaginativeness in overcoming limits and the attention to details required to make a satisfactory product.

Two main problems of leadership in a progressive multipersonality firm are supplying communication links and ironing out frictions between the discoverers and the fine-tuners. For example, in chemical companies, a crucial problem is said to be finding people who can act as intermediaries between the chemists and the chemical engineers. AT&T has an entire organization that specializes in helping pave the transition between fundamental advances in technology and detailed engineering design.

Notice that the function of performing as an intermediary is *not* to act as a coordinator. The system that finally emerges is not a happy compromise between the initial ideas of the developers and those of the production engineers. At some point in its evolution an airplane must be designed to be producible, as must a new microwave system. Nevertheless, in any reasonably progressive firm the developers do not begin with detailed constraints; they are not managed by the production people. Rather, the production people must learn to accept the inevitable uncertainties involved in creating a new product as it progresses through development. The more predictable the production people try to make their lives, the smaller will be the probability that the firm in question will be able to generate a significant advance.

It can be seen, therefore, that the main difference between competitive and noncompetitive firms is in the diversity of their people and organizations. In competitive industries a wide diversity of people is required with respect to their thresholds for dealing with the risk and uncertainty inevitably involved in dealing with feedback suggesting new opportunities. The more basic reason dynamic efficiency is considered a process is that without institutional arrangements to keep people working together the result would be chaos: a high degree of disorganization is required for a cross-fertilization of ideas, and a sense of mission—beating a rival to a larger market share—is required to keep internal conflicts impersonal. On the other hand, firms lacking that diversity are specialized for fine-tuning: to make progress in a slow and painful way.

Chemists say that to relate their micro- and macroworlds one must be able to visualize the molecules singing and dancing. And although our micro- and macroworlds are entirely different, more or less the same is true in economics. When looking at data concerning industries that are in the top group of productivity performance, you will find that the firms in question undoubtedly possess a wide diversity of people; and the task of making their efforts add up to fairly steady advances is a never-ending process. In such firms the employees always ask questions; humor, especially the kind that involves dealing in contradiction, is very common; and, above all, people tend to be self-critical. When productivity performance in an industry doubles in a decade, you can be quite certain that a wider diversity of people is being tolerated, and to make this possible the personality of the firm has been greatly changed. This success indicates that *self-responsibility* is being fostered. People of very different personality characteristics can work together only if they believe that their tasks are important in their own right. Conversely, when the rate of productivity gain declines substantially in an industry, self-responsibility is eroding. In fact, a productivity decline can be defined as an erosion of personal responsibility in which people become humorless and blame all misfortune on events beyond their control. People in such firms excel at fostering internal bureaucratic procedures so, if anything does go wrong, no one person can be blamed. Nearly all firms with a low or rapidly declining productivity performance are programmed to say "yes" or "no"—but never "maybe."

TYPES I AND II FLEXIBILITY

The following discussion is based on a continuing study aimed at a better understanding of the relationship between machine-tool firms and machine-tool users, the most important of which is the automobile industry. It must be emphasized that this project has not yet been completed. The aim is to be able to rank various companies in terms of types I and II flexibility (without, of course, revealing company names) and, as information is obtained, to learn more about the costs and benefits associated with both kinds of flexibility. Type I flexibility always involves giving up something in scale and specialization economies. To what extent can modern technology be employed to minimize the cost of making significant shifts in the composition of output? Type II flexibility, which is intimately associated with dynamic efficiency, inevitably involves a loss in static efficiency. To what extent do the gains exceed the losses?

A substantial research effort will be required to provide satisfactory answers to these questions. The reason for beginning with Japanese firms is that, on the basis of previous research, I simply could not believe that the Japanese productivity miracle in the field of automobiles could not be accomplished without a high degree of type II flexibility—without which, I am convinced, no firm can hope to be highly dynamic. I was unprepared, however, to find the great extent to which Japanese firms also featured type I flexibility. If firms are to prosper in the longer run, they obviously must be able to survive in the shorter run.

Keep in mind that the following discussion is not intended to describe the activities of any single firm. Actually, X, Y, and Z theories of Japanese management notwithstanding, Japanese automobile companies differ substantially. According to conversations with Koichi Shimokawa (professor of business administration, Hosei University, Japan), who has delved deeply into the histories of both the United States and Japanese automobile firms, Japanese auto firms are no more alike than the Ford Company of 1908 was like the Nash Company of 1920, or the Nash Company of 1920 was like the Chrysler Corporation of 1930.[1] Yet, describing their activities under the labels of two broad operational concepts may do no serious injustice to the facts. And these concepts, in turn, may be very helpful in explaining why Japanese automobile firms have surpassed U.S. firms in terms of the absolute level of productivity.

There seems to be little doubt that Japanese auto firms are producing automobiles with fewer workers per car. Estimates made by James E. Harbour, a former director of corporate manufacturing and engineering at Chrysler, who worked closely with Mitsubishi Motors, indicate that Japanese compact or subcompact cars are assembled in 14 worker-hours as compared with 33 for comparable cars in the United States; comparable engines in Japan and the United States require 2.8 and 6.8 hours respectively; and the figures for stamping out body parts are 2.9 and 9.5 hours respectively.[2] William J. Abernathy, Kim B. Clark, and Alan M. Kantrow provided detailed estimates in a recent article, indicating that Toyo Kogyo produced a comparable car to Ford's compact with about 60 percent fewer man-hours.[3] Although initially very skeptical of these estimates, I have found that in at least two Japanese firms the numbers were in the same ballpark as those cited. In one firm, the number of cars produced per employee per year (i.e., the standard way of keeping productivity statistics in Japan) was increased from 33 in 1972 to 98 in 1982. Included in the definition of *car* are not only assembly but also engine and transmission.

Japanese automobile firms subcontract to a larger extent than their counterparts in the United States; and for this reason the above comparisons overstate the actual productivity differences. Although precise comparisons are virtually impossible to make, little doubt exists that there is a gap highly reminiscent of that developed during the nineteenth century when American steelmakers went into the production of Bessemer steel. Although highly protected by tariffs, they were selling to Scottish shipyards by 1900.[4]

Type I Flexibility

A point not well understood by people unfamiliar with machine operations is this: a flexible tool is not necessarily a general purpose tool. To be sure, it might seem that *flexible* and *general purpose* are concepts that go hand in hand. For example, with a radial saw in your home workshop you can perform a variety of operations. From that point of view it seems like a flexible tool. In reality, it is flexible in only one domain, sawing. Suppose that you trade it in for a seemingly more flexible tool, one that can be used as both a saw and a drill press. You will find that, while both saws can be used quite as effectively for rather simple operations, the saw that was built to be a saw—the more dedicated tool—can provide a higher degree of accuracy over a much wider range of operations. Therefore, if you want a home workshop equipped to operate in more than one domain, with tools that can be used for making high-quality furniture, you must buy a dedicated radial saw and a dedicated drill press.

Next, let us consider an example of a flexible tool that might be seen in a factory: a flexible boring machine. A diagram of such a machine looks like this:

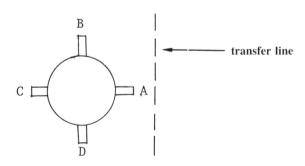

It is controlled by a computer; that is, after it bores holes in some parts, the cylinder rotates from A to B, so equally precise holes can be made in a new part. This machine is both dedicated and flexible; and it can be connected to other machines on stations downstream that operate in entirely different domains.

Let us consider, now, a transfer machine. A transfer machine is one in which parts are automatically transferred from station to station, with quite different operations performed at each station. Suppose that you observe one. How can you tell whether it is or is not a flexible transfer machine? A Harvard Business School professor would probably say that once you have seen one transfer machine you have seen them all; but, in fact, unless you actually observed the objects emerging from the machine you would not know. An eight-station machine might produce only water faucets—or it might produce, simultaneously, water faucets and padlocks, with some stations dedicated to water faucets and others to padlocks. What is the purpose of such a machine? From one point of view, it can be looked upon as a machine that produces a given output at a given cost for lower investment costs than otherwise would be required. For example, two firms in two quite different industries might own such a machine jointly—a machine whose initial cost is in the neighborhood of two million dollars. From another point of view, when a machine such as this is owned by a single firm, ownership can be looked upon as a way to diversify its investment portfolio.

Our focus will now be on the automobile business and, in particular, on assembly-line flexibility. First, consider an assembly line where various X-model cars might be manufactured, whether in the form of a Buick, Chevrolet, Pontiac, or Oldsmobile. If Buick's sales are higher than forecasted and Pontiac's lower, General Motors can reprogram its production mix; but, from our point of view, such a minor variation in the product mix is not to be regarded as type I flexibility, because it provides only a nominal degree of insurance against inaccurate market forecasts. Every other car coming down the line in a U.S. automobile company is also different, because of the unbelievably large number of options provided. Again, however, options provide little type I flexibility: even if they can choose among dozens of instrumental dials, many buyers seem to be mainly concerned with higher-level optimizations, such as repair costs. For example, if all the early X- model cars have serious reliability problems, the company cannot shift without serious penalties. In fact, a recently built General Motors plant in Oklahoma seems to reflect this lesson: on the same line the now more seasoned X-model cars as well as the newly introduced A-model (which is larger than the X-model, but smaller than the older Oldsmobile Cutlass and Buick Regal models) can be produced. From a Japanese point of view, even that kind of portfolio choice would be considered very narrow. On a Japanese assembly line you might see the counterparts of X-models, A- or J-models, a relatively small truck, or a small van—all moving down the line in very quick succession. Inasmuch as this assembly line permits investment in a wider portfolio of cars, it is characterized by a higher degree of type I flexibility.

A rough picture of the difference between more and less flexible assembly lines is shown in figure 5.2. The flatter cost curve is the average for several different cars produced on a typical line. If the plant operates at a substantially smaller production rate than the optimum, the penalties are relatively large, whether one or several cars are produced on the same production line. This cannot be avoided. The object is to get the curve as flat as possible for an assortment of cars. The flatness results from the fact that the proportion of different cars produced on a flexible production line can be changed with no penalties. Given the technology, the cost of such flexibility will obviously depend on the diversity of cars produced on a single production line. But the costs also depend on the technology. Consider, for example, a succession of robot welding machines, where each robot welds a car in a dozen to two dozen different places: the conventional practice. Or suppose that a single robot machine designed to simultaneously make one thousand welds were also designed in much the same way as the boring machine discussed earlier, namely, to be flexible. With that kind of technology, type I flexibility obviously costs less.

Inasmuch as Japanese companies are producing automobiles on more and less flexible lines, engineers from these companies are in a good position to know the cost difference between flexible and nonflexible production routes. According to recent Japanese information, the cost difference between a production line which

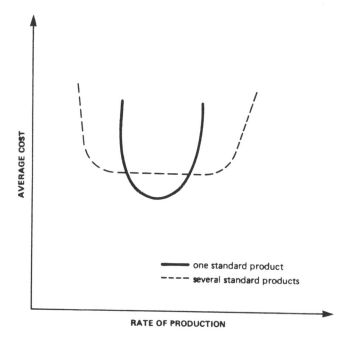

Figure 5.2. Type I Flexibility.

can produce three or four quite dissimilar cars versus a single car is in the neighborhood of ten percent. In fact, the cost of obtaining a given amount of diversity on production lines can be looked upon as a measure of type I flexibility.

Is ten percent a relatively small or large cost for hedging one's bets? It all depends on your point of view. To the U.S. production engineers, who for many years lived in an environment in which different firms made similar cars at similar prices, such a cost would seem very large. On the other hand, suppose that one out of three cars turns out to be such a poor bet that plants are either run at 50 percent of capacity or have to close down. In that case, ten percent is a relatively small cost. Or suppose that during the first two years of operation a new car turns out to have serious reliability problems and very disappointing sales. Again, ten percent is a relatively small cost for hedging one's bets, because with a flexible plant new cars can be produced in relatively small quantities during the earlier years, and, later, when demand builds up, output can be increased.

In summary: One reason that Japan leads the United States in auto productivity is that it has a relative advantage in type I flexibility, which means that production is less frequently interrupted than it is in more specialized plants. High-volume output, the key to low-cost operation, is easier to maintain for a variety of cars. However, as will become apparent, a more important reason, and one not so easy to imitate, involves type II flexibility. In fact, type I flexibility is only a means to an end: building a bridge between the present and an even more uncertain longer-run future.

Type II Flexibility

The principal difference between types I and II flexibility is that, whereas the first is designed to deal with feedback suggesting short-term changes in market demand, the second is designed to assure dealing with more ambiguous feedback as a requirement for maintaining the longer-term competitiveness of firms; for example, feedback suggesting new process discoveries. United States firms are not lacking in either kind of flexibility when technologies are young, when the firms in question are relatively small, or when the industry in question happens to be the chemical industry—which has long engaged in fierce, and sometimes not so fierce, international rivalry. But, when firms become large and preoccupied with taking maximum advantage of scale economies to fully exploit various opportunities for specialization, they tend to lose both types of flexibility. For example, the work of Abernathy and Utterback has shown that not only in the automobile industry, but in others as well, a phase of rapid product innovation was followed by a phase of rapid process innovation; and both types of advances died out when specialization was carried further and further.[5] The evolution, in other words, is one in which firms become increasingly incapable of dealing with feedback. The main lesson to be drawn from the Japanese experience is that this one-way evolution, which can be offset only by the establishment of entirely new industries, is by no means as inevitable as it might seem on the basis of American experience.

To the extent that firms enter international competition, they cannot afford to become highly inflexible; VW did, and almost went out of business. What is unique about Japanese automobile companies is not so much their continuing press for advances in the product (although there have been very impressive improvements in reliability), as the fact that they have concurrently brought about very impressive changes in the production process. The difference between the two approaches is shown in the following diagram:

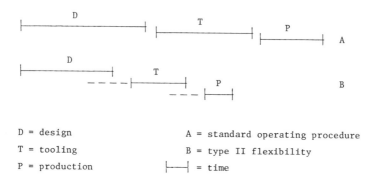

D = design   A = standard operating procedure
T = tooling   B = type II flexibility
P = production   ├──┤ = time

Consider, first, the top bars, which represent standard operating procedure in firms that have lost their dynamism. After the design concept has received the stylists' stamp of approval, the engineers devote meticulous attention to working out all of the detailed technical problems; and this phase usually ends with the building of a few prototypes constructed with soft tooling. Following this stage, detailed designs are given to the tooling department so precise specifications for the tools to be supplied by various machine tool firms can be composed. Afterward, in stage three, production preparations are initiated, usually during a two or three week period, at which time the plants are closed.

The principal character of this highly routinized process is that it leaves little leeway for the introduction of new tools. If the design of the automobile involves a substantial change, the tooling people are seldom allowed to take risks with the introduction of new production technology. If the design is not changed, automobile firms are not willing to invest significant sums on new tooling. Consequently, the United States machine tool industry, insofar as it is engaged in supplying tools to the automobile industry, is not only a feast or famine industry, but it is also in no position to benefit from feedback provided during the development of various autos.

Next, consider firms that have an impressive degree of type II flexibility, whose planning process is represented by the second set of bars on the above diagram. In this case each of the bars is shorter, indicating that the time taken is shorter; the dotted lines indicate an overlapping of activities. What permits the bars to be shorter and to overlap is that each activity is carried on simultaneously. Thus, those in design and development work do not wait for cues from the stylists; they work on new product designs almost continuously. To do this there are often fierce internal design competitions. A unique feature of both Japanese and Swedish automobile firms is that the tooling people do not sit at a desk and write specifications. They have a substantial in-house capability not only for testing new types of machines developed by machine tool firms, but also for developing new machines that might prove to be of special advantage. Several Japanese automobile firms have more than two thousand people in their tooling departments, which, in U.S. terms, makes them relatively large machine tool companies.

How long does it take the Japanese to normally develop a new transfer machine? Providing the project is not held up by U.S. suppliers, about a year, which is actually less than the time taken by a U.S. company to deliver an older-type transfer machine. However, to do that, the people in the tooling department must experiment with and test new tools almost continuously; and although mistakes will be made, it is only from their mistakes that they can learn.

Indeed, it is precisely this kind of activity that permits the design, tooling, and production functions to overlap. On the one hand, because the toolmakers have previously done their homework, they have a great deal of know-how to draw on when planning concepts for new machines. So, detailed final drawings from the design people are not needed before toolmakers commence their work. On the other hand, the activities of the machine-building and testing departments also help insure that plant managers need not be kept in the dark as far as new machines are concerned, because they can observe the testing of the machines before their introduction. And not only that: the tooling people are always working with the plant managers to benefit from feedback received from workers after the tools have been introduced. Indeed, one can often see parts of an old production line and a new section being operated and debugged simultaneously. At times, but not always, in Japan such changes result from the quality circle method of management; more commonly, they result from informal close-working relationships between the tooling people and workers on the line.

In short, the entire operation can be looked upon as experiments that will be revised on the basis of feedback. What it really means to heed feedback is to exercise *self-responsibility*. In a highly centralized system, in which everyone is trying to cover up mistakes, feedback tends to be ignored. But, in a highly decentralized system, in which making mistakes is regarded as an essential aspect of bringing about rapid progress, sensitivity to feedback and self-responsibility are merely different ways of saying the same thing.

Keynes emphasized the necessity of keeping a significant proportion of one's assets in liquid form in order to be prepared for both good and bad surprises. Obviously, in an entirely predictable world there would be no such requirement. The same proposition also holds for a world in which firms hope to make rapid progress. To take advantage of new opportunities, and quickly abandon poor investments, firms need to hold their physical assets in a relatively liquid form. It is understandable, therefore, that the same habits of thinking are associated with making rapid advances in the United States. For example, Donald Douglas, Sr., insisted that the DC-2 be designed in such a manner that if the engine programmed for it was not successful another could be readily substituted. This turned out to be a very fortunate decision, because, if the two-engine airplane had had to operate on the basis of the engine initially programmed for it, the airplane would never have been able to meet the safety requirements (i.e., to fly with one engine). I recently asked an official from one of the U.S. makers of commercial airplanes this question: "How important is it for you to tool in such a manner that, if an opportunity arose to make a new kind of airplane, it would not be necessary to completely retool for its production?" His answer, "It is the way decisions like this are made that either makes or breaks companies!"

Are there clearly recognizable features of dynamic efficiency that can be found in industries of quite dissimilar characteristics? We know the commercial airplane business is very different in scope from the automobile business. For one thing, large volume production is not nearly as important in the commercial airplane industry as it is in the automobile industry. If types I and II flexibility do not take the same form, are there similarities? In that which follows, types I and II flexibility will be examined, including their similar and dissimilar applications.

To an even greater extent than in the automobile industry, it is difficult to predict the short-run demand for particular commercial airplanes, especially during economic recessions. However, by having the ability to adjust to changing demand estimates, the aircraft industry has one clear advantage over the automobile industry; that is, inasmuch as aircraft assembly is a highly labor-intensive operation, it is relatively easy to switch workers from one assembly line to another. On the other hand, millions of components are used in commercial aircraft which are made by highly capital-intensive processes; and, to a far greater extent than in the case of automobiles, they need to be specialized for particular airplanes. Consequently, in this respect the aircraft industry is at a clear disadvantage. To meet the need for type I flexibility, transfer machine technology has been developed (i.e., so-called group technology) to permit an entire group of dissimilar components to be made on the same machine. Therefore, flexibility that automobile manufacturers can achieve by making dissimilar automobiles on the same production line, aircraft manufacturers can attain by making diverse components with a single machine. It can be noted that much the same practice can be found in the farm machine industry. This means that when such companies are confronted with economic adversity, it is not necessary to lay off as many workers. Moreover, I understand that in this case, too, the cost of such flexibility is, in relation to its benefits, rather nominal.

In the following discussion of type II flexibility, the policies of a commercial airplane company, which is the most progressive in the industry, will be used as an illustration. One similarity of American aircraft companies and Japanese auto companies concerns the amount of tooling that is done inhouse; in fact, one firm in the U.S. commercial aircraft industry has had as many as four thousand people engaged in designing and making new tools. Moreover, as in Japanese automobile companies, it is strictly against company policy to optimize tools for particular end products; instead, I was told, "Tools are designed for an entire envelope of airplanes." While some airplanes (e.g., flying boats) could not be produced with these tools, the tooling preparations, nonetheless, contemplate a much wider spectrum of airplanes than those which are either now in production or on the drawing board. Holding such physical assets in relatively liquid form has a real advantage: those responsible for designing new tools have no way of predicting what will emerge from the aircraft design and development shŏp. They have learned, as a result of bitter experience, that it is dangerous to tell one of the vice-presidents, "We cannot produce that airplane unless you give us all the money needed for new tools." Taking such an attitude could easily cost an executive his job.

In progressive aircraft companies tooling is also in a more or less continuous state of evolution. For example, except for the substitution of plastics on wing and tail surfaces, an airplane designed fifteen years ago may be essentially the same one being produced today (although not the newest airplane in production). Yet, as a result of making some fairly impressive process discoveries, the airplane will not be produced in the same manner as it was initially.

For quite understandable reasons, the employment of such procedures requires a high degree of decentralized decision making in which one group does not wait for others to complete its tasks. Officials from one U.S. aircraft company jokingly refer to their firm as a "Japanese" company—in that it also uses the "consensus" method of decision making; that is, workers are often consulted when changes in production processes are considered. And bonuses are given to workers for suggestions that will reduce the weight of airplanes by *one* pound. When a new technology, such as computer-aided design, is added, there is a good deal of consultation throughout the company about how to make best use of it, which results in a common philosophy.

Finally, one of the most striking similarities is the method employed for dealing with subcontractors. During my visit to Japan, automobile executives described at length how they had to use a "carrot-and-stick" method for subcontractors who were making both components and machine tools. To make technological progressiveness possible, subcontractors were provided with a great deal of technical assistance. Those who refused to comply were likely to find that they had lost an important customer. And, when I heard officials from two aircraft companies describe their problems with subcontractors, they used almost the same words.

When shown production processes in both the Japanese automobile industry and the American aircraft industry, I was puzzled by one question. I knew that the production processes were always in flux, but I also had the feeling that everything I saw might have been designed initially as a harmonious whole. Given the fact that decision making is highly decentralized, how was this possible? Although this particular subject will require more research, my present conclusion is that there is no real inconsistency between the decentralized decision making and integrative functions. The latter requires that those involved have some commonly shared goals with respect to the general characteristics of the factory of the future. But there is little doubt that pleasant and unpleasant surprises occurring after the introduction of new equipment keep them continuously involved in question-and-answer activities. For example, in an automobile company the current key questions might be: How can a transfer line be made more flexible? How can a robot more ably perform some highly specialized tasks? In an aircraft company one key question might be: How can computerized machine tools be made to perform comparably to highly dedicated tools? How can we develop a dynamic programming tool with one part able to probe for unusual problems, and when finding one will be able to send a message back to the computer to slightly alter the angle of the hole?

One rude shock all commercial airplane companies experienced after World War II was that, whereas prototype airplanes had been previously made with soft tooling, the tolerances in modern aircraft required that they be developed on the basis of hard tooling that greatly increased the cost of development. The initial reaction to this problem was to build aircraft on *expandable* tooling. To make changes in prototype aircraft relatively inexpensive, the wings were first constructed using one assembly fixture and, later, after the bugs had been worked out of the wings (a fairly typical problem) and orders mounted, the process was made more specialized by using up to four assembly fixtures. Needless to say, production engineers in the aircraft industry, who during World War II had learned to operate like those in the automobile industry, were not overjoyed to go to this method of operation. However, computerized machine tools and computer-aided design now make possible the achievement of the same goal in a less expensive manner. In particular, the role formerly played by prototypes is now played by much less expensive mock-ups, and provision to make inexpensive changes in tooling is built into the production process.

To return to the main question, what is the connection between having a sense of vision and being able to take advantage of feedback? I think there are reciprocal forces at work. Involvement in a continuing series of challenges improves an entrepreneur's sense of vision; and better vision provides a greater ability to deal with challenges. Without vision, disappointment is likely to be regarded as nothing more than noise: it is vision that converts noise into valuable feedback.

An even more certain conclusion is that the "cultural" differences between firms are far greater than the cultural differences between nations. This means that a Japanese automobile executive could go to work in an American airplane company, and after learning the English language, he would feel quite at home. The same is true of an American aircraft executive who might choose to work for a Japanese automobile company. But, if either one chose to work for Ford, General Motors, U.S. Steel, or the Anaconda Copper Company, he would find himself in an entirely different culture: a far greater degree of adaptation would be required than that involved in learning a new language. Indeed, if a U.S. commercial airplane engineer decided to work on military airplanes, that would involve going to an entirely different culture.

In addition to making possible the use of a highly flexible procedure, a firm's capability to do its own tooling has other advantages. For example, people from a U.S. company engaged in making transfer machines sold some of their machines to a Japanese company that had been able to get the running (uptime) of the machine to a figure of 82% as compared with 60% for American automobile manufacturers. In the past, U.S. firms' standard operating procedure consisted of running a machine until it broke; then it was repaired. But, as a result of experimenting with machines before introducing them into operational use, a Japanese procedure evolved in which it was found that better uptime could be obtained by running a machine for ten hours, and then engaging in two hours of preventive maintenance.

When firms take an active role in their own tooling preparations, people are encouraged to think for themselves. Initially, all Japanese companies used general-purpose robots. But one firm found that when both workers and machines were looked upon as a system, workers could provide valuable insights on how the robots might be most advantageously used. As a result, it was decided that robots should be developed as specialized instruments, with no two looking alike. (People, it was said, already provide good general purpose machines, so why try to build that capability into robots?) From what I gather, other firms are rapidly moving in this direction. As was emphasized in an earlier chapter, when firms take risks and are successful, the payoff, as far as the whole industry is concerned, can be very impressive.

In graphic terms, the picture is as shown in figure 5.3. The steeper sloping curve generates more cost curves; that is, due to the fact that production technology is more or less continuously improved, costs can be pinned down only during a period of six months or so. It is this fact of life that leads to a steeper path. On the other hand, optimal plants at particular points in time by no means assure an optimal path. So, again, there is a trade-off between static and dynamic efficiency: if it were assumed by the Japanese that opportunities for technological progress had been exhausted, it would undoubtedly pay to build larger and more specialized plants instead of those that are only one-third to one-quarter the size of comparable U.S. plants.

How large can plants become, and still remain flexible? Technologically speaking, there is no close relationship between size and flexibility. The diseconomies of scale relate to the entire relationship between management and employees. At some point, which is difficult to precisely pin down, increasing the degree of specialization, which is inevitably involved in exploiting scale economies, will destroy the intimate relationships and the degree of trust required for type II flexibility. Representatives of both Japanese and Swedish firms em-

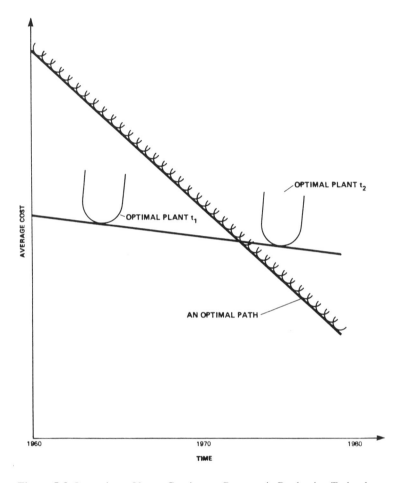

Figure 5.3. Intermittent Versus Continuous Progress in Production Technology.

phatically stated that their plants are already as large as they can be to continue to engage in flexible operations. Therefore, the prescription, if output must be increased substantially, is not to build bigger plants but more plants, each operated as a decentralized profit-making center.

This is not to suggest that if automobile companies of the United States were to imitate Japanese companies in tooling preparations, the difference in their personalities would disappear. Other and more fundamental factors are also at work. One is a Japanese principle that can be best described as the scrupulous avoidance of redundancy, because it jeopardizes the reliability of the component parts of a system. For example, the just-in-time approach to keeping inventories down in Japanese auto companies not only supplies an incentive to build equipment in such a way that a cushion of inventories will not be needed; it also encourages suppliers

to design highly reliable components. There are other applications of this principle. For example, the headquarter staffs of some Japanese automobile firms are
kept so lean that sometimes there are not enough secretaries to go around. Hence,
there are not large staffs whose main aim is the diffusion of responsibility.

Even more basic factors are necessary to make type II flexibility possible. The
first is that there is in Japanese automobile companies a relatively small gap
between management and workers. All dress more or less alike when at work, eat
in the same cafeteria, play baseball together on Saturdays, and so forth. In short,
Japanese firms are not plants, they are integrated communities. Furthermore, the
income gap between workers and top management is, by American standards,
relatively small. Automobile workers in the United States receive about twice the
wages of their Japanese counterparts. And top management incomes of $100,000
are almost unheard of in Japan. So, even without taking quality differences into
account, there is something like an 8-to-1 difference in managerial compensation.

"Was it always like this in Japan?" I asked again and again. And the answer was
invariably, "No." Apparently, before World War II, feudalistic capitalism (i.e.,
capitalism that promotes the *artificial* rather than the *natural* aristocracy) was far
more developed than it is in the United States today. General MacArthur evidently
believed that by breaking down large agricultural estates and feudalistic industrial
empires an important cause of war would be removed. However, while MacArthur
is no doubt the personification of the change that occurred, I have the feeling that
when such momentous social revolutions unfold they do so because people want
them. It is a well-known fact that after World War II there was a revolt against
tyrannical leaders in Germany that affected all aspects of German society. For
example, attend a Bach concert during Easter in Berlin and you will find that not
only members of the choir rise when singing a solo part, but so do solo-performing
members of the orchestra. Why? It is said that this symbolizes the importance of
the individual; and something like that also may have happened in Japan.

The second important difference between Japanese and United States auto firms
concerns the degree to which people are shifted from job to job. In Japan, workers
are shifted on the production lines about every three months, and after reaching the
age of thirty they are often shifted into administrative work. There is no clear line
between a white collar and a blue collar worker. In some companies, engineers
must serve a tour of duty on the production lines before being rotated into other
activities. Managers are shifted around every five years or so—from accounting to
marketing, from engineering to marketing and accounting, and from marketing
back to accounting. Consider this example: despite the fact that he had no
engineering background, a person in marketing in a Japanese auto company was
given the assignment of being in charge of building a new auto plant. Now, that
certainly encourages the development of the individual and evidences trust.
Because he was known to ask questions the so-called experts would not ask, it was
not blind trust. This example also should serve to indicate why it is difficult to pin
down the diseconomies of scale in a flexible firm. In an operation of a certain size
there is a fairly high probability of recognizing such talent. But make the operation

three times as large and how can you compute the reduction in the probability? In fact, it is precisely the inability to make such calculations that causes executives to worry over the penalties involved in operating large plants.

What is the difference between operating a nonspecialized and a highly specialized labor force? Consider, for example, the task of replacing a teakwood deck on an aircraft carrier. Because no two carriers are built alike, this is a nonroutine operation. Though before World War II, carrier decks were almost always replaced by firms in the United States, afterward it became the practice to have them replaced in Japan, because the work was better, faster, and done at a far lower cost. From what I have been able to gather, the chief difference between the procedure in the United States and Japan was this: in Bremerton, the workers engaged in replacing the deck were separated into teams, each with fairly definite responsibilities (as was required by union work rules). Consequently, when unexpected problems arose there were long conferences between team leaders, and long coffee breaks, before it was determined how to proceed. But to the great amazement of the admirals, in Japan nobody seemed to be in charge; when a worker ran into difficulty he simply signaled with a nod and someone came rushing to help him. Roughly speaking, these two procedures illustrate the difference between a flexible and nonflexible labor force. But, note, it is not necessary to adopt Japanese culture in order to adopt such a procedure. During World War II, American GIs could be observed spanning the Rhine more quickly with British bridge-building equipment than could the British, who approached the task in more or less the same spirit as the U.S. firms engaged in replacing carrier decks.

As far as automobiles are concerned, I was aware of the difference between highly specialized and nonspecialized operations long before my visit to Japan. I visited the Ford Motor Company at the time that Honda engineers and general-purpose mechanics were busily engaged in equipping one hundred Pinto cars with stratified charge engines and modifying them as the test program progressed. Engineers and general-purpose machinists worked together so closely that it was impossible to distinguish one from the other. Again, the entire process was one that featured quick and uncoordinated decision making.

Why did Ford subcontract to Honda for this undertaking? According to my host from Ford, the essential reason is that the Honda procedure could accomplish in a few days what would have required six months on the basis of the traditional Ford procedure. In the case of Ford, parts could not be fabricated until detailed drawings had been released to the production department, and changes in parts could not be made without bringing a full-fledged committee system into operation. It should be noted that the Honda tradition is not altogether new to the Ford Company; it is the same procedure employed during the development of the Model-T Ford.

In *The Wealth of Nations* (written in 1776), Adam Smith observed:

> The common ploughman, though generally regarded as the pattern of stupidity and ignorance, is seldom defective in his judgement and discre-

tion. He is less accustomed, indeed, to social intercourse than the mechanic who lives in the town. His voice and language are more uncouth.... His understanding, however, being accustomed to consider a greater variety of objects, is generally much superior to that of the other, whose whole attention from morning to night is commonly occupied in performing one or two operations.[6]

Why were manufacturing procedures of the United States once the flexible operations that characterize Japanese organizations today? The fundamental reason, it would seem, is that entrepreneurs were recruited mainly from farms. (On the eve of the American Industrial Revolution, which began in the late nineteenth century, 50 percent of the American population was still living on farms.) And the kind of flexibility commonly possessed by American firms during the nineteenth and early twentieth centuries was undoubtedly transplanted from the farms. But in the promotion of self-responsibility, the emphasis on providing managers and workers with a diversity of experiences, and providing workers with life-time jobs, Japanese firms behave as if they were still operating farms.

In the *Wealth of Nations*, Adam Smith was worried about the danger of Britain remaining a colonial power, fearing it would eventually lose its ability to compete in foreign markets. The danger of the monopoly of colony trade was, in his words: "The industry of Great Britain, instead of being accommodated to a great number of small markets, has been principally suited to one great market."[7] In other words, the danger was a lack of type I flexibility. And the United States has had all the disadvantages of a large colonial power without actually being one: a large homogeneous market and almost unlimited resources. "Fortress America," in the form of firms so large that no nation could hope to match the prowess of the United States, is no longer a viable concept.

Chapter 6
A MODEL OF DYNAMIC PROCESSES

This chapter is based on two related models: an *incentives* model and a *dynamic efficiency* model. The incentives model corresponds to a Nash dynamic equilibrium: an equilibrium in which firms adopt mutually consistent policies with respect to risk taking. Two distinct activities are involved: (1) providing better technological building blocks, and (2) utilizing them to bring about productivity gains. The dynamic efficiency model is concerned with the *ability* of firms to utilize R&D resources to make progress in bringing about the largest possible productivity gains and technological advances. The relationship between these two models is simply this: the more pressure there is on firms in an industry to engage in risk taking, the greater will be their emphasis on those organizational qualities associated with the achievement of a high degree of dynamic efficiency. To survive in an uncertain environment, firms must be highly sensitive to the possibility of receiving negative feedback from competitors and positive feedback suggesting new opportunities. To benefit from good luck as a means of survival, members of firms must be constantly alert to ask new searching questions, while at the same time acting in a manner to minimize the consequences of bad luck: this requires firms which feature both types I and II flexibilities.

The purpose of this chapter is to show how these two concepts can be integrated into a predictive theory. The first two sections will be concerned with a detailed explanation of the PERK diagram described in chapter 1. It will be seen that there is a definite mathematical relationship between the value of PERK and the rate of progress. Furthermore, this mathematics can be used for making predictions when it is assumed that the availability of technological inputs for bringing about productivity gains remains constant. Suppose that the needed technological inputs do not remain the same. Is it luck and luck alone that determines outcomes, or are other important factors at work?

In many industries steady-state progress occurs in the form of more or less steady improvements in the rate of productivity advance. Consider, for example, figures 6.1, 6.2, 6.3, and 6.4, which are examples of various degrees of progress over a span of twenty years. Of the 375 industries included in the BLS data, something like 100 provide pictures similar to these. Although there were also cases in which the rate of productivity advance decelerated, altogether there were about 275 cases in which the rate of productivity gain was, so to speak, quite orderly. On the other hand, there were other cases in which productivity gains moved in cycles: these will be discussed in chapter 9.

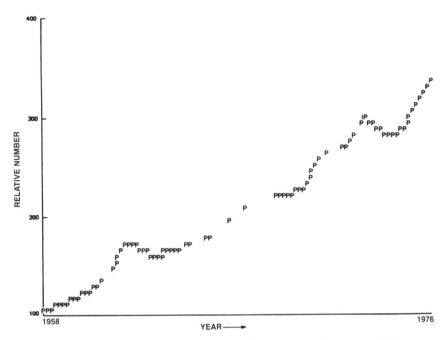

Figure 6.1. An Example of Linear Progress: Tufted Carpets and Rugs.

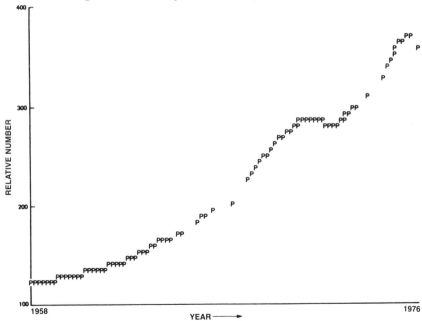

Figure 6.2. An Example of Rapid Linear Progress: Hosiery.

Prices, Wages and Business Cycles

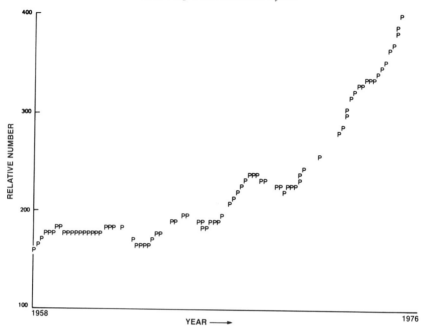

Figure 6.3. An Example of Accelerating Progress: Organic Fibers.

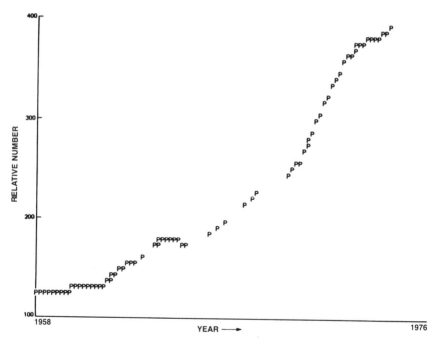

Figure 6.4. An Example of Rapid Accelerating Progress: Radios and Television.

Consequently, we can assume that steady-state progress, accelerating or decelerating progress, actually occurs, and is not a figment of our imaginations. My aim is to devise a falsifiable theory to explain such phenomena.

THE NATURE OF TECHNOLOGICAL ADVANCES: THE PRODUCT CURVES

Figure 6.5 shows two pairs of s-shaped curves illustrating the mental processes involved in overcoming discontinuities. On the vertical axis is shown the performance of a technology measured, say, in cost-effectiveness terms. It is not assumed, however, that entrepreneurs know beforehand the height the curve will reach; the more creative the innovations, the more uncertainty will be involved. On the horizontal axis both time and dollars are measured. But this is not to imply that diminishing returns in both a temporal and an economic sense occur simultaneously.

It will be noted that, mathematically speaking, curve A, which has a higher initial curvature, grows to a greater height. From an economic point of view, what determines the initial curvature? As we already have seen, limits are overcome as a result of a process of ideological mutations; that is, new concepts are discovered for either broadening the definition of a technology (as in the case of computerized machine tools) or for imposing new rules on the game (as in the case of flexible machine tools).

However, there are some concepts that are of a more general nature than others and, as such, have a greater growth potential. For example, the concept of an automobile with front-wheel drive and a transversely mounted engine obviously is a broader concept than that of a new transmission. Generally speaking, the take-off speed is determined by the breadth of the concept and the degree of preparedness of the firms in question to exploit the potential. It also may be noted that, while curves A and B can be described as discontinuous advances, the essential difference between them and incremental advances is that the latter take the concept as a given and are tacked on to already-made discontinuous advances.

Thus, it is no accident that Alfred Marshall was both an admirer of Darwinian biology and a great believer in marginal incrementalism.[1] In Darwinian biology an environment is taken as a given, which is tantamount to taking a concept as a given. This is not to say, however, that the paradigm which emerged from Darwinian biology was inappropriate for describing a habit-bound society such as late nineteenth-century Britain—or the United States today. Unfortunately, Marshall went wrong by assuming that the Darwinian model applied to all countries at all times.

However, the curves will not necessarily have the same paths shown in figure 6.4. A developer may begin a project, find that his expectations are disappointed (which is to say, the curve will drop), and still later find ways to make the curve rise again by generating new ideas (which is, in fact, quite common). Consequently, we do not really care about the shape of these curves. Rather, our interest is in the height and slope when development is completed. The only assumption needed is that at some point diminishing returns will be encountered.

These curves can be looked upon as representative of PERK. While a relatively high-PERK industry may be making incremental and discontinuous advances simultaneously, which bring relatively strong pressures on other firms in the industry, low-PERK industries feature incremental advances, which create less pressure on others.

THE KEY PARAMETERS REQUIRED TO GENERATE PRODUCT CURVES

As shown in figure 6.6, two key parameters are needed to describe s-curves associated with particular products. The first is *gamma*. Gamma is the height the curve would reach if an infinite amount of money and time were spent on the perfection of a product. The second is *tau*, where, it so happens, the slope of a new s-curve is at least as great as the previous one. It should be noted that when performing at tau the developer will be operating beyond the point of diminishing returns. Diminishing returns set in at the inflection point on the curve, that is, at tau/2. The third parameter is *lambda*, the exploitation parameter. Technically speaking, lambda is defined as the performance measured at tau divided by progress made between the plus and minus asymptotic values of gamma. However, for our purposes lambda is an unimportant parameter.

The following discussion intends to explain the economic reality behind these curves. The definition of tau does not necessarily imply that new curves will begin with a particular slope. All that is necessary to assume is that when firms undertake new projects they will begin them with the expectation that profits from risk taking will not decline. Tau is an important parameter, because, if we think of the productivity of R&D expenditures as the amount of progress per dollar, why spend a good deal on elaboration when generating a new product will result in greater gains? Bringing about progress by making a product carefully optimized for a particular application (which is the essence of static efficiency) is worthwhile only when it is assumed that opportunities for discontinuous advances have become exhausted.

There are genuine risks involved in either stopping well before or going beyond tau. In the latter case, the firm in question risks having a market stolen away. In the semiconductor industry, for example, delaying the introduction of a new product a month longer than absolutely necessary after it has been tested is regarded as a grave risk. To take another example, according to de Tocqueville, in the 1830s Americans built steamboats that were not nearly as durable as those of the British. Part of the reason was that American builders assumed more or less continuous progress would be made with steam engines. But it may also be true that there were greater risks of being overtaken by a rival in the American steamboat industry. And, no doubt, a combination of these reasons explains why today Japanese steamships are designed according to the same philosophy as were those of the United States in the 1830s.[2]

On the other hand, inasmuch as productivity of R&D dollars decreases after tau/2, why go beyond that point? The reason is simply this: on the basis of flying an experimental airplane you, the developer, might feel that you have a marvelous new product—but when turned over to the airlines the airplane might not be successful from a reliability point of view. As when writing a book, you begin with many nifty ideas, but, if not well worked out the concepts will not fly.

In short, operating in the neighborhood of tau minimizes two risks: the technological risk involved in developing an unreliable product and the competitive risk of having a market stolen away. The developer has no alternative but to walk a narrow tightrope between these two incalculable risks. This is not to say, however,

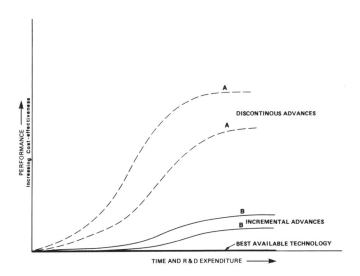

Figure 6.5. Discontinuous Versus Incremental Advances: s- curves.

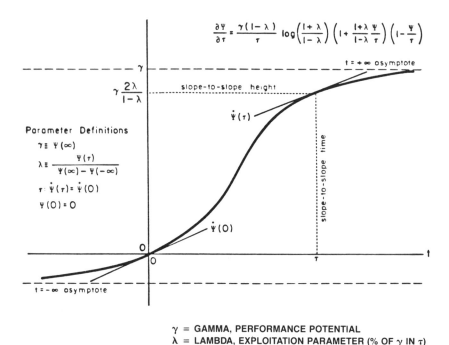

$$\frac{\partial \Psi}{\partial \tau} = \frac{\gamma(1-\lambda)}{\tau} \log\left(\frac{1+\lambda}{1-\lambda}\right) \left(1 + \frac{1+\lambda}{1-\lambda}\frac{\Psi}{\tau}\right) \left(1 - \frac{\Psi}{\tau}\right)$$

γ = GAMMA, PERFORMANCE POTENTIAL
λ = LAMBDA, EXPLOITATION PARAMETER (% OF γ IN τ)
τ = TAU, DEVELOPMENT DURATION

Figure 6.6. The Key Parameters.

that tau cannot be shortened in calendar time; for example, the use of computerized machine tools to shorten the process of making changes.

The definition of tau may seem ambiguous because it depends on knowing when a project is initiated. Indeed, because ways to overcome limits are typically discovered before the development of a system, it is unclear when the ideas are actually initiated. However, it is also true that, inasmuch as it involves committing a relatively large volume of resources with a more definite notion of the payoff than occurs in exploratory development projects, the decision to develop a new system can be described as a unique event—quite as unique as making an investment.

The preceding discussion describes, in a general way, how competitive pressures can affect the size of either innovations or technological advances. And, as was indicated in an earlier chapter, there is no clear-cut line between an innovation and an invention. The only two parameters that will enter the discussion in the next section are tau and gamma. They may either be generated in firms making productivity advances, borrowed from other firms making technological advances, or, more realistically, partly borrowed and partly generated. Consider, for example, a production process for making tractors which may consist, in part, of American machine tools and, in part, of Italian computerized tools, plus some clever ways of combining them. In such cases it is very difficult to say which is the innovation and which is the invention. All we really can say is that competitive pressures drive firms to be ingenious in one way or another. By trying to neatly dissect the process, we risk not seeing the forest because our attention is on the trees.

If we assume that opportunities for bringing about progress remain constant in various industries, and that the larger the value of gamma sought, the wider will be the distribution of outcomes, then, by using a Poisson distribution (a distribution in which the time of arrival of new products is highly discontinuous), it would be relatively easy to show the requirements for different rates of steady-state progress. To maintain steady-state progress gamma cannot decline, and products must be released in the neighborhood of tau. Since stochastic forces are at work, steady-state progress also requires that a sufficient number of products be under development so, statistically speaking, these requirements can be met. As a rough guess, if the number were below three or four per time period, the probability of maintaining a high rate of progress would be low; and, if the number were greater than ten, the probability would not be significantly increased by adding to that number.

If the performance of different subsets of firms were compared within the same industry—the rate of progress in the Japanese auto industry versus the rate of progress in the American auto industry; the rate of progress made in reducing the per-seat mile costs of U.S. and European airplanes; or the relative rate of progress made in reducing steel costs in Britain and the United States during the nineteenth century— it would be quite proper to reason from rates of progress to the values of PERK. In such cases it can be assumed that the basic technological opportunities were more or less the same in all the various countries, and a greater rate of progress occurred due to the willingness to take risks to exploit those opportunities.

This, however, is obviously not a reasonable assumption for predicting the productivity performance of a variety of domestic industries. Needed, therefore, is a way to make statistical inferences about the rate of productivity gain, when it is assumed that opportunities for maintaining various rates of progress do not necessarily remain constant. If they are to lead to a testable theory, such inferences must be made on the basis of assumptions relating to the behavior of individual firms, which can then be tested against industry data. For this purpose, a Gaussian distribution is more promising. These gains are usually made by the incorporation of both large and small advances. Hence, it can be assumed that such advances will ascribe to a normal probability distribution.

A MODEL FOR PREDICTING PRODUCTIVITY PERFORMANCE

First, I will briefly contrast two ways to think of a dynamic equilibrium. One consists of a situation in which productivity gains are not limited by the availability of technological inputs. Consider, for example, a *family* of industries, such as computer games and semiconductors. In this particular case, the ability of the electronic-games industry to make good use of technological advances brought about in the semiconductor industry may not be limited so much by advances brought about in semiconductors as by the ability of the computer-games industry to make good use of them. There must be some limit on how far the concept of type II flexibility can be carried; in principle, at least, one can imagine a firm so flexible that it could never produce anything.

When technological advances are supplied at a rate they are demanded, the factors of necessity and luck work for each other. In the case of the computer-games industry, the factor of necessity is a very high degree of dynamic competition, with wide differences between more and less successful products during any time period. On the other hand, the factor of luck consists of the ability to become nearly saturated with technological innovations. But, from the point of view of the semiconductor firms, the necessity of computer-games companies is their luck; that is, they have a ready market in which to sell relatively large advances.

It is safe to assume, however, that the vast majority of industries are not nearly so fortunate as to have their luck ready-made for them. The industry may be in an equilibrium in the sense that the average rate of productivity gain is steadily increasing. But it would be wrong to assume that productivity rates of individual firms will not be highly dispersed around an industry trend line. Typically, the activities of no single firm in the industry can be said to represent *best* practice. Like professional golfers, they try in a variety of ways to improve their scores. Nevertheless, from the point of view of individual firms, a dynamic equilibrium exists, because, with competitive pressures remaining the same, the momentum of the search process will be maintained.

In other words, dynamic equilibria can be looked upon as games that can be played at faster or slower rates, depending on the degree of necessity. For any value of PERK, firms are assumed to be involved in parallel games: the greater the values of PERK, the faster moving will be the parallel games; and the faster moving the game, the greater will be the ability of an industry to maintain a previous rate of productivity advance.

In the following discussion, some quite specific hypotheses will be set forth; afterward, it will be shown how a statistical theory, devised on the basis of assumptions with respect to the behavior of firms in more and less competitive industries, can be tested against industry data. The first part of the discussion will concern predictions which might be made if we could measure the value of PERK, and the second will involve predictions which can be made when we have only industry data for price, productivity, and output changes.

Gamma will be measured with respect to its potential or actual contribution to productivity gains, depending on its stage in the development process. Furthermore, it will be assumed that, as we move from exploratory development aimed at discovering relatively high values of gamma to the later stages of development, costs will rise very sharply. A team can, of course, minimize R&D costs by searching for lower values of gamma. But, if it does, the stage of diminishing returns will be encountered more quickly, because firms will be going well beyond tau, and the s-curves will evolve more slowly over time.

Also assumed is that a ten percent improvement in productivity during some particular year can be achieved by either one fairly impressive innovation or ten innovations which individually made only a one percent contribution to productivity gains. In other words, for purposes of the following discussion, gamma can be thought of as an *average*: an average whose value will be greater when more impressive innovations are incorporated into the production process.

Maintaining a high degree of dynamic efficiency has two aspects; one consists of searching for relatively large values of gamma, and the other, of minimizing the risks associated with bringing about particular innovations. In other words, dynamic efficiency can be thought of as a ratio of the ex post height of the weighted value of gamma to the ex post width of the distribution. If a firm searched only for minor innovations while its rivals searched for major ones, it could be forced out of business. However, if the firm gambled everything on a few seemingly promising innovations, it could also go out of business.

To clarify the distinction between dynamic efficiency and the minimization of risks, consider figure 6.7. Efficiency when searching for higher values of gamma

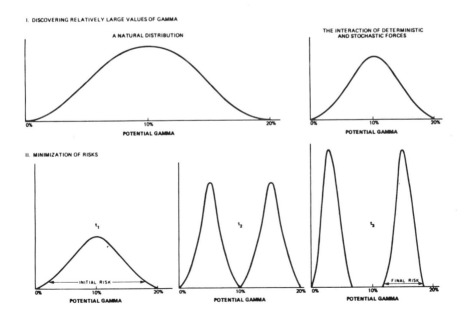

Figure 6.7. The Two Aspects of Dynamic Efficiency.

consists of acting on the basis of relatively subtle feedback. As the top panel of the figure indicates, the width of the distribution is shrunk by something like 50 percent, indicating that by asking penetrating questions, rewarding innovative behavior, maintaining highly interactive organizations with a relatively small gap between management and workers, firms can put good luck on their sides. Indeed, the key idea in dynamic economics is that the respective roles of necessity and luck are not completely independent; and the basic question to be answered in this chapter is this: Can a competitive economy do better than one in which outcomes are decided by God throwing dice?

The second panel of figure 6.7 shows a likely outcome of a sequential search for relatively large values of gamma. In the first period (t_1), pressure from competition results in a wide search to uncover large gammas. Then, to discover whether a seemingly promising gamma looks as good ex post as it did ex ante, the team will engage in a process of risk minimization aimed at obtaining better estimates of the actual value of gamma. As the figure shows, in the second time periods (t_2), the distribution could peak at either a relatively small or large value of gamma; beforehand there is no way to know. If, as the drawing shows, the team had only one promising innovation underway, in the third period (t_3), it could end with making not a ten percent contribution to productivity gains, but less than a five percent contribution. This is the primary reason why, during a particular time period, there will be wide differences in the fortunes of individual firms, even if all were dynamically efficient. Notice that the search process seeks to make the average value of gamma as large as possible, and the risk-minimization process narrows the width of the distribution. That, essentially, is efficiency in research and development.

In principle, the probability of the distribution peaking at relatively high values of gamma, rather than low values, would be the same whether the search were conducted by a similar number of competing teams within one firm or in several competing firms. For example, when IBM featured a good deal of internal competition, it was, in effect, acting to increase the probability of uncovering relatively high values of gamma: if one division was more successful than another, the participants would be rewarded accordingly. However, even in this case, new entrants into the market discovered many possibilities overlooked by IBM. It seems safe, therefore, to assume that the probability of uncovering relatively large gammas will be proportional to the number of firms in an industry, up to some number like ten. If the number is very small, say three, the only way that firms can collectively minimize the risk of going out of business is to operate at relatively modest values of gamma. If they do not do that, the number will sooner or later shrink as a result of stochastic forces. Hence, it can be predicted that impressive productivity gains are not likely to occur in concentrated industries unless they are challenged by foreign competition. On the other hand, it also can be safely assumed that, if the number of firms is more than, say, ten, additional efforts to increase the value of gamma will have a relatively small effect on increasing the probability of maintaining a particular rate of progress.

To bring us closer to making some definite predictions, two pairs of distinctly different cases will be contrasted. The word *family* will be used to describe a pair of industries engaged in making necessity and luck for each other. From this point of view, the semiconductor and computer industries can be considered a family, as can the tooling and production departments of Japanese automobile companies. The two families are considered to be in different situations, because it can be assumed that the first family operates at higher values of PERK—and, by so doing, it plays a faster-moving and potentially more risky game than the second.

By contrast, an *ensemble* describes a collection of industries operating at similar values of PERK, which may either sell technological advances to a variety of industries that will utilize them to bring about productivity gains or will buy them from industries engaged in generating such advances. Now, it is true, in terms of an input-output matrix all industries are members of families. But, if the demand for higher rates of productivity gain on the part of some industries is not reflected in sharply improved technological inputs— in improved possibilities for making substitutions—then, for all intents and purposes, the so-called *family* is not operating as a real family. The purpose of the following discussion is, on the one hand, to contrast the difference between families and ensembles, and, on the other, to illustrate the differences between families and ensembles that operate at different values of PERK.

It should be apparent that there are two principal differences between families and ensembles. In the first place, because they provide a ready market for innovations, members of families are at an advantage in being able to discover relatively high values of gamma. Only by the formation of new families can outsiders hope to be as lucky as they might like. For example, several German firms engaged in making cotton textile machinery became interested in utilizing a new technology to greatly reduce costs. But, inasmuch as German cotton textile firms specialize in producing very fine quality products, there was no basis for a marriage in that country. So, what they did was to form a new family by recognizing that competition between American synthetic fibers and cotton textile plants provided a good market for their machines. At the present time the supply side of the family includes not only German machinery firms but also Japanese firms, which, from the point of view of a cotton textile firm, makes the probability of uncovering a relatively large value of gamma even greater; and modest further improvements have been made by combining features of both German and Japanese machines.

While a member of an ensemble which is hard pressed to bring about productivity advances may turn up with a 20 percent gamma, the probability is much smaller than it is with respect to a similar member of a family. This may seem to suggest that if a particular member of an ensemble wants to generate relatively steady productivity gains, it can allow its dynamic efficiency to fall by searching for relatively small values of gamma. However, until we actually consider the differences between members of ensembles operating at higher and lower levels of PERK, this must be left as an open question.

A second advantage of families over ensembles is that their members can be expected to enjoy a more steady rate of productivity gain, because their luck is being made for them. By contrast, individual members of ensembles have a more uncertain market in which to buy and sell their advances.

A comparison of families and ensembles operating at different values of PERK is shown in figure 6.8; at the bottom of the figure the differences between both ensembles and families are described. The statistical distributions shown on the figure are constructed on the assumption that in the first year all firms began a relatively wide search for gammas. The essential difference between the higher- and lower-PERK industries is that they are centered on a greater value of gamma. It is assumed that all industries engage in a process of minimizing risks, whether they begin at relatively high or low values of gamma. To be sure, cases can be found in which low-PERK industries do sometimes engage in desperate gambles, and, not actually realizing that they are involved in such speculation, they fail to minimize risks. However, these cases occur so infrequently that they are not likely to affect the overall statistical results.

There are two principal questions brought out by figure 6.8. First, the lower-PERK families engaged in bringing about productivity gains are centered on lower values of gamma; yet, according to the bottom of the figure, there is no significant

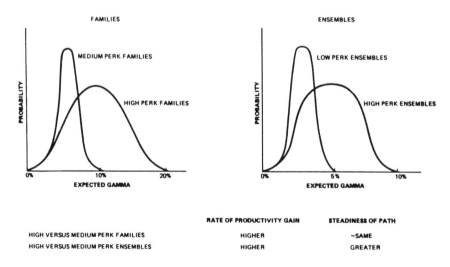

Figure 6.8. Families Versus Ensembles: The Initial Distribution.

difference between high- and low-PERK families with respect to the steadiness of their long-term productivity gains. Second, while the distribution is narrower for the low-PERK ensembles, they are, nevertheless, described as being at a disadvantage with the high-PERK ensembles in the steadiness of productivity gains. Why do the PERK ensembles have a double advantage in long-term productivity growth?

As far as families are concerned, the explanation for assuming that low- and high-PERK industries will have an equal advantage with respect to the steadiness of their long-term productivity gains is relatively simple. The low-PERK industries search more narrowly (i.e., have a lower dynamic efficiency), but they literally have no need to possess a greater dynamic efficiency inasmuch as their ability to make good use of innovations is already saturated. For example, in Japanese automobile plants, plant managers are probably operating at a point where they cannot profitably employ more process innovations during any time period. Indeed, to make good use of innovations they must be willing to consider gammas whose gestation period will be several years.

On the other hand, members of ensembles engaged in bringing about productivity gains must, to a greater degree, live by their wits. However, if my main proposition is correct, the forces of luck and necessity are not independent, which means that the members of high-PERK ensembles should have a relative advantage in *both* unearthing large values of gamma and in the steadiness of their productivity gains. If hard pressed to reduce costs, it would seem that almost everyone in firms which manage to survive in such an industry—from highly creative engineers to workers on the production lines—will be searching for ways to bring about productivity advances. Moreover, it also would seem that, if harder pressed by domestic and foreign competition, those firms which manage to survive in a more competitive environment will have to broaden their search processes. In either case, the deterministic and stochastic forces would not be completely independent. But, to be frank, there is another reason for making this aassumption: it is needed to make sense out of the data!

How can we determine if the theory actually works? Let us say that we have data on prices and productivity for a period covering twenty years for a large number of industries. And, during that period, the average prices in manufacturing as a whole may have been rising or falling. For purposes of this discussion, it really does not matter, because, at this point, we are only interested in *relative* price changes. If prices in a particular group of industries have been declining relative to those of manufactured products in general, such changes will be treated on a par with actual price reductions. There is, however, an important difference between a single change in relative prices (when, at a particular date, the price of coffee declines relative to that of tea) and an entire series of relative price changes (when, during an entire decade, prices in particular industries increase half or twice as fast as manufacturing prices in general). Single changes in relative prices may occur for a number of reasons. But protracted changes, as measured in terms of rates, are unlikely to occur for capricious reasons. When industries observe a high degree of price restraint by a continuing reduction in prices relative to the average in manufacturing as a whole, the reasons are invariably to be found in keen domestic competition (e.g., sporting goods), intense international rivalry (e.g., television sets), or both. Conversely, when industries observe a low degree of price restraint by continuing increases in their relative prices, almost invariably the reasons are to be found in their being directly or indirectly protected from foreign competition— directly, when industries like steel are protected, and indirectly, when protection of steel also results in the protection of close substitutes (e.g., lumber products).

One point to be emphasized here is that observing such price changes can, at best, be regarded as only a very rough proxy for PERK. Two groups of industries might be equally pressed by price or quality competition to generate productivity gains, but, because of differences in the nature of the technologies, there is no reason to suppose that they will generate equal productivity gains. To imply that there are equal opportunities for reducing costs in all industries would be absurd. It may turn out that, on the whole, the group of industries that is reducing its prices most rapidly is also bringing about productivity gains most rapidly. But the theory developed here does not purport to account for differences in the rate of productivity gains across industries. Rather, my interest is in the second derivative of productivity indices, because the steadiness of productivity gains is the main determinant of longer-term growth.

Another key point concerns the direction of causality. If price and productivity behavior are compared, how can we be sure whether price competition or quality competition, within tight price constraints, drives productivity gains, or whether the price behavior is merely a reflection of productivity performance? According to the price indices, the prices of radios and televisions declined substantially relative to the prices of other manufactured products during the 1960s and the 1970s. The productivity data indicate that these industries were among the top U.S. performers, with an average rate of productivity gain during both decades of eight percent. Was the price behavior a cause or a result of the productivity performance? It seems safe to assume that among radio and television manufacturers there is no code of honor requiring the conversion of lower costs into lower prices. If firms in any industry employed a standard markup procedure, and automatically translated reductions in costs into reductions in prices, they would indeed be guilty of highly irrational behavior. Undoubtedly the price and quality competition from Japanese imports, as well as from Japanese firms established within the United States, has provided the pressure for productivity performance.

At the other end of the spectrum, U.S. sawmills increased prices one standard deviation above the average, and their rate of productivity gain declined from 3.2 percent during the 1960s to 1.3 percent during the 1970s. Was their price escalation merely a reflection of rising costs? Firms may or may not be able to increase prices with no penalties, depending on whether their expectations with respect to the elasticity of demand are confirmed. But, if expectations of an inelastic demand curve are confirmed, they are under no pressure to maintain a particular rate of productivity gain. And with negative feedback long absent, as it was in the case of sawmills, we can expect productivity performance to erode.

Now consider a situation in which one group of industries maintains the highest degree of price restraint in both the 1960s and the 1970s, and another maintains a somewhat lower degree of price restraint during both periods. According to the above argument, the first group should be expected to enjoy a greater degree of stability in its long-term productivity gains. Suppose that another group of industries is forced to observe a greater degree of price restraint during the 1970s than it did during the 1960s. It can be predicted that, quite irrespective of their previous rate of productivity gain, those industries which have been dealing with a greater degree of dynamic competition, as measured by their degree of price restraint, will do the best job in responding. To be sure, the second situation can be described as a movement away from a dynamic equilibrium. It is the question-raising activity and the diversity of responses that provides firms with the greatest degree of stability in either maintaining or exceeding a previous rate of gain. This activity plays the same role in economic evolution as does genetic diversity in biological evolution; that is, in both cases, the elements of necessity and luck are not completely independent. Thus, when necessity increases, it can be predicted that, on the average, productivity gains will rise, and when it diminishes, they will decline. However, I am not claiming that the role of necessity completely dominates that of stochastic forces. Because stochastic forces are always present, highly accurate predictions about the impact of either strong or weak competitive forces on a specific industry cannot be made. To test the theory, therefore, it must be asked, to what extent is the median rate of productivity for, say, 50 industries likely to be affected?

Testing the Model

As was indicated in the previous section, the principal hypothesis to be tested is whether the degree of price pressure provides a reasonable predictor of the steadiness of productivity gains over reasonably long periods. If the theory is correct, families should have a distinct advantage over ensembles in not only the rate of productivity gain, but the long-term steadiness of such gains.

The price-pressure statistics were calculated by dividing all BLS four-digit industries into four groups. The A group includes those industries which increased prices one standard deviation or more *less* than the average (on the average, prices declined about 1 percent annually during the 1960s and increased only about 3 percent during the 1970s). Conversely, the D group includes those cases in which prices increased one standard deviation or more *above* the average (on the average, they increased about 3.5 percent annually during the 1960s and 11 to 12 percent annually during the 1970s). The B and C groups were obtained by splitting the middle of the distribution (while increases for the B group averaged less than 1

percent annually during the 1960s and about 6 percent during the 1970s, the
respective figures for the C group were about 2 percent and 8 percent).

To state the principal hypothesis more succinctly, imagine a diagram with the
1959-1969 rate of productivity gain shown on the vertical axis and the 1969-1979
rate shown on the horizontal axis. A 45 degree line sloping upward from the left
corner of the diagram indicates an equal probability of productivity gain during
both periods. The dots on the diagram represent the productivity performance of
individual industries: if a dot is above the line, there was a decline in the rate of
productivity gain (i.e., the second derivative) between the two periods; if it is
below the line, there was a gain. If stochastic elements alone were involved, the
distribution of the dots would be roughly the same for all industries.

If the hypothesis cannot be disproved by the data, then, relatively speaking, the
median gains in the rate of productivity advance should exceed the losses to a
greater extent for the A group than for the B group, because it is assumed to be
operating at a higher dynamic efficiency. I say, "relatively speaking," because
there is no way of knowing beforehand whether the technological inputs required
to generate relatively large gammas were as plentiful in the 1970s as during the
1960s.

As far as the C and D groups are concerned, it can be predicted that to a much
greater extent the median losses will exceed the median gains for two reasons.
First, with less pressure to restrain price increases, there will be a lower degree of
dynamic efficiency. Second, it is safe to assume that if a high degree of preparedness is not required for long periods of time, firms will become more centralized
and less able, therefore, to recognize genuine opportunities for productivity gains.
Or to put the point in another way, the longer the factor of necessity is absent, the
more myopic firms will become in terms of their profit-seeking ability.

This is not to say that the Cs and Ds cannot be motivated to increase their
preparedness—their ability to respond to hidden-foot feedback—if this is to occur,
they must be confronted with a greater degree of challenge.

In this chapter I will only be concerned with the cases in which competitive
pressures remained the same during both of the decades 1959-1969 and 1969-1979.
The statistical test employed to check the accuracy of the predictions is Wilcoxon's
Signed Rank Test: a test which is said to provide quite accurate results even when
the number of observations is as small as 16. The test is based on a symmetry
hypothesis (i.e., a uniform distribution of points around a line). If we predict that
group A industries will be more likely to conform to the symmetry hypothesis than
group B industries, on the basis of conducting the test at the 5 percent confidence
level, this means that the hypothesis cannot be falsified if the group A industries are
found to be keeping up their previous rate of productivity gains to a greater degree
than the B group.

The actual statistical results are shown in figure 6.9. It is not altogether
surprising that the statistical tests conform to what is actually seen in the figure.
Keep in mind, however, that only the *relative* productivity performance of various

industries is being tested. Whether the technological inputs for productivity gains increased or decreased between the 1960s and 1970s we do not know. What can be said is that not one of the predicted results is falsified by the test. The A group fell into the acceptance region (76 as compared with an acceptance region of 30 to 106). The B group fell short of meeting the acceptance test (1089 as compared with an acceptance region of 537 to 1004); and the C and D groups were much shorter (1329 as compared with an acceptance region of 635 to 1144 for the C group; and 63 as compared with an acceptance region of 11 to 55 for the D group).

As it happens, the average rate of productivity gains in the A group was about 50 percent greater than the B group (6 percent as compared with 4 percent). The primary reason is that the A group had the highest proportion of families (over 50 percent as compared to less than 5 percent for B) whose average rate of productivity gain for both decades was about 8.5 percent. Moreover, to a much greater degree, families were operating at compound interest rates. Even so, in both the A and B groups there were industries that were not members of families which accelerated their rates of productivity gain.

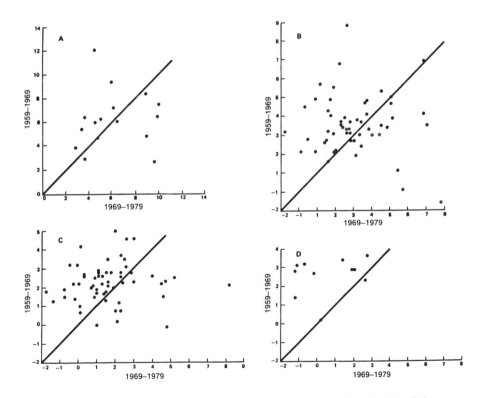

Figure 6.9. Constant Changes in Relative Prices: Distribution of Productivity Gains.

At the other extreme, motor vehicles and machine tools are, technically speaking, in the same family; that is, a very significant fraction of the U.S. machine-tool industry specializes in work for the auto industry. Yet, in the auto industry, the average rate of productivity gain over the two decades was only about 3 percent—and it failed to accelerate. According to this line of reasonsing, U.S. machine-tool firms interested in protecting their longer-run interests should switch to more demanding families.

Risk minimization was computed by comparing the year-to-year fluctuations in productivity gains to the trend line, and then computing the square of the deviations for each industry. On the basis of sample computations for about two dozen A and B industries, there were no large differences. The single industry which did best on this basis was malt beverages, which was in the B group and had an average productivity gain over the two decades of almost 7 percent. The deviations from the trend line were very large, but these resulted primarily from economic downturns. For example, while the sum of the squares of the deviations for radio and television was greater than that for malt beverages, the former industry was more seriously affected by economic downturns than the latter.

In my book, *Dynamic Economics*, the concepts of microstability and macrostability were introduced; and I argued in general terms that it was unpredictable behavior at the microlevel (i.e., the antithesis of microstability) which led to *smooth* performance at the macrolevel.[3] In terms of that argument, what do the above statistical conclusions show? Quite clearly, the industries which generate the highest rate of productivity gain also demonstrate the greatest degree of smooth performance at the macrolevel. And, as we just have seen, it is the search aspect of dynamic efficiency—as compared with the risk minimization aspect—which leads to the steadiest productivity performance.

PERFORMANCE OF THE INDIVIDUAL INDUSTRIES

The purpose of this section is to describe the individual industries in the various price performance groups. This discussion will make it clear that good or bad price performance is a reasonable proxy for the strength of dynamic competition.

The A Group

Some industries included in this group (electronic computing equipment or radio and television, on the one hand, and semiconductors, on the other; hosiery or tufted carpets and rugs, on the one hand, and synthetic fibers, on the other) can be looked upon as closely related families that provide the element of necessity. So it is not surprising that productivity gains for these families tend to run well above the average for the entire group (about 6 percent annually). Between the 1960s and 1970s, the annual average rate of productivity gain for electronic computing equipment increased from about a 4.5 percent to a 9 percent annual average rate, tufted carpets and rugs from about 3 percent to 7 percent. At the same time, the increase in the annual rate of productivity gains in semiconductors went from about 6.5 percent to 10 percent, and organic fibers from 2.5 to about 10 percent.

Inasmuch as improved performance in computers is not taken into account in the productivity estimates, the gain in the rate (i.e., the second derivative) between the 1960s and the 1970s is, indeed, very impressive. In the semiconductor industry a 40 percent annual average improvement in performance must be added to an 8 percent average rate of productivity gain for the entire period.

A major conclusion running through the statistical analysis is that the industries which performed well in generating better quality products also did well in achieving a high rate of productivity gains. When competition is keen, better quality means quality competition within tight price constraints.

Because they were not members of families, other industries in the A group did not fair so well in generating increasing productivity gains. These included service industry machinery, electric housewares and fans, distilled liquor, and vacuum cleaners. The A group of industries not only did best in its productivity rate relative to the other industries, but the weighted average annual increase in the rate of productivity gain (about 35 percent annually) was the best of the four groups.

The B Group

The single most important industry in this group is the automobile industry which, starting in the mid-1960s, had to exercise a higher degree of price restraint due to competition from foreign imports. Between the 1960s and 1970s, its annual rate of productivity gain actually slipped by about 10 percent. Trucks and mobile homes also fell in this group, and slippage in their productivity gains was somewhat greater. On the other hand, there were industries in the B group whose plants were much smaller, and, therefore, inherently more flexible. These included malt beverages, whose calculated dynamic efficiency was by far the greatest for the entire group; wines; knit underwear mills; metal household furniture; plumbing fixtures; metal foil; hard surface floor coverings; burial caskets; sewing machines; and lighting fixtures.

It must be acknowledged that the impact of environmental and safety regulations on the B group was somewhat larger than on the A group. This is not to say that the A group was unaffected; for example, regulations certainly affected the rate of productivity gain in the pharmaceutical industry. However, it seems reasonable to assume that the automobile industry was more seriously affected, and, therefore, the difference between the A and B groups would not have been quite so pronounced had it not been for environmental and safety regulations. As a rough guess, productivity performance of the B group of industries might have been, at the most, 10 percent greater. But, relatively speaking, it would be difficult to argue that the B industries did as well in keeping up their rates of productivity gains as the

As. In fact, there were a number of industries in the B group which had even greater productivity declines than the automobile industry, notwithstanding the fact that they were less seriously affected by environmental and safety regulations; these included marking devices, sewing machines, ophthalmic goods, artificial flowers, needles, pins, and fasteners.

The C and D Groups

The C category is dominated by industries engaged in making intermediate products of one kind or another: iron and steel foundries, paperboard boxes, concrete block, fabricated and structural metal, and internal combustion engines; footwear is also included. Prices in the C category went up more or less the same as shoes—about 8 percent annually during the 1970s. It can be safely assumed that in these industries firms were operating on the assumption that demand was relatively inelastic; that is, in nearly every case increases in prices far outweighed declines in output.

Case C is perhaps the most interesting, because, while, as might be expected, in only 14 out of 59 cases was the rate of productivity gain up in the 1970s, the distributions of both the gains and losses in productivity performance were highly bimodel; that is, while the median gain in productivity performance was about 100 percent, the median productivity loss was in the neighborhood of 75 percent. In about a dozen cases the productivity gains turned negative during the 1970s (meaning that decline in output was so great as to render an inefficient use of plants). However, there obviously is no way of knowing whether the fourteen industries which achieved the gains were operating at a higher preparedness parameter, or whether they were just plain lucky.

Finally, the important industries in the D group were also mainly engaged in making primary industrial products: industries such as logging camps, sawmills, primary lead, zinc, secondary nonferrous metals, and several types of machinery. By increasing their prices one standard deviation more than the average during both the 1960s and 1970s, these were the industries that clearly sparked an inflationary fire which did not begin to blaze until the steel industry engineered its protection from foreign imports beginning in the late 1960s.

Quite understandably, in the case of the D industries the results were even more lopsided; only one experienced a modest gain in productivity performance, and the others, fairly sharp declines, which means that the median loss for this entire group of industries was about 40 percent. But, completely take away the role of necessity as supplied by the hidden foot, and dynamic efficiency obviously will decline. In short, while there are relatively modest differences between the productivity performances of industries falling in the A and B categories, observing the behavior of the C and D industries is like going to an entirely different world. This occurred because, as PERK goes toward zero, firms in tight oligopolistic industries switched to raising prices, which, given the uncertainty of generating significant productivity gains, was a far more viable alternative.

I find it difficult to believe that, in the absence of regulation, productivity gains would have been more than 10 to 15 percent greater than they were during the 1970s. For example, while the C category contains industries, such as paper mills and steel foundries, that were certainly seriously affected by regulation, it also includes industries upon which the impact was relatively modest, such as cookies and crackers, chocolate and cocoa products, and machinery. But, in such cases, the data clearly show that large price increases were commonly associated with large productivity declines. Likewise, while the D category contains a small number of metal industries, it also includes other industries less affected by regulation, and behavior of prices and productivity was more or less the same. Consequently, while adjustment for the impact of regulation would make the contrast with the A group a little less sharp, it would not make a significant change in the overall picture. Quite clearly, the impact of environmental and safety regulations has been greatly exaggerated. It is as if steady productivity gains in all industries were preordained, and only regulation mattered!

Chapter 7
THE DYNAMIC RESPONSE TO FOREIGN COMPETITION

Nearly all economists favor free trade, because the fewer the restrictions on commodity flows, the greater will be the gains in static efficiency. In terms of this argument, trade does not increase the size of the pie, but, when countries can specialize in activities in which they have a relative advantage, a more efficient international allocation of resources is possible.

In this and the next chapter, I intend to make a more powerful argument for international dynamic competition, namely, that it provides a means for making lower-cost alternatives. This means that the consumer gains because real incomes can become larger; dynamic competition, in other words, increases the size of the pie. Conversely, restrictions on international dynamic competition have the effect of making real incomes smaller in countries which impose such restrictions. These restrictions can contribute to the stability of particular industries, but they do so at the expense of reducing per capita income.

As was pointed out in the last chapter, it can be predicted that, when a greater degree of price constraint is made necessary, productivity gains, on the average, will rise. This chapter shows that the principal element of necessity, which made industries exercise a greater degree of price restraint during the 1970s than the 1960s, was foreign competition. Compared with the reference group of industries discussed in the last chapter, this caused productivity gains to shift to the left of the 45 degree line. Chapter 8 will demonstrate that the price paid for imposing restrictions on foreign imports can be very high, indeed.

The first part of this chapter will address this important question: Does foreign competition make employment opportunities smaller than they otherwise would be, or is it the avoidance of such competition which penalizes employment opportunities? To answer this question, I shall consider all industries, whether they observed constant, increasing, or declining degrees of price restraint during the 1970s. In the second part of this chapter a more detailed analysis of the industries which exercised a higher degree of price restraint will be made.

Before turning to the main discussion, a point to be emphasized is that, contrary to the common wisdom, a higher rate of productivity gain is not to be regarded as an end in itself. It is true that when such gains occur as a result of price or quality competition with tight price constraints (which is involved in most quality competition), the consumer will benefit. On the other hand, productivity gains can come about simply because firms in an uncompetitive industry happen to obtain a "free ride" on advances in technology generated by a more competitive industry.

As figure 7.1 shows, the correlation coefficient between changes in prices and productivity across industries is unimpressive; and it is evident that quite a few industries not loath to raise prices do benefit from the free-ride phenomenon. Moreover, it can be seen that merely driving up the rate of productivity advance by a few percent annually would have no significant impact on the rate of inflation.

RESPONSE TO VARIOUS DEGREES OF PRICE RESTRAINT: AN OVERVIEW

In chapter 6 our concern was with industries whose changes in relative prices remained fairly stable during the periods 1959-1969 and 1969-1979. For a more general picture, now also consider industries which operated under either higher or lower degrees of price constraint during the 1970s than they did during the 1960s. The four categories of price performance are those already described in chapter 6. An industry exercising the highest degree of price constraint during the 1960s could move down three steps from A to D. Conversely, an industry exercising the lowest degree of price constraint during the first period and the highest during the second could move up three steps (i.e., from D to A). However, as it turns out, though some industries moved down three steps in price performance, none moved up three.

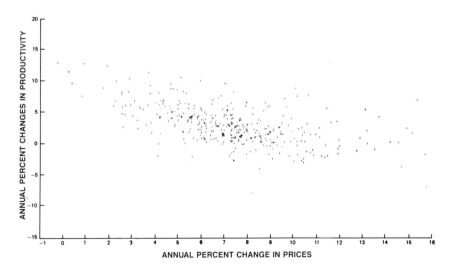

Figure 7.1. Productivity Versus Prices: 1969-1979: All Industries.

Since the industries which increased their relative prices by the same percentage during both periods have already been discussed, in the following they will be used only as reference points. As table 7.1 shows, the major factor involved in either pushing up the rate of productivity advance or allowing it to decline was a greater or lesser necessity to restrain price increases. In particular, increasing pressure (as reflected in declining relative prices) resulted in a 30 percent average step-up in the rate of productivity gain; and declining pressure, to a 40 percent average reduction. A greater interest in keeping costs down is also evidenced in smaller increases in input costs and wage rate increases between the two decades.

On the other hand, the essential reason costs and prices escalated as they did in the declining pressure groups is that no penalties were involved. As the last column of table 7.1 shows, during the 1970s each group of industries increased its output less rapidly than occurred during the 1960s, and industries whose price increases were greatest exhibited the largest reductions in output growth. It also should be noted that the last three groups in the table incurred no penalties whatsoever; that is, the average rate of price increase between the two decades outweighed the reduction in the rate of output by a factor of about ten.

One apparent anomaly in the table is that the 32 industries involved in a two- or three-step decline in price performance did not experience as sharp reductions in productivity gains as those involved in only a one-step decline. However, during the 1960s, productivity gains for this group were 60 percent higher than for those involved in only a one-step decline. Apparently, if industries have been dealing with a very high degree of challenge, the response to a lower degree will be somewhat slower. At the same time, while the response was not quite as drastic, every one of the ten industries involved in the three-step decline in price performance experienced a significant reduction in the rate of productivity gain.

Table 7.2 is intended to pave the way for a more detailed discussion of apparent differences in dynamic efficiency within those industries subjected to a greater degree of challenge. In the first column of the table is shown the percentage of industries which, in that particular group, experienced the same or an increasing rate of productivity gain during the 1970s. The second column shows the percentage of industries within a particular group that did not experience a gain in the productivity rate between the decades. Nevertheless, these industries managed, by making substitutions, to keep their input costs from rising more rapidly than occurred during the 1960s. It can be noted that even those groups subject to increasing pressures did not score nearly as well as they might have.

While decreasing pressures did not result in a decline in performance (considering, again, both productivity gains and input costs) of about one-fifth of the industries that moved down only one notch, as the pressures dropped off further the performance of all industries rapidly declined to zero.

The moral: Assume for the moment that a greater degree of restraint in raising prices can be equated with increasing competitive pressures, and a smaller degree, with diminishing pressures. Then, it can be predicted that, while in something like

Table 7.1. Increasing, Constant, and Declining Pressure Groups.

PRESSURE GROUP	(1) AVERAGE PRICE CHANGE (%) 1959–1969	(2) AVERAGE PRICE CHANGE (%) 1969–1979	(3) (2)/(1)	(4) AVERAGE PRODUCTIVITY INCREASE (%) 1959–1969	(5) AVERAGE PRODUCTIVITY INCREASE (%) 1969–1979	(6) (5)/(4)	(7) INCREASE IN INPUT COSTS 1969–1979/ 1959–1969	(8) INCREASE IN WAGE RATES 1969–1979/ 1959–1969	(9) RATIO OF OUTPUT GAINS
Three-step increase	—	—	—	—	—	—	—	—	—
Two-step increase (32 industries)	3.0	5.7	1.9	2.4	3.4	1.4	1.3	1.7	.9
One-step increase (104 industries)	2.2	6.5	2.9	2.5	3.3	1.3	1.9	1.7	.9
Constant pressure (145 industries)	1.3	6.8	5.3	3.2	3.0	1.0	1.7	1.9	.7
One-step decline (74 industries)	.5	8.1	17.9	3.6	2.4	.7	2.2	2.0	.7
Two-step decline (22 industries)	.6	12.9	22.1	3.6	2.0	.6	4.1	2.6	.5
Three-step decline (10 industries)	-1.6	11.8	—	5.9	3.6	.6	2.7	2.3	.5

Source: Derived from Bureau of Labor Statistics data, 1982.

seven out of ten cases there will be a positive response to increased competitive pressures, in about eight out of ten cases reduced pressure will result in a negative response. This is the first general conclusion. The second is that the industries subject to increasing pressures do a better job of creating employment opportunities than those subject to diminishing pressures. Thus, as table 7.1 shows, whereas the increasing pressure industries experienced growth rates that were only 10 percent below those of the 1960s, for the entire group of industries subject to diminishing pressures the decline in output growth was about 40 percent!

A third important conclusion concerns the relationship between equipment expenditures, on the one hand, and productivity and output growth rates, on the other. According to conventional wisdom, investment in new equipment and productivity growth are highly correlated. More savings, we are told, will mean more investment, and more investment, better productivity performance. Moreover, according to most growth models, there is a tight relationship between

Table 7.2.   Industry Responses to Feedback (Percentage).

PRESSURE GROUP	PRODUCTIVITY RATE REMAINED THE SAME OR INCREASED	PRODUCTIVITY RATE DECLINED, BUT INPUT COSTS DID NOT INCREASE SIGNIFICANTLY	TOTAL PERCENTAGE
Increasing 3 (none)	—	—	—
Increasing 2 (32 industries)	56	28	84
Increasing 1 (104 industries)	51	14	65
Constant (145 industries)	28	29	57
Declining 1 (74 industries)	16	5	21
Declining 2 (22 industries)	4	4	8
Declining 3 (10 industries)	0	0	0

Source: Derived from Bureau of Labor Statistics data, 1982.

Table 7.3. Productivity and Output Growth Versus Growth in Equipment Expenditures: Decade-to-Decade Changes (weighted averages).

	PRODUCTIVITY RATE	OUTPUT GROWTH	EQUIPMENT EXPENDITURE GROWTH (CONSTANT DOLLARS)
Industries whose relative prices declined	+30%	−10%	−34%
Industries whose relative prices increased	−40%	−40%	−24%

growth in output and growth in investment. But as the following tabulation shows, these contentions are not borne out by the facts.

Apparently industries which are hard pressed to restrain price increases are not only indifferent to savings on capital and labor inputs, but, when faced by competitive threats, will minimize capital growth in the face of rising demand. In other words, the notion that American industry can be revitalized by increasing investment expenditures does not stand up under close scrutiny. Revitalization is a matter of motivation, and not of preserving the appearance of a successful firm.

A DETAILED ANALYSIS OF THE INDUSTRIES SUBJECT TO INCREASING PRESSURES TO RESTRAIN PRICE INCREASES

The dynamic efficiency of industries consists of their ability to improve the competitiveness of their products when subjected to increasing pressures; and it can be measured by their ability to either retard or reverse a decline in output. Firms can respond to increasing pressures by (1) reducing costs (i.e., measurable productivity gains and input costs), (2) improving the quality or performance of their products (i.e., immeasurable productivity gains), or (3) by a combination of these. The main purpose of this section is to discuss, in quantitative terms, the importance of the first response. The discussion will include a description of the importance of foreign competition as a source of increasing pressure and the combined role of necessity and luck.

Table 7.4 summarizes the record of the 136 industries subject to increasing pressures to restrain price increases during the 1970s in terms of the relationship between their productivity and output responses. It will be recalled that the entire group of 136 industries enjoyed an average 35 percent increase in productivity gains during the 1970s. Yet we find that the productivity response to moving up in price performance was very diverse, indeed. In the first category are 13 industries whose productivity gains slipped slightly, while at the same time their output increased greatly: the mildly lucky industries. In the second category are 49 industries, about one-third of the total, which experienced declines in both output and productivity growth, despite the fact that many had generated productivity gains at a four percent or better rate during the 1960s: the unlucky industries. In the third category are 36 industries which responded by generating productivity gains at a more rapid rate; in many of the cases the gains in the rate were absolutely fantastic. Though able to retard but not reverse a decline in output rates, these industries were much luckier than the preceding group. And, finally, in the fourth category are 38 industries, about one-quarter of all those involved, which managed to turn adversity into opportunity; that is, quite remarkable increases in productivity performance were rewarded by significant increases in output: the luckiest industries of all. Thus, while there were wide differences in the rate that productivity performance improved, generally speaking, the most spectacular improvements were accompanied by the largest gains in output growth.

What happened in the case of the first group of 13 industries is not difficult to explain. With very few exceptions, industries do not achieve sizeable gains in productivity unless faced with *both* greater pressure to restrain price increases and output penalties. But, while these industries were faced with the necessity of narrowing the gap between their prices and those of substitute commodities, the gap was already so large that a highly determined effort to further reduce costs and prices was not required. Included in this group were products such as prefabricated wooden buildings, wood office furniture, cereal breakfast foods, and men's and boys' work clothing (principally blue jeans).

On the basis of the data shown in the table, it would seem that the second group of industries was not responding to a greater degree of necessity to generate productivity gains. Yet wage rates for this group of industries rose no more rapidly than did wage rates for the entire group of 136 industries, and input costs rose a good deal less. Such evidence suggests that the industries in the second category possessed the incentive but not the dynamic efficiency to sustain a high rate of productivity gain. Included in this group are industries such as commercial printing, copper rolling and drawing, newspapers, and a variety of clothing products (mostly men's).

Considering their competition, some of the industries in the third group were literally fighting with their backs to the wall. For example, the button industry quadrupled its rate of investment in equipment during the 1970s, increased its productivity performance from four to eight percent annually, permitted wage rate increases which were only 33% more rapid than during the 1960s, and yet, caught between competition from the zipper industry and foreign imports, it experienced a decline in output of about four percent annually during the 1970s. Other industries in much the same position included watches, clocks, brassieres, and men's and boys' separate trousers (as distinct from blue jeans). What this means is

Table 7.4. Analysis of Industries Subject to Increasing Pressure.*

Output response category	NUMBER OF INDUSTRIES		MEDIAN RATE OF PRODUCTIVITY INCREASE (%) 1959–69		MEDIAN DECADE-TO-DECADE CHANGE IN PRODUCTIVITY PERFORMANCE (%)		MEDIAN DECADE-TO-DECADE CHANGE IN OUTPUT RATE (%)	
	A	B	A (< 2%)**	B (> 2%)**	A	B	A	B
I Productivity rate down, output rate up (13)	0	13		2.0		−20		+60
II Productivity rate down, output rate down (49)								
< 50% Decline in output rate	5	13	1.0	4.0	−50	−30	−70	−30
> 50%	8	23	1.0	4.0	−30	−60	−50	−70
III Productivity rate up, output rate down (36)								
< 50% decline in output rate	9	14	1.0	3.0	+200	+35	−35	−25
> 50%	7	6	1.0	4.0	+200	+70	0	−75
IV Productivity rate up, output rate up (38)								
Output rate > 100%	10	10	.5	3.0	+900	+100	+150	−500
< 100%	9	9	1.0	2.5	+200	+40	+30	+25

Source: Derived from Bureau of Labor Statistics data, 1982.
* All results rounded.
** Average productivity rate during decade.

that, while the size of a firm and its financial ability to conduct R&D may not be of decisive importance in determining results, it is nonetheless a factor which should not be left out of account: if the industries in question had not been so pressed for funds, they might have generated more rapid productivity gains.

On the other hand, as table 7.4 shows, about two-thirds of the industries in the third group were able to keep their declines in the *rate of output gain* to 50 percent, which is certainly an impressive record. Among top performers, whose output increases were within 25 percent of what they were during the 1960s, were office machinery, costume jewelry, bottled and canned soft drinks, and photographic equipment.

Even more spectacular, however, was the performance of industries in the fourth group. For example, the sporting goods industry, which generated productivity gains at less than a one percent average rate during the 1960s, managed to speed up its dynamic performance to a five percent rate during the 1970s. Such a highly discontinuous change is not made without altering the culture of the firms involved; other examples are metal coating, millinery, and processed textile waste. During the 1970s, the median increase for industries whose productivity rate was three percent during the 1960s was about 100 percent.

It should be noted that the output response of the industries in the fourth group was not dependent upon only impressive productivity gains. For example, the engineering and scientific instruments industry managed to turn a negative growth rate during the 1960s into a positive growth rate during the 1970s. And it is quite unlikely that such an increase can be accounted for by a doubling of its productivity performance; as is generally known, substantial improvements in scientific instruments were made. While the productivity performance of the optical instruments industry more than doubled, this alone cannot explain why output growth increased from about one percent annually during the 1960s to almost 13 percent during the 1970s. Similarly, sales in the doll industry, which in real terms increased three times more rapidly during the 1970s than during the 1960s, were certainly responding to improvements in their products (e.g., the Star Wars dolls) as well as in their relative prices. Others in this group included farm machinery, fluid milk, phonograph records and tapes, power hand tools, and smoking tobacco. While the cigar and cigarette people acted on the expectation that demand for their products was quite inelastic, the same was not true with respect to smoking tobacco.

So, leaving out of account the 13 mildly lucky industries, what determined which industries would appear in the second, third, or fourth categories? The technologists will say, of course, that the technological bent of the industries is all-important. But it should be apparent that past productivity performance is a very poor predictor, indeed, of current productivity performance. Consequently, to explain the mystery, we must return to the proposition that the respective roles of luck and necessity are not independent.

As a first approximation to a reasonable answer, consider the data shown in table 7.5, whose matrix shows both the price performance category a particular industry

Table 7.5. Output Response Versus Previous Price Performance.

OUTPUT RESPONSE*	PRICE PERFORMANCE CATEGORY			
	D TO C OR D TO B	C TO B OR C TO A	B TO A	TOTAL
2	17 (45%)	29 (49%)	3 (11%)	49
3	13 (34%)	15 (26%)	8 (31%)	36
4	8 (21%)	15 (25%)	15 (58%)	38
Total	38 (100%)	59 (100%)	26 (100%)	123

Source: Computed on the basis of Bureau of Labor Statistics data, 1982.
D = worst price performance during the period 1959–1969; A = best.
* See table 7.3.

was in during the 1960s and the four productivity versus output categories it fell in during the 1970s. Quite clearly, firms in industries in which competitive pressures resulted in a continuous question-raising process had a greater probability of emerging in the fourth category, and those which were apparently sleeping, in the second category. Thus, of the industries that began in the B price performance category, only 11% ended in group 2 and 58% in group 4. Conversely, of those that began in the D price performance category only 21% ended in group 4 and 45% in group 2.

It must be remembered, however, that all of these industries were subject to increasing pressures to restrain price increases during the 1970s. How can we be sure, therefore, that their ability to raise sharp questions did not improve? To be more specific, if the distribution of productivity rate outcomes during the two decades is plotted around a 45 degree line, then on the basis of the arguments made in the last chapter, we can be quite certain that the distribution will shift.

To make it easier to judge the extent of the shifts, figures 7.2 and 7.3 show both the constant- and the increasing-pressure cases. Consider, first, the Ds in the reference group. When pressure to restrain price increases was equally weak during both the 1960s and 1970s, only one of the D group ended on the right side of the 45 degree line. But, in the increasing-pressure case almost half reached or crossed the line—and the median increase was almost 100 percent! Consequently, it is not at all surprising that as many as one-fifth of the industries shown in the best output category were recruited from a D under-pressure population. True, the distribution is highly bimodal. However, it is better to draw from a population in which something like half of its members are awake than to draw from one in which nearly all are sleeping.

Next, consider the C category. Here, out of 54 industries more than half had greater productivity gains during the 1970s; and, as was true with respect to the Ds, the median productivity increase was about 100 percent. On the other side of the

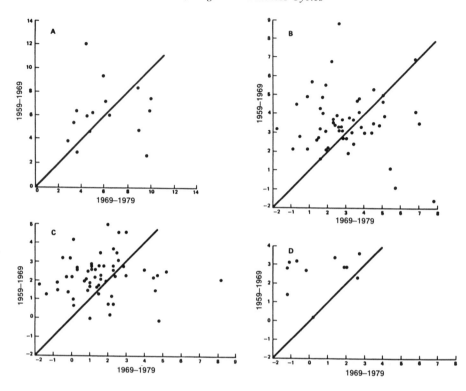

Figure 7.2. Constant Changes in Relative Prices:
1959-1969 versus 1969-1979 Productivity Gains.

coin, the median decline was about 60 percent; and since the gains in the productivity rate more than offset the losses, as the figure shows, this was actually a much better outcome than for the B group that was subject to constant pressure.

Finally, the B group that moved up to As during the 1970s actually did a good deal better than the As in the reference group.

Next, I will compare these conclusions with those resulting from the application of Wilcoxon's test. It will be recalled that for the reference groups, the following results were obtained:

A: score = 76; acceptance region, 30 to 106. B: score = 1089; acceptance region, 536 to 1004. C: score = 1329; acceptance region, 625 to 1145. D: score = 63; acceptance region, 11 to 55.

For the groups that exercised a higher degree of price restraint, the calculations are as follows:

Bs which moved up to As: score = 48, acceptance region, 81 to 219.
Cs which moved up to Bs or As: score = 1329; acceptance region, 625 to 1145.
Ds which moved up to Cs or Bs: score = 63; acceptance region, 11 to 55.

Again, the results are in accordance with the information gleaned from the diagrams. The Bs did better than even the As in the reference group; the Cs did better than the Bs in the reference group; and the Ds did better than the Cs in the reference group.

It would be nice if we social scientists had the ability to perform a controlled experiment in which precisely the same industries that had been operating at constant pressure for, say, two decades were subjected to increasing pressures in a third. Then we would have a controlled experiment for determining to what degree necessity changed the shape of the distributions. As of the moment, I cannot explain why some industries crossed to the right side of the diagram while others remained on the left. It is conceivable that of those that did or did not cross, some

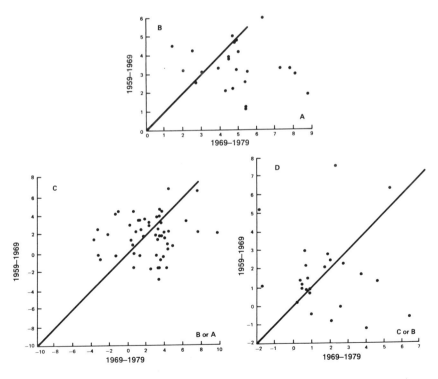

Figure 7.3. Declining Relative Prices: 1959-1969 versus 1969-1979 Productivity Gains.

were lucky to obtain the needed technological inputs, and others were not. But it is also conceivable that in the more successful industries basically different processes were at work.

Assume that in all of the C and D industries bringing about more rapid productivity gains is primarily a matter of imitation. If that were actually the case, when one firm in an industry discovered a combination of inputs needed to bring about a rapid increase in productivity gains, others under pressure would rapidly follow suit. On the other hand, if no firm were lucky, the industry would not be lucky.

Another plausible assumption is the following: Assume that firms making low rates of productivity advance have the choice of either imitating others or of doing better by developing ideas of their own. In other words, assume that, at a low level of productivity advance, a genuine short-term bifurcation develops in which firms can attempt to improve their situation either by imitation or a wide variety of means (including management and organizational changes) to generate more rapid productivity gains.

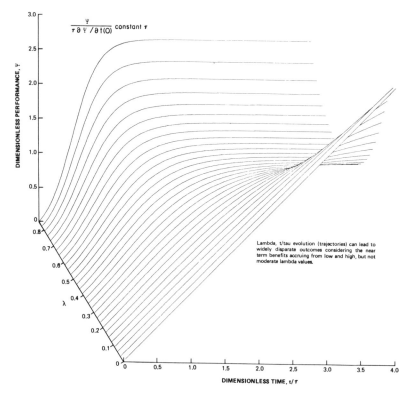

Figure 7.4. A Bifurcation of Short-Run Performance in Lambda Space.

The short-term trade-off in question is shown in Figure 7.4. The vertical axis indicates performance measured in dimensionless terms. The depth axis measures time and dollars, again, normalized. Note that this diagram involves no coupling of s-curves over time. The fact that the curves begin at the same slope means that all of the firms in an industry are assumed to start with the same opportunities for improving performance. The curves to the left of the point, where lambda = .5, do an increasingly better job of manufacturing their own opportunities. On the other hand, the phenomenon of diminishing returns is not exhibited in the curves on the right side of the diagram, because it is assumed that the firms on the right are importing most of their ideas. When lambda = 0, this is the limiting case of pure imitation (which seldom, if ever, occurs in the real world). The bifurcation results from the fact that at some point, in this single family of s-curves, a modest lambda-value curve must intersect a curve whose value of lambda is lower, but which does not exhibit diminishing returns to the same degree. In brief, rather than trying to climb up the left bank, there may be an already proven concept to copy. Our common sense should tell us that manufacturing ideas and importing them are alternatives; and, in the short run, firms sometimes can do a good deal better by importing them.

How can anyone operating on the right side of the ravine hope to catch up in the long run? The point is that, if firms cross to that side, they are likely to be stuck there: while in some periods they might enjoy good luck, in others they can expect to encounter bad luck. The irrationality involved is illustrated by figure 7.5. The ticks in the diagram demarcate each new generation of products. It will be noted that in the long run the bifurcation completely disappears, with the higher lambda operators always having a clear advantage over those who put their emphasis on short-term profits. Why, then, does the bifurcation disappear? Under two assumptions it would not: if either progress came to a halt, or the firm could be certain of finding the needed technological inputs. The first assumption is unreasonable, because rival firms usually do not act to make such a prophecy self-fulfilling. The second assumption is unreasonable, because there is no guarantee that there will be successful ideas to imitate.

Now, there is no way of knowing whether the C and D groups, which greatly improved their productivity performance in the 1970s, did so because, following the imitation route, they were lucky to find good ideas to imitate, or whether they developed the ability to be more self-reliant. Or it might be found that, while the right-side model was working in some industries, the left-side model was working in others. The question that remains to be answered is whether greater pressures provided by foreign competition had a long-term effect in increasing the values of gamma.

It also should be kept in mind that, even if imitation were initially employed, it might be used as the springboard for dynamic processes. There are many cases in which new firms have copied and then improved a technology. Thus, while newly founded U.S. steel firms at first religiously copied the process utilized for making

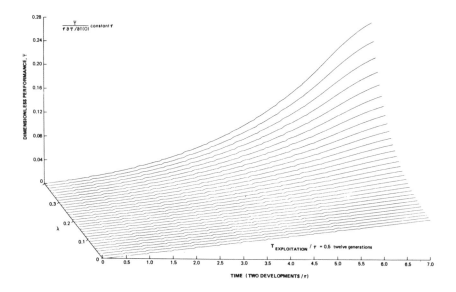

Figure 7.5. The Bifurcation Disappears.

Bessemer steel in Britain, apparently this was not regarded as an end in itself: by 1900, both United States and German firms were selling steel to Scottish shipbuilding firms. Nor was copying allowed to become a habit, as when German cutlery manufacturers began copying Sheffield steel or Japanese camera makers began copying German cameras. To consider a quite different kind of case: when children imitate other children, the construction of the mental images involved in such imitation can result in the first required step toward genuine creativity. But, in either event, understanding the long-term impact of international competition is very important.

In *The Prince*, Machiavelli sought to give advice to ancient princes on the basis of the information he collected. On the basis of the statistical information just discussed, my advice to modern-day princes is as follows:

1. Firms in industries that are unwilling to keep PERK high enough to generate productivity gains at more than two percent annually are neither being fair to themselves nor to their competitors. When caught by adversity, highly discontinuous change and a great deal of good luck will be required to stem a decline in output.

2. Firms in industries whose productivity performance is in the range of five percent do not require highly discontinuous changes to deal with negative feedback, but, to give themselves the best chance, the members of those

industries ought to be thinking that good luck favors a continuously questioning firm.

In other words, my advice to modern princes is (1), if you are going to satisfice, do not satisfice at a low level of performance, and (2), if you are going to satisfice at high levels, be a worried satisficer. Most of the industries in the second category of table 7.5 were satisficing on the basis of a four percent annual productivity gain, and from that seemingly favorable position, their fortunes declined.

THE ROLE OF FOREIGN COMPETITION

The principal reason 136 industries exercised a higher degree of price restraint during the 1970s than they did during the 1960s was foreign competition. About two-thirds of these industries were involved in a significant amount of import competition, export competition, or both. The more detailed matters to be considered in this section are (1) the difference in the output penalties of those industries involved and not involved in foreign competition, and (2) the importance of previous price performance as a predictor of how well particular industries will fare in international competition. To do this, the following procedure was employed: for each industry in the first three output-response categories, shown in table 7.5, approximately one out of five was selected at random, and, because of its special interest, two out of five in the last group were randomly selected. The reason for this procedure is simply that matching BLS data and international trade data is a very laborious process.

Table 7.6 lists groups I, II, and III industries that are subject to increasing pressures (one out of five industries in these categories); and table 7.7 lists the group IV industries subject to increasing pressures (two out of five in this category) in order of importance of the industry, as measured by contributions to total output. The numbers in parentheses refer to their productivity gains during the 1960s.

As far as group I industries are concerned, not only those shown in the table, but all 13, were not subject to a significant degree of foreign competition. Had they been, no doubt their productivity performance would have been better.

About half of the group II and III industries were affected by foreign competition: they were either subject to a significant degree of import competition or were subjecting other countries to a significant degree of import competition (or both). But the interesting conclusion is that, with the exception of copper rolling and drawing, which was in the lowest price performance category during the 1960s, the industries involved in foreign competition had smaller output penalties than those not involved. It is safe to assume that the primary reason industries such as toilet preparations, products of purchased glass, and primary batteries did so well is that they were fairly competitive even in the 1960s. Is this a robust conclusion or did it simply result from having chosen this particular group of industries? To answer this

Table 7.6. Performance of Particular Industries: Groups I, II, and III: 1969–1979/1959–1969.

INDUSTRY	PRICE PERFORMANCE CATEGORY	OUTPUT GAINS	PRODUCTIVITY GAINS	WAGE INCREASES	INPUT COST INCREASES	EQUIPMENT EXPENDITURE INCREASES (CONSTANT DOLLARS)	IMPORTS AS A PERCENTAGE OF DOMESTIC SUPPLIES	EXPORTS AS A PERCENTAGE OF SALES
GROUP I								
Prefabricated wooden buildings	C/B	2.8	.3 (2.0)	1.5	3.0	1.3	< 1	< 1
Cereal breakfast foods	D/C	1.6	.7 (3.0)	2.0	3.2	4.5	< 1	< 1
Cheese	D/C	1.4	.8 (3.0)	1.7	1.8	5.0	4	< 1
GROUP II								
Toilet preparations	C/A	.9	.9 (4.0)	1.8	1.1	.5	< 1	35
Products of purchased glass	C/A	.8	.2 (1.0)	2.1	1.4	.2	4	< 1
Newspapers	D/C	.6	.4 (1.0)	1.7	1.8	1.1	< 1	< 1
Commercial printing	C/B	.8	.6 (2.0)	1.7	2.1	1.7	< 1	< 1
Primary batteries	C/B	.7	.7 (5.0)	1.6	1.7	.5	7	14

Coper rolling & drawing	D/B	.1	.5 (3.0)	2.0	1.1	.5	5	4
Frozen fruits	C/B	.7	.8 (3.0)	1.8	1.5	.6	<1	<1
Canned fruits & vegetables	C/B	.4	.8 (4.0)	1.7	1.9	.1	<1	<1
Hardware	C/B	.4	.5 (4.0)	1.9	1.7	.4	3	3
Cutlery	C/B	.2	.2 (1.0)	1.8	2.1	.2	2	<1
GROUP III								
Asbestos products	C/B	.8/−1.3	4.5 (1.0)	2.3	3.4	.5	9	7
Tobacco stemming	C/B	.6	3.6 (1.0)	1.9	13.2	1.5	N.A.	<1
Watches & clocks	B/A	.2	1.1 (4.0)	2.4	.8	.6	40	8
Creamery butter	C/B	.3	1.1 (7.0)	2.0	2.0	1/−5.7	<1	<1
Photographic equipment	B/A	.7	1.1 (6.0)	1.9	1.0	.2	10	15
Men's & boys' separate trousers	B/A	10.3/−.4	1.1 (3.0)	1.8	1.4	17/−2.4	15	3
Buttons	C/B	1.1/−4	1.9 (8.0)	1.3	.3	1.7	17	>1

Source: Derived from Bureau of Labor Statistics data, 1982; 1982.

Table 7.7. Performance of Group IV Industries: 1959–1969/1969–1979.

INDUSTRY	PRICE PERFORMANCE CATEGORY	OUTPUT GAINS	PRODUCTIVITY GAINS	WAGE INCREASES	INPUT COST INCREASES	EQUIPMENT EXPENDITURE INCREASES (CONSTANT DOLLARS)	IMPORTS AS A PERCENTAGE OF DOMESTIC SUPPLIES	EXPORTS AS A PERCENTAGE OF SALES
Farm machinery	C/B	2.3	2.6 (1.0)	2.1	2.9	1.2	13	21
Fluid milk	C/B	2.6	1.9 (3.0)	2.1	2.9	−3.4/1.1	<1	<1
Women's & misses' blouses & waists	B/A	1.2	1.1 (4.0)	1.4	1.4	.6	22	<1
Flat glass	B/A	2.3	1.8 (3.0)	2.6	4.7	.9	3	8
Ceramic tile	B/A	3.8	1.5 (3.0)	1.5	13.9	.3	50	<1
Phonograph records	B/A	1.1	4.9 (1.0)	2.6	1.4	.5	2	9
Paints & allied products	C/B	1.1	2.1 (2.0)	2.0	3.0	.8	<1	3
Power hand tools	C/B	1.1	2.2 (1.0)	2.0	1.8	1.0	4	8

Optical instruments	B/A	11.6	2.3 (3.0)	2.1	-2.6/16.3	.6	18	36
Dolls	B/A	3.3	2.2 (3.0)	1.8	9.8	.8	6	3
Chewing & smoking tobacco	D/C	1.9	3.5 (1.0)	1.6	3.4	1.0	9	< 1
Engineering & scientific instruments	C/B	-1.3/2.5	2.0 (2.0)	2.3	3.0	2.3	< 1	34
Sporting goods	C/B	2.2	6.9 (1.0)	2.4	3.0	3.6	19	12
Brass, bronze, & copper foundries	C/B	1.1	3.0 (0)	2.0	1.5	2.4	NA	NA
Metal coating	D/B	2.1	5.0 (0)	2.4	2.6	1.1	NA	NA
Women's & misses' suits & coats	C/A	2.1	2.0 (2)	1.2	2.0	.1	14	< 1

Sources: Derived from Bureau of Labor Statistics data, 1982; *1982 U.S. Industrial Outlook* (Dept. of Commerce); *U.S. Exports* (FT 610/Annual 1979) (Bureau of the Census); and *U.S. Imports* (FT 210/Annual 1980) (Bureau of the Census).
Note: Numbers in parentheses are productivity gains 1959–1969.

question, I picked, at random, from group II industries, another sample of 20 industries, matched them with the foreign trade statistics, and found that the result was much the same.

With respect to the 16 group IV industries shown in table 7.7, notice, first, that more than one-third of this group was in the second price-performance category during the 1960s, and the two industries which began in the fourth price-performance category were forced to climb to the second price-performance category. With the principal exceptions of fluid milk, paints, and dolls, all of these industries were significantly involved in foreign competition. (Because foreign trade statistics are not available for brass, bronze, and copper foundries or metal coatings, there is no way of knowing what accounted for the increased degree of price pressure on these particular industries.)

The main point brought out by figure 7.7 is that, while a much larger proportion of those listed participated in foreign competition than those in table 7.6, a number of these industries performed spectacularly in turning adversity into opportunity: notably, farm machinery, flat glass, ceramic tile, optical instruments, dolls, engineering and scientific instruments, sporting goods, and women's and misses' suits and coats—all industries in which, judged by previous price behavior, there is a good deal of domestic competition. To test whether this was a robust result, again, I picked another group of 16 industries and matched them with the foreign trade statistics. This second group of 16 industries did not have as many spectacular gains in output as the first group. But the overall conclusion is much the same; when industries, already competitive, engage in foreign competition, the results can be highly beneficial.

Tables 7.6 and 7.7 also bear out an important point reached earlier, namely, there is no close relationship between investment in equipment and productivity growth. Thus, in the group IV industries, which registered the highest gains in output growth, only six out of sixteen cases indicated increases in investment outlays; in the other ten industries, reductions commonly were about 50 percent. And much the same is true of the group III industries.

There are three important conclusions which emerge from the analysis of the entire group of industries subject to increasing pressures. First, while foreign competition was not the only source of increased price pressure, the industries forced to deal with greater pressures did better outputwise than those which dealt with smaller pressures; that is, while output for the entire group of higher-pressure industries declined by less than ten percent between the two decades, output in the lower-pressure groups declined by about 40 percent. True, many labor union leaders view foreign competition as their main threat. But job opportunities are threatened even more by industries that do not engage in domestic or international competition and, instead, raise their prices several times more rapidly.

The second conclusion is that, almost without exception, plants in these competitive industries are relatively small as compared with, say, automobile or steel plants, and are generally more labor-intensive. The same is true of the constant high-pressure industries, such as computers and semiconductors, which were also involved in a substantial amount of international competition. Does this mean that small is beautiful? Not necessarily. As compared with U.S. doll, semiconductor, or computer plants, Japanese automobile plants are relatively large operations. My best guess is that in the United States only relatively small plants possess a high degree of type II flexibility.

In any event, we can certainly conclude that Schumpeter's argument (taken up by Galbraith and, more recently, by Nelson and Winter) that large firms have an inherent advantage over smaller ones in bringing about progress is wrong.[1] Certainly, large firms have an important advantage in financial ability, and if only R&D spending mattered they could always win the game. But motivation matters even more in dynamic performance. The results of the above analysis clearly show that there is nothing like a hidden foot to supply that motivation.

The third conclusion is that, if we consider all of the highly dynamic industries in America—those in the increasing pressure group and the high-performance constant pressure group—then, with the exceptions of fluid milk and computers, it hardly can be said that the most dynamic part of the U.S. manufacturing economy is currently engaged in producing the basic necessities of life. On the contrary, American capitalism works best when consumers' demand response is highly uncertain, either because competitive forces within particular industries are working or because other industries are providing substitutes. For example, competition from the television news media undoubtedly caused newspapers to exercise a greater degree of restraint in raising subscription prices during the 1970s than during the 1960s. Or, in still another case such as cutlery, demand may be elastic simply because it is relatively easy to defer the consumption of the item in question. Contrary to the common wisdom, prices are determined by costs only when producers assume the demand for their products is inelastic, that is, only when they have no incentive to discover ways to reduce costs.

THE FIRST DYNAMIC LAW OF ECONOMICS ✣

To be more specific, according to the first static law of economics, supply curves always slope upward, with output determined at that point where the supply and demand curves intersect. However, this law applies only at a given time, when the supply curve can be taken as a datum (PERK = 0). In other words, the static law is a special case of the first dynamic law, which states that when firms act on the expectation of elastic demand curves—price elastic, quality elastic, or both—costs will be determined by dynamic efficiency. The essence of dynamic efficiency, it will be recalled from an earlier chapter, is to put good luck on the side of the entrepreneur while minimizing the consequence of bad luck; and this requires firms with a high degree of randomness in their internal and external communications. In addition to providing less expensive or better alternatives, firms may also discover entirely new products. Assuming that demand curves are sloping downward before and after inventions, according to the second law, such events are described as discovering loopholes in the law of supply and demand. The essential difference between the static and dynamic laws is that, whereas the first applies to situations in which firms act on the assumption that they are confronted with little risk and uncertainty, the second does not. Firms' attitudes toward risk and uncertainty enable them to take advantage of feedback that otherwise would be ignored.

As an illustration, consider having a house built by a contractor. Before you sign the contract, the builder may make many constructive suggestions to reduce costs or improve quality: this is second law (dynamic) behavior. But, make any changes after construction has started, even just to leave out a closet, and the price will rise astronomically: this is first law behavior (after the contract is signed the contractor is a monopolist).

The dynamic law does not contradict the classical law of supply and demand; on the contrary, it is needed to protect it. Assume that the cost of all alternatives were not given as of the time the economic universe was created, and that, when pressed, firms in some industries were able to reduce costs (or improve the quality that can be provided on the basis of a given cost). If we know that such events actually do occur, the first dynamic economic law must be used to explain them, because, if we did not, the effect would be to bring the static law into disrepute, which, since it can make very good short-term predictions, would be very unfortunate. And the same would be true if we refused to admit the possibility of firms' discovering loopholes in the law of supply and demand, when they, in fact, do so to exempt themselves from the harsh penalties provided by that law. Suppose that some inventions, such as the zipper or inside plumbing, could not be made because they invalidated the classical law of supply and demand. If this were the case, mankind could not improve its well-being. So, to permit the occurrence of such events, the first dynamic law is needed to protect the static law!

Chapter 8
DEADWEIGHT DRAG

Deadweight drag occurs when a relatively few industries generate supply shocks for a wide variety of industries, thereby exposing the latter to a continuing series of artificial shortages. The effect is described as a *drag* rather than a *loss* because, as long as the effect continues, it results in a series of losses. As a consequence, sales in both domestic and foreign markets are smaller than they otherwise would be. Dynamic efficiency is jeopardized because, if measured against gains in total factor productivity (including capital and input costs, as well as labor hours), both capital and input costs are increased. It is generated when firms act on the assumption that they have the ability to pass on cost increases to consumers with no penalties to themselves; the effect is much the same as would occur if some strategically important resources were to be progressively denied to an economy. During the 1970s, the two main sources of deadweight drag were the large increases in the costs of steel and energy inputs, which contributed equally to rising manufacturing costs.

RESPONSE TO DIMINISHING PRESSURES

Data for the twenty-five most important industries, measured in terms of their contributions to manufacturing output, are shown in table 8.1. The numbers in the first column show for both periods the actual rate of price increase and the number of grades an industry slipped in its price performance. While increasing prices by only .2 percent annually during the first period placed the petroleum industry in the B group, raising them by 17 percent annually during the second period placed it in the D group; hence, it slipped two price-performance grades. The data in the remaining columns represent changes between the decades. The table includes all major industries in the declining pressure groups; those which generated dead-weight drag are marked with asterisks.

Before turning to a discussion of these data, one general point should be made about their interpretation. It should not be assumed that all industries listed in table 8.1 will continue to exercise the lack of price restraint in the 1980s that they did in the 1970s. The cases in which a greater degree of price restraint might be expected in the future will be dealt with in the discussion of the role of foreign competition.

Table 8.1 illustrates vividly two points that were made in the last chapter: *First*, when betting that a decline in price pressure will result in a productivity decline,

Table 8.1. Responses of Twenty-Five Largest Industries to Declining Pressure: 1969–79/1959–69.

INDUSTRY GROUP	PRICE CHANGE	PRODUCTIVITY GAINS	INPUT COST INCREASES	WAGE RATE INCREASES	OUTPUT CHANGES
Petroleum Refineries*	0.2 to 16.9 B to D	.5	6.6	2.0	1.0
Blast furnaces & steel mills*	1.0 to 10.6 B to D	1.0	2.7	3.5	.9
Plastic & rubber*	–.2 to 7.2 A to C	.7	2.0	2.2	.7
Radio & communications equipment	–.8 to 4.7 A to B	1.4	1.0	1.6	.3
Refrigeration & heating equipment	–.8 to 5.0 A to B	.6	1.1	2.5	.6
Prepared animal feeds	0.7 to 8.1 B to C	.5	2.6	1.8	.7
Roasted coffee	0.9 to 10.6 B to D	.2	4.2	1.8	.2
Plastic material resins*	–2.3 to 10.7 A to D	1.1	2.5	2.4	.4
Aluminum rolling & drawing*	0.2 to 8.8 B to C	.9	1.9	2.3	.7
Paperboard mills*	–.3 to 7.1 A to C	.7	1.8	2.1	.4
Ready mixed concrete*	1.1 to 8.9 B to C	.4	3.4	2.9	.9
Shipbuilding	1.3 to 8.0 B to C	1.4	1.8	2.2	.9

Industry					
Cyclic crudes & intermediates*	−1.2 to 13.3 A to D	.3	3.3	2.3	.3
Plywood*	.9 to 8.5 B to C	.6	2.0	2.1	.5
Ball & roller bearings*	−1.0 to 7.9 A to C	.6	2.0	2.0	.3
Cotton weaving mills*	.3 to 8.7 B to C	.4	−1.4/7.2	1.8	.3
Sheet metal works*	.5 to 10.1 B to C	.2	2.8	1.5	.6
Motors & generators*	0.1 to 7.7 B to C	.5	1.9	2.5	.4
Railroad equipment*	1.2 to 9.2 B to C	.5	1.2	2.4	.5
Industrial inorganic chemicals*	1.2 to 8.8 B to C	.5	2.9	2.0	.9
Fertilizers*	0.2 to 8.8 B to C	.9	2.8	1.7	.8
Bags	.4 to 9.0 B to C	1.0	3.6	2.3	.5
Primary aluminum*	1.0 to 9.4 B to C	.9	1.9	3.5	.7
Metal doors*	0.6 to 8.1 B to C	.3	4.7	1.9	0
Iron & steel forgings*	1.9 to 11.6 C to D	2.9/−1.3	2.1	2.0	3.3/−1.0

Source: Computed on the basis of information supplied by the Bureau of Labor Statistics, 1982.
Note: The numbers in parentheses show the change in ranking with respect to price performance.
* Industries generating deadweight drag.

one cannot count upon winning every bet—but, in the case of major industries the odds are something like four out of five. According to the new supply-side economics, which draws heavily on ideas contained in classical microeconomics, when it comes to generating a higher rate of productivity gain only positive incentives matter; that is, the chance of making higher profits is all important. However, negative incentives, in particular the risk of having a market stolen away by a competitor (i.e., hidden-foot feedback), are just as important; and any analysis which leaves negative incentives out of account is, at best, an analysis engaged in telling only half of the truth. In fact, very large drops in the rate of productivity gain occur when firms are not "taxed" by their competitors. *Second*, while the speedup in price increases certainly undermined the stability of the economy during the 1970s (with many industries in this category experiencing half of the output gains enjoyed during the 1960s), they were eminently rational from the point of view of the firms involved. Thus, as the table shows, in almost every case, prices rose to the extent that, even at reduced rates of output growth measured in constant dollars, the total sales of products increased. It also can be seen that, though wage rates and input costs of the industries shown in table 8.1 increased more rapidly than those of industries subject to increasing pressures, on the whole, prices rose more rapidly than either wage rates or input costs. In short, during this period, at least, the industries in question can be described as cost-plus industries; that is, they engaged in much the same behavior as defense industries. Of course, in defense industries, output must be curtailed when the sum of the overruns threatens to exceed the defense budget. Nevertheless, inasmuch as particular contractors do not know if theirs or another program will be cut, it pays to behave as if the demand for their systems is quite inelastic. Much the same is true of the industries shown in table 8.1: the leaders of the firms cannot be sure that one or another of the industries in question will not have to deal with a greater degree of price constraint in the future. But as long as their expectations are confirmed, it can be assumed that they will continue to behave the same.

Assuming for the moment that more rapid increases in relative prices during the 1970s were caused either by the absence of foreign competition or an increasing degree of protection from foreign competition, to what extent did the distributions of productivity advances move to the left instead of the right side of the 45 degree line? Again, we have no way of knowing how this same group of industries would have fared if they had been subject to increasing pressures to hold prices down rather than to reduced pressures. Nevertheless, statistically speaking, the results were very much as might have been predicted; that is, whereas increasing pressures to hold prices down resulted in distributions which were to the left of those industries that observed constant degrees of price restraint during both periods, declining pressures had just the opposite effect. Figures 8.1 and 8.2 indicate quite clearly that the differences between being subject to greater and lesser degrees of pressure were, indeed, quite spectacular. According to Wilcoxon's test, the As that fell to Bs (whose score was 142, and whose acceptance region was 46 to 143) did slightly poorer than the As in the reference group (whose score was 77, and whose acceptance region was 30 to 106). The Bs that declined in price performance (whose score was 792, and whose acceptance region was 295 to 608) did much poorer than the Bs in the reference group (whose score was 1089, and whose acceptance region was 536 to 1004). On the other hand, there were too few cases (11) in the Cs to meet the requirements for the test.

What these conclusions suggest is that, when industries are subject to greater or lesser competitive pressures, the results are asymmetric; that is, the gains in productivity performance, when the pressures become greater, exceed the losses when they become smaller.

Are people from the firms involved actually aware that they are suffering from an acute shortage of hidden-foot feedback? I talked to some high officials from a firm which is in one of the most important industries included in table 8.1. Not only were they aware of the lack of challenge, but they described at length how difficult

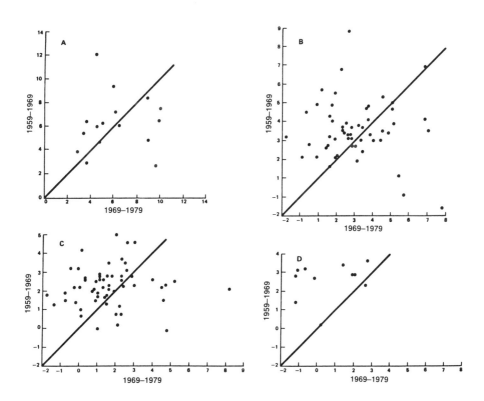

Figure 8.1. Constant Changes in Relative Prices: 1959-1969 versus 1969-1979 Productivity Gains.

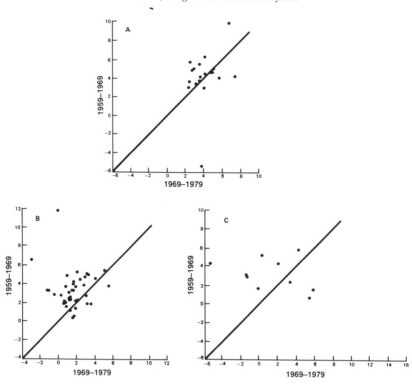

Figure 8.2. Increasing Relative Prices: 1959-1969 versus 1969-1979 Productivity Gains.

it is to reorient the efforts of a firm suffering from a prosperity they believed was temporary. Apparently, polite and cozy relationships develop that are almost impossible to change as long as the firm is making a great deal of money. They asked me, "Do the politicians really understand what is happening?" I replied that, since they probably talked only to presidents of companies, the politicians did not understand the terrible economic predicament of the United States. One of the officials present retorted: "Professor, if you or I were president of this company, we wouldn't be talking like this, either!"

THE ROLE OF FOREIGN COMPETITION

In a few cases, high transportation costs impede workable international competition (e.g., cement and glass containers). Next are the industries in which there are tight domestic oligopolies, but which are not challenged by import competition to restrain domestic price increases. The aluminum industry, wherein four firms account for three-quarters of domestic output and imports amount to less than ten percent of domestic consumption, comes within this category. Moreover, once steel prices started to increase ten percent annually, why should aluminum producers refrain from increasing their prices by nine percent annually? The paperboard industry is highly capital intensive and features little dynamic competition in any country. The newspaper industry is one of its largest customers, and lack of competition in final-products industries commonly leads to unprogressiveness on the part of the firms engaged in supplying technological inputs.

A third category of industries includes those in which there is a good deal of foreign trade, but not much foreign competition. For example, in the field of commercial fertilizers, imports and exports exceeded ten percent; but, judged by price behavior, the competitive forces were very weak. In the field of industrial inorganic chemicals, imports increased from 10 to 15 percent during the 1970s. However, in this case it is a well-known fact there is a high degree of international specialization in imported and exported inorganic chemicals. The plywood industry provides a similar case; that is, the imports are primarily hardwoods whose prices have risen by almost as much as domestically produced softwoods.

Finally, there is a fourth category of industries which, by the late 1970s, had reason to be more cautious in raising prices. For example, although there was a lapse of competition with respect to cyclic crudes and intermediates (a branch of the petrochemical industry), by the late 1970s price increases had slowed down. Refrigeration and heating happen to be cases in which the United States obtained a substantial export advantage by being one of the first to pioneer the technologies. While this provided the industries with an advantage to raise prices during the 1970s, apparently it is an advantage that will not last; that is, the Japanese have targeted air conditioning for a large export market. A similar case, in which Japanese imports are rapidly increasing but have not reached a level to change the expectations of domestic producers, is ball bearings. Ball bearings are produced according to universally accepted tolerances. By the late 1970s, price competition began developing in the ball-bearing industry. Another such case is plastic materials; the Japanese are currently building plants in Saudi Arabia to produce lower-cost plastics.

In short, the general picture which emerges is this. For reasons that cannot be understood without additional research, some industries were threatened by foreign competition; but, because it did not result in a constraint on price increases, the results cannot be defined as workable competition. There are other industries in which foreign competition cannot be expected to work very well because of large transportation costs; and there are still others which have been lucky, not having been targeted earlier by the Japanese.

However, the two industries which provided the principal sources of deadweight drag, because of their importance and impact on a variety of industries, are the first two shown in table 8.1: petroleum refining and steel. They are also likely to be the two most persistent sources of deadweight drag in the future because, in the first case, OPEC is a cartel that the United States is powerless to control; and, in the second case, the steel lobby has made itself so powerful that the government seems to have as little control over it as it has over OPEC.

Because of the recent declines in gasoline prices, many people have assumed that the petroleum industry is unlikely to provide the shortage problem in the future that it did during the 1970s. To be sure, it is probably unlikely that gasoline prices will again increase at the rate they did before the 1974-1975 downturn. For one thing, there is a continuing shift to smaller cars; for another, there has been a significant decline in the proportion of oil output accounted for by the Arab countries. Nevertheless, Saudi Arabia continues to have an awesome ability to punish cartel violators—and cartel discipline is easier to enforce during economic upturns. When unemployment is prevalent, people become wary about taking long motoring vacations. With rising gasoline costs, many, who otherwise would drive their own vehicles to work, take buses or join car pools. Moreover, the domestic petroleum industry, which has had a long record of government support, can hardly be said to provide a shining example of robust competition. While entry into the petroleum refining business would have helped prevent the large price increases shown in table 8.1, obtaining the financial backing needed to enter this industry is virtually impossible as long as the refinery in question does not have an assured supply of crude oil.[1]

On the other hand, in the case of the steel industry, an increasing freedom of choice to raise prices is clearly traceable to increasing import restrictions which began in the late 1960s. I will summarize briefly only those measures which were taken to exempt this industry from the full impact of foreign competition. I do not propose, however, to deal in detail with the phoniness of the arguments which claimed that, were it not for Japanese and European steel firms selling to the United States at less than full cost, the American steel industry would be in good shape.[2]

During the 1950s, the average annual price increase for steel rose significantly, and the industry was then regarded as a principal source of cost-push inflation. But, by the mid-1960s, the steel industry was not able to maintain its near static equilibrium, because the boundaries of the system were no longer stable. This helps to explain why, during the 1970s, productivity in the steel industry did not decline from the already low level of 1.5 percent annually. During the 1960s, the steel industry was forced to increase outlays on equipment at the fabulous rate of more than ten percent annually (while adding very little to total steel-making capacity); and a significant part of this investment did not begin to bear fruit until the 1970s. Only then, when there was a sharp decline in competitive pressures, did the rate of investment decline. This does not mean that the steel industry became less ambitious in its investment plans; in addition to acquiring a petroleum company, there have been a number of other unrelated acquisitions. Protection, therefore, meant that, from an investment point of view, once freed of the necessity to invest in their own industry, steel firms were far less constrained in the ways they might diversify their investment portfolios.

Until the mid-1960s, the position of the U.S. steel industry was a very familiar story: an industry basking in its glory because the United States was still the largest steel producer of the world, and its imports had not exceeded 6 percent of domestic consumption. However, by 1968, imports had risen to about 18 percent. Moreover, the sleeping giants were challenged not only by foreign imports. Due to the discovery of the electric process by a small steel firm located in Illinois, so-called mini steel plants were able to produce steel at around the same cost as blast furnaces which cost something like ten times as much to build.

The story of trade restrictions began in 1969, when the American Iron and Steel Institute and the United Steel workers joined forces to prevail on the Johnson administration to restrict imports as a means of providing the breathing space for making productivity improvements required to make American steel products once again competitive in international markets. This led to voluntary restrictions of imports by Japanese and European producers, and to a 23 percent increase in the price of steel between January and August 1971,[3] when President Nixon, whose ability for dealing with difficult problems was not markedly different from the presidents who preceded or followed him, imposed general wage and price controls. Consequently, while the increase in steel prices was almost brought to a halt in 1974, when price controls on steel were finally abolished, steel prices rose by 28 percent.[4]

In any event, as of the mid-1970s, price and wage controls on steel were no longer needed, because, in the face of a serious worldwide recession, Japanese and European producers returned to their old habits of dumping steel at relatively low prices. As a historical footnote, it may be added that Japanese and European steel firms did not begin the practice of "dumping." At the turn of the century, when the American steel industry was still highly competitive, Scottish and English company executives accused American and German steel firms of doing the same thing![5] Given the undisputed technological superiority of English and Scottish steel-making firms, how else, except by engaging in unfair competition, could they undersell their competitors? What distinguishes the far greater entrepreneurial ability of U.S. steel companies when it comes to interfering in the political process? Though a high tariff on British steel was not imposed until the time of the Great Depression, as early as 1974 a congressional steel caucus was formed; and the 1974 Trade Act required foreign producers to increase their prices whenever a recession prevented domestic producers from earning a profit. Following this, a trigger-price mechanism (TPM) was adopted which, in the name of preventing unfair competition, had the effect of raising steel prices in all countries. To be sure, officials in the Carter administration did muster enough courage to temporarily abolish the TPM. But the compromise finally reached was one in which trigger prices were 12 percent higher than before.[6] And, while as of this date it is too early to say what particular measures the Reagan administration will take to cloud the issue, a very safe prediction is that the ultimate effect of U.S. policy will be the formation of some kind of international steel cartel. If Japanese and European steel firms are to fall in line with respect to protecting the interests of the United States, assurance will obviously be needed that they can charge what the traffic will bear at home. Curiously enough, in the foreword to a Department of Commerce publication, *1982 U.S. Industrial Outlook*, Malcom Baldridge, the Secretary of Commerce, made the following whimsical statement: "Lean and hungry management is as necessary today as it was when this Nation was formed."[7] Yet, in the section of the report on the steel industry, it is said:

> In spite of TPM, the trend of steel imports remains upward, and their share of the U.S. market is increasing. In late 1981, with imports rising sharply and likely to exceed the 1980 total by one-sixth, the effectiveness of the TPM was under close scrutiny by government administrators and steel company officials.[8]

What, then, does it mean to keep an industry lean and hungry? According to information supplied by Adams and Mueller, during the 1970s Japanese steel firms not only surpassed U.S. firms in labor productivity, but their costs were currently something like one-third less.[9] In addition, according to a General Accounting Office study, the quality of Japanese steel is significantly better; and Japanese steel producers have shown a greater willingness to meet the demands of American steel users for special kinds of steel.[10] As of 1980, wage rates in the U.S. steel industry were almost twice those of steelworkers in Common Market countries, and more than twice what they were being paid in Japan.[11] Apparently, what it means to keep such an industry lean and hungry is to keep it in business without going quite so far as to guarantee its rate of profit in bad times.

THE IMPACT OF PRICE SHOCKS

The last topic to be taken up in this section is the quantitative effect of deadweight drag. Deadweight drag is caused by supply shocks; that is, by relatively large price increases of basic commodities used in a variety of industries. To be sure, if only the price of oil rose as a consequence of OPEC's actions and not the price of coal, the supply shock would not have been as great. But evidently there was not enough competition in coal mining to prevent this from happening. Likewise, instead of deterring large price increases for steel, the sizeable increases in the prices of various steel products permitted the prices of substitutes to rise. As we already have seen, while the price of aluminum rose about nine percent annually during the 1970s, the price of steel rose by 11 percent. Consequently, prices for aluminum could be increased more rapidly while at the same time providing an attractive substitute for steel. And much the same is true of plastic and lumber products where competition has never been robust.

Were it possible to obtain annual estimates for the amount of steel consumed in manufacturing industries, there would be no need to be concerned about substitution effects, because they already would have been taken into account in their steel consumption figures. But, because such information is unavailable, it was assumed that steel consumption was proportional to changes in real output in manufacturing. This was equivalent to ignoring substitution effects; however, as was already pointed out, the cost of steel substitutes rose almost as much as steel prices. Moreover, it is safe to assume that the short-run substitution effects were mainly felt in construction, rather than in manufacturing.

On the basis of the above assumption, calculations of deadweight drag were made as follows: First, on the basis of data contained in the *1977 Census of Manufacturers*, it was found that the cost of steel inputs used in all manufacturing industries accounted for 7.7 percent of total manufacturing costs, while fuel inputs accounted for 4.1 percent.[12] This means that manufacturing costs were almost twice as sensitive to increases in the costs of steel inputs as they were to increases in the prices of fuel inputs. Second, increases in the cost of steel were adjusted to remove the impact of rising energy costs. Third, on the basis of indices of fuel costs contained in the *Census of Manufacturers* and BLS data, adjusted to take into account rising energy costs to the steel industry, the impact on manufacturing prices was computed. The following table gives the percentage of change due to each of these resources for the two overlapping periods, 1967 to 1977 and 1971 to 1977.

In short, it would appear that steel had quite as large an impact on manufacturing costs as did fuel. And, when a single industry can drive up costs by ten percent in the entire manufacturing sector of an economy, it should be apparent that this is a quite different story from that involved in the deadweight loss from monopoly power. Involved here is a simultaneous misallocation of resources and a penalizing of the more competitive industries.

Given the fact that both wages and prices were rising very rapidly during the period 1974-1977, a ten percent impact on manufacturing prices may not seem very significant. But let us assume that during this period Milton Friedman had been the Chairman of the Federal Reserve Board; and, by practicing some kind of monetary

Table 8.2. Percentage of Cost Increases in Manufacturing Attributable to Rising Costs of Steel and Fuel Inputs.

RESOURCE	1967–1977	1971–1977
Steel	10.8	11.6
Fuel	8.2	9.7

Source: Computed on the basis of the data contained in *1977 Census of Manufacturers*: "Fuels and Electric Energy Consumed," vol. 1, chapter 4; "Primary Metals Industries," Parts 2 33-A-1.

Table 8.3.   Price and Wage Increases in the
Steel Industry, 1969–1979.

| YEAR | PERCENTAGE INCREASES | |
	HOURLY WAGE	PRICE
1969	6.8	4.7
1970	5.7	6.7
1971	10.4	8.1
1972	14.4	5.9
1973	8.1	2.6
1974	15.4	28.3
1975	16.6	18.2
1976	11.9	5.5
1977	9.4	9.1
1978	9.5	11.0
1979	10.7	10.0

Source: Derived from Bureau of Labor Statistics,
1982.

wizardry, he had been able to keep the overall price level absolutely stable—he still could not have prevented a ten percent annual increase in steel costs. Even during the heyday of the 1960s, profits on sales in manufacturing came to less than ten percent. So the impact would have put profits in manufacturing as a whole in the red; and this, of course, would have spelled a slump in investment and a recession which, according to Friedman, simply could not occur with a firm hand on the monetary throttle.

The above calculations only tell part of the story. All economists who live in the real world know that the absence of dynamic competition and a push for rapid wage increases (combined with the imposition of highly restrictive union work rules that diminish the possibility of significant productivity gains) go hand in hand. As table 8.3 shows, in such cases it is by no means clear whether prices are pushing up wages or vice versa.

Let us assume for the moment that, during the 1960s, wages in the competitive industries were increasing no more rapidly than productivity gains. Can anyone imagine such generous wage increases in the steel industry with the more competitive industries being able to hold the line on their wage increases? You are the manager of, say, a firm in the machinery industry. How do you explain to the union officials involved that what is good for workers in the steel industry is not good for them? Although there is no accurate way to calculate the secondary impact on wages induced by deadweight drag, it seems safe to assume that this effect would have been at least as great as the primary effect.

The conclusion? It should be apparent that, even without the impact of OPEC, what happened in steel would have been enough to bring about a first-rate downturn.

A FURTHER CONSEQUENCE OF DEADWEIGHT DRAG

A second consequence of deadweight drag is that it slows down industries which become attached to a basic industrial culture that has become obsolete. In particular, for many years the U.S. machine tool industry has been geared for making tools for high volume and specialized operations. I have been able to gather from historians that this occurred not because the machine tool industry itself took a leading role in pioneering such operations; rather, it tailored its practice to suit the needs of the automobile industry, which was long regarded by the leaders of many mature industries as the model to follow. Indeed, as long as industries have neither a good deal of internal competition nor are challenged by foreign competition, *Fordism* makes good sense.

On the other hand, as was brought out in an earlier chapter, the strategy employed by the Japanese in their automobile industry is the very antithesis of Fordism; that is, it is a combination of types I and II flexibility. However, we can be quite certain that these practices also characterize other Japanese industries. We know that, since the mid-1960s, Japan has become the world's leading exporter of numerically controlled machine tools that can be employed for either type I or II flexibility. Indeed, the fact that Japan is the world's largest producer of numerically controlled machine tools probably says a good deal more about the nature of Japanese management than all of the books that have been written on that subject.

The general picture of what has happened to the U.S. machine tool industry is a very familiar story. As of 1960, there was a bare trickle of machine tool imports, and the United States was the world's principal exporter.[13] But during the 1960s, imports increased very rapidly—probably, at first from Germany—with the consequence that, by the late 1960s, imports were more or less equal to exports.[14] However, by 1980, metal-cutting and metal-forming machine tool imports exceeded exports by about 30 percent.[15] And, as of 1981, almost 50 percent of machine tool imports came from Japan.[16]

One interesting question is: Which U.S. firms are buying Japanese machine tools? Did the highly competitive industries that made fabulous productivity gains turn to Japanese numerically controlled machine tools? Or, as one would like to believe, is the U.S. machine tool industry so diverse that, if some parts of it are not responding to the challenge to escape from Fordism, others are?

One cannot ignore the fact that during the past fifteen years Britain's machine tool industry almost went down the drain, no doubt, as a reflection of the fact that, except for the British chemicals industry, competition in that country has been weak. Nor can one ignore the fact that a country which relies mainly on other countries for its machine tools simply cannot hope to remain a major industrial power. Commodities such as steel can be entirely imported with no consequence whatsoever with respect to a country's industrial might. But a country which comes to rely mainly on others for its machine tools is one that has to rely on other countries for its thinking.

Indeed, there is no better way of indicating how little common sense people use when they say: "If we could only cut the government back to the size it was when Herbert Hoover was president, American industry would be in great shape!" The government has not jeopardized the future of the American machine tool industry; sadly, the blame lies instead with the inaction of machine tool users, whose principal concerns when ordering a new piece of equipment are to avoid changing the specifications of parts and the delivery date. The lack of steady competitive pressures makes the machine tool industry, at best, a feast-or-famine industry. Ironically, whereas at least some machine tool makers are aware that, by tying their fortunes to the U.S. automobile industry, they have hitched themselves to a falling star, public officials seem to have no comprehension about what is happening. Unwisely, all is blamed on foreign subsidies.[17] Whatever role subsidies may or may not have played in the case of Japan, the fact remains that numerically controlled machine tools were developed on the basis of a contract from the U.S. Air Force, and in the form of defense contracts the U.S. machine tool industry has been highly subsidized.

Furthermore, United States firms are doing very well, indeed, in the export of farm machinery and power hand tools. And, if machine tool firms are not doing nearly as well, how else is this to be explained other than that they are being dragged down by highly uncompetitive major industries?

Chapter 9
DEADWEIGHT DRAG AND BUSINESS CYCLES

The last three chapters were concerned with decade-to-decade changes in the rates of productivity advance. This chapter will deal with explaining why, during the 1970s, economic downturns became far more serious than they were during the earlier postwar period. The common thread running through all of these chapters is the difference made by the lack of steady competitive pressures. Such lack not only resulted in many industries becoming increasingly subject to deadweight drag during the 1970s, but it also resulted in ever larger economic downturns. The industries which accelerated deadweight drag during the 1970s also pushed the economy into larger downturns by initiating price shocks that could be controlled only by pursuing a highly restrictive monetary policy. As will be pointed out in this chapter, the essential reason productivity gains in these industries exhibited a highly cyclical form is that negative feedback was supplied to them only during economic downturns. It also will be shown that industries which had to respond to price shocks during the upturn were driven into even deeper downturns than those engaged in initiating the price shocks. Because the initiators of supply shocks suffered less from the consequences of their actions than did other industries, this form of behavior continued.

Industries whose behavior can be described in terms of the first static law of economics act to make business cycles more severe; and those whose behavior can be described in terms of the second law play no role whatsoever in generating more serious cycles.

Before turning to a more detailed discussion, two general statements are in order to minimize the risk of having my arguments misconstrued. First, although I am convinced that strong and steady competitive pressures promote economic stability—even though they cannot completely eliminate the business cycle—my position is entirely different from the University of Chicago rational expectations school. According to that argument, cooling down inflation and returning to a state of far less serious business cycles is mainly a matter of dampening workers' expectations for higher wages. That argument, as I will show, is complete nonsense. It is not the rational expectations of the worker with respect to price increases that drives inflation during an upturn; rather, it is the rational expectations of firms which act on the assumption that the demand for their products is quite inelastic. Under present policies, major industries which generated deadweight drag during upturns in the past will do so in the future. The problem, therefore, is not one of changing workers' expectations, but, rather, one of providing management of firms in industries with the expectations associated with an elastic demand curve for their products.

I would also like to make it clear that by making these arguments I consider myself to be a good Keynesian. One of Keynes's major messages was the need for deficit financing when nations are involved in serious depressions. I not only agree with that prescription, but I also think that the idea of a constitutional amendment requiring a balanced federal budget is absolutely ridiculous. It is like telling someone that he dare not become ill with pneumonia, because if he does there is nothing that can be done for him. I am entirely in agreement with the proposition that taxes should be raised under conditions of excess aggregate demand; for example, they should have been raised during the war in Vietnam.

Being a good Keynesian does not require that the logic of Keynesian economics be stretched so far that microactions never can have any macroeffects. Keynes himself argued that the savings habits which may be good for the stability of the individual may not be good for the economic stability of a nation. By arguing that the generators of deadweight drag may be engaged in highly rational actions from their own point of view, but not from the point of view of the nation, I am merely carrying the logic of Keynes's argument one step further.

Being a good Keynesian means more than just believing that what is true of the parts is not necessarily true of the whole. Keynes's great genius consisted of raising questions which economists had never thought about before. Real Keynesians, therefore, are in agreement that whenever difficult economic circumstances arise new questions need to be raised.

In particular, a trade-off is involved between steady pressure to generate productivity gains (via the mechanism of dynamic competition) and intermittent pressure (via the business cycle): a trade-off where the less steady the competitive pressures, the more serious the downturns. This trade-off can be observed not only within the U.S. economy but among various economies, such as the United States and Britain, or West Germany, Japan, and Sweden. It also will be argued that, while the intermittent-pressure option can result in very significant productivity gains on the part of industries that must respond to deadweight drag, it is not a choice that can be pursued indefinitely.

To understand the reasoning behind this conclusion, consider the following three economies: (1) an economy composed of many small industries whose value of PERK is close to zero when their business is booming, but which have only a negligible influence on each other; (2) an economy in which the value of PERK is high in all industries; that is, due to more or less continuous competitive challenges, firms receive negative feedback (i.e., hidden-foot feedback) quite regularly; and (3) a mixed economy composed, in part, of not only economies 1 and 2, but also major industries that, by raising prices substantially during upturns, generate a cyclical form of deadweight drag.

Case 1: Independent Cycling. As an illustration, consider the "pea-coat cycle" in Britain. Pea coats, which are both warm and highly water repellent, were developed first for British sailors. Shortly after World War II, the British manufacturers of these coats offered a version for the civilian market, and output of pea coats increased greatly throughout the 1950s and part of the 1960s: a period of "local prosperity." A local recession occurred when other European countries introduced more competitive products which were less expensive and more stylish. However, a new period of local prosperity developed when, in Swedish department stores, well-made and elegant British manufactured pea coats were offered for sale at a 35 percent lower price than those made either in Sweden or other European countries. This is the pea-coat cycle about which I learned from talking to a British banker, whose firm had made loans to the manufacturers of pea coats. It is this clue that finally enabled me to understand that cycles in productivity can be caused by intermittent competition. As far as the United States is concerned, I have no way of explaining what particular events caused the irregular cycles. I can only say that they occurred in about fifty relatively small industries (e.g., manufactured ice, dehydrated fruits, canned vegetables, soups, shortening and cooking oils, and tobacco stemming and redrying), and the pattern was strikingly similar to that which occurred in the pea-coat cycle, namely, a dying out of productivity gains when output rates peaked, and there was a resumption of an upward trend only when output rates sagged and prices declined. It should be kept in mind that the main increases in the *absolute* level of productivity were made only when coming out of those cycles.

It is not certain that the cycles brought about by irregular competition will always cancel. We cannot discount the possibility that several of these cycles will combine to produce a modest economic downturn. For statistical reasons alone, it is not surprising that no country has been able to completely avoid even modest economic downturns. When major industries, such as automobiles or steel, are suddenly confronted with a greater degree of foreign competition, this obviously will produce larger cycles: the larger the industries involved, the smaller will be the probability that the cycles will cancel.

Similar cycles can be caused by flexible exchange rates. When a country devalues its currency which, in turn, makes its products more uncompetitive, this puts pressure on firms in other countries to reduce costs. While studying U.S. data, I found that in something like 100 industries, where no such cycling had occurred before 1970, up to three clearly defined cycles occurred after 1970. This is not to imply that it was wrong to adopt flexible exchange rates. In the first place, while there was a bunching of productivity declines in 1970 and 1971 (after which President Nixon set up the U.S. Productivity Commission!), in the following years, as might be expected, the cycles spread out and acquired a highly random character. Second, although this particular conclusion is subject to further examination, I found on the basis of rough calculations, that in a majority of the cases the trend in productivity advances was actually higher after the introduction of flexible exchange rates. Though this may not have been what the proponents of flexible exchange rates had in mind, intermittent shocks apparently can have the effect of driving up a trend. Since the early 1970s this cycling has tended to be highly random and has had no significant impact on increasing the amplitude of the business cycle.

Case 2: Strong and Steady Competitive Pressure. Consider an economy composed entirely of industries with a high value of PERK, e.g., the computer, semiconductor, doll, smoking tobacco, and scientific instruments industries. Unlike the pea-coat example, in these industries, firms are challenged by their rivals almost continuously, which is to say, hidden-foot feedback occurs regularly. A snapshot of such industries taken at any one moment will reveal that while some firms in an industry are suffering from local recessions, others are experiencing local recoveries. If we assume that when workers are laid off by firms suffering from local recessions they are hired by firms experiencing local prosperities, then the only unemployment that can exist in such an economy is frictional unemployment. In many such industries, total output and employment increase while at the same time individual firms experience both local upturns and downturns. Consequently, the conclusion is the same as for case 1 above: business cycles occurring in this economy have to be initiated by outside forces.

Case 3: A Mixed Economy. Some industries in this economy are also included in cases 1 and 2. In addition, a mixed economy includes industries which are like those described in case 1 in one respect— they are subject to very irregular negative feedback. They differ because their impact on the rest of the economy cannot be ignored; that is, by generating supply shocks which drive up prices in a number of industries during a business recovery, they bring about price increases that can be throttled only by a serious downturn. Moreover, unlike the pea-coat example, they generate productivity cycles which are highly consonant with general business conditions. Thus, during the upswing of the business cycle, when prices and output are rising, the *rate* of productivity gain in these industries declines—and begins to increase again only when, during a general economic decline, they receive negative feedback in the form of declining sales and increasing pressures to restrain price increases.

Examples of industries exhibiting such behavior during the 1970s are petroleum refineries, steel mills, aluminum foundries, nonferrous metals, and sawmills. Single major industries, for example, petroleum or steel, have the ability to generate such large price shocks during an upturn that inflation can be brought under control only by a major downturn. It is safe to assume that had the steel industry engaged in the same price behavior during the 1960s as it did during the 1970s, the business cycles during that period would not have been as minor.

The main reason a trade-off is involved is that the balance of forces between industries, which do or do not generate deadweight drag, need not always remain the same. In particular, if major industries are not protected from foreign competition during one time period, but are protected during the next, the cycles will become larger; which is to say, the economy will become less stable from a dynamic point of view. In an economy in which there is such a shift, we can expect a changed pattern of price, output, and productivity behavior. However, in economies which are dynamically stable we can predict distinctly different patterns.

One reason the trade-off cannot be pursued indefinitely is that, as the economy is pushed into ever larger cycles, at some point the capability of many industries to deal with negative feedback will be exceeded. Another reason is that, as the more competitive industries are pushed into large cycles, their ability and motivation to make continuing huge investment outlays are weakened; in fact, one of my major statistical findings is that industries contributing least toward causing business cycles suffer most from them. This, in turn, is the primary reason self-correcting mechanisms are not at work.

How can these conceptual observations be related to statistical findings? Let us assume that because the case 1 industries generate cycles at random intervals they can be safely ignored. With respect to case 2 industries, a picture of the relationship between price and output changes and productivity gains is shown in panel 1 of figure 9.1. Note that prices show no significant tendency to cycle, because it is assumed that competitive forces are more or less continuously working. It cannot be assumed that these competitive industries will experience no cycles in output and productivity. Although such industries may play no role in precipitating

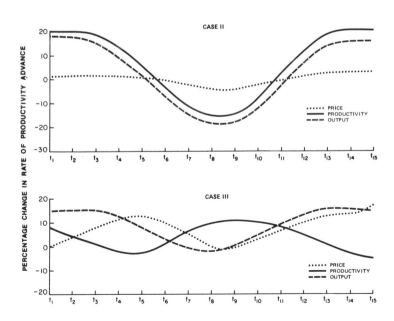

Figure 9.1. Cases 2 and 3 Profiles.

economic downturns, they certainly will be affected by them; and when capacity is less fully utilized, there will be penalties in productivity—with sharper penalties the more that scale economies are emphasized. In this case, we should expect output and productivity changes to occur more or less concurrently, with no significant lags between the series.

A picture of the relationship between prices, productivity gains, and output changes for uncompetitive industries is shown in the bottom panel of the figure. Note that the productivity rate peaks before the output rate; and the rate of productivity advance quickens only after there have been sharp output and price penalties. In contrast to the industries shown in panel 1, the cycling is very sharp. In short, figure 9.1 shows the difference in behavior between industries which are subject to continuous competitive pressures and those in which pressures are highly intermittent. As economists have long observed, in prosperous times capacity tends to be overutilized and skilled workers are in very short supply. While this view can explain changes in absolute productivity around a trend line which has a zero rate of increase, it cannot explain differences in the *rate* of productivity growth. The industries in question improve their absolute productivity at the greatest rate when emerging from downturns.

STATIC VERSUS DYNAMIC THEORIES
OF THE BUSINESS CYCLE

According to the monetarists, an economic world in a static equilibrium is the natural state of the economy. Hence, in their view, only actions of the monetary authorities or exogenous price shocks can bring about economic downturns. But, according to the neo-Keynesians, quite unpredictable changes in spending decisions can result in either inflationary or recessionary gaps. To them the appearance of these gaps is to be regarded as the natural state of the economy.

I believe that, during long periods of prosperity, the natural state of the economy will be one of increasing predictability and decreasing stability. However, from a dynamic economist's viewpoint, even under the best circumstances, complete economic stability is neither attainable nor desirable. For two reasons my views differ from those of the neo-Keynesians. First, while I do not deny that business cycles can occur for the reasons they suggest, I also believe that microforces can increase inflationary pressures during upturns and the severity of downturns. Second, I do not assume that the role of private firms is purely passive. Their actions not only affect the severity of downturns, but their behavior can be affected by government policies. For this reason I do not subscribe to the view that, short of major economic downturns, the government should attempt to prevent all minor downturns. Assume an economy in which downward pressure on prices due to strong competitive forces and upward pressure due to deadweight drag roughly offset each other: a situation which was approximated throughout most of the

1960s, when the relative prices of some products increased while others declined, with prices in manufacturing remaining relatively constant. Under such circumstances, when the *demand* for money is relatively stable, the supply should be managed accordingly—and President Kennedy should have acted as firmly in opposing a tax cut as he did in the Cuban missile crisis.

Keep in mind, however, that a classical equilibrium did not prevail during this period. On the contrary, there were some industries which assumed that the demand for lower-cost products was quite elastic: they acted in terms of the second economic law. This meant that the shifting of production functions, which competitive pressures induced, was causing economic motion away from an equilibrium. Conversely, even during the early 1960s, there were a few industries that increased prices and allowed productivity gains to slip: the lack of competitive pressures was causing motion toward a static equilibrium. When these two forces cancel, it can be assumed that inasmuch as the demand for money will be stable so should the supply. There might be relatively small economic fluctuations for a number of reasons. Assuming there are uncompetitive major industries that generate productivity gains only during downturns, such downturns can produce some positive results. By contrast, suppose that it were possible via a policy of fine tuning to completely iron out even minor economic fluctuations. Would this be desirable? By no means. Those industries receiving negative feedback only during downturns would raise prices even more during upturns; instead of declining, the amplitude of the cycle would increase! While strong and continuous competitive pressures in all industries are to be preferred over intermittent pressures resulting in relatively small economic fluctuations, these fluctuations are to be preferred over ever larger ones.

Do these arguments move me out of the camp of the Keynesians and into the camp of the monetarists? By no means. Keynes was not interested in preventive medicine; he was interested in finding ways to make the patient recover from the Great Depression. Trying to remove even minor cycles with compensatory and fiscal policies can result in very poor preventive medicine.

To carry the discussion one step further, suppose that competition were so robust in one country that the sum of prices times output declines. Such an economy can be described as one with a high degree of motion, and under these circumstances the monetary authorities should allow the money supply to contract. Trying to keep the money supply stable would be equivalent to increasing it in a country in which movements toward and away from a static equilibrium canceled each other.

Finally, consider a situation in which deadweight drag becomes so serious that prices begin to rise. If the monetary authorities either respond or fail to respond to such pressures, they will be either validating an unwarranted change in relative prices, thereby making it easier for unfit industries to survive, or jeopardizing the survivability of the more fit. From the point of view of maintaining the dynamic stability of the economy, it is imperative that measures be taken to assure that a relatively small number of industries are not given the freedom of choice to subject an entire economy to larger and larger cycles. To maintain approximate economic stability, the maintenance of appropriate producer expectations with respect to the role of the hidden foot is all important.

From what I have been able to gather, the reasoning behind the above propositions does not entirely accord with the University of Chicago Economics Department's position. To be more specific, Milton Friedman has propounded the view that there is a "natural" rate of unemployment which resembles a razor-sharp equilibrium. If actual unemployment is above the natural rate (i.e., an equilibrium condition under which workers' expectations are geared to a zero rate of inflation), real wage rates will continuously decline and, if unemployment falls below the natural rate, wages and prices will spiral upward with no breaking point.[1] This spiraling is caused by expectations of becoming adjusted to higher and higher rates of inflation and workers bargaining in terms of real, instead of money, wages. The only way to dampen a vicious inflationary spiral is to have a stern monetary policy aimed at cooling down workers' expectations and allowing unemployment to rise to whatever figure is required to prevent prospects of further inflation from developing.

Given Friedman's basic assumption—a static general equilibrium world in which production functions never change and dynamic competition is forbidden to occur—it cannot be argued that there is anything logically wrong with his conclusion. Imagine an island completely isolated from the rest of the world, where the natives are free to specialize in whichever fields their talents are best suited. They mutually agree never to tamper with the production functions handed down to them at time of the creation of their economic universe. On Friedman Island so many substitutes are included in its natural endowment that no native can hope to raise the price of a product without the fear of instant retaliation. To assure that markets will clear daily, Robinson Crusoe acts as auctioneer.

Of course, on this island, Friedman acknowledges there is "stochastic variability in demands and supplies."[2] To avoid the penalties involved in leaping before they look, by acting on the basis of best estimates, the natives must perform as Bayesians by buying information to determine the divinely preordained stochastic variability of the economic universe. (According to the logic of Bayesian probability theory, new prior probability estimates need never be discovered; that is, an endless number of experiments will reveal the true picture.[3]) Chimpanzees have demonstrated an amazing capability to do what Bayesians cannot do: when food supplies are denied, they can be observed inventing tools to assist in obtaining their food: thus they establish new hypotheses. However, the natural endowment of Friedman Island is so bountiful that the natives need not be as imaginative as chimpanzees. To make the point in another way, since the sea is always perfectly predictable around Friedman Island, and every other aspect of life quite as predictable as the tides, sailors need never observe the feedback required to deal with an unexpected shifting of the winds. No one need make guesses about an uncertain future on the basis of ambiguous feedback, because life has been so beautifully arranged for the natives that they never have to exercise that particular freedom of choice. Information may be lacking to make optimal choices; but, in that event, the natives could buy information just as they could any other commodity.

The three fundamental propositions underlying the religion propounded by the Chicago School would seem to be these: First (Frank Knight notwithstanding), the economy is always seen to be either in a static equilibrium or tending toward such an equilibrium. Second, a static equilibrium is inherently stable (presumably, because of its mathematical properties). Third, competition is defined in such a mechanical manner that it can play no role as an economic stabilizer.

On the basis of these assumptions, the Friedman Island model is correct. The economy is made to be dynamically stable by assumption. According to this model, producers have absolutely no control over their prices; but workers have an unlimited ability to increase their wages! Therefore, only action on the part of monetary authorities can prevent inflation from developing. Because all unexpected events have been completely outlawed, no economic disturbances can occur, except for unwarranted action on the part of the monetary authorities; only they can rock the boat.

There are economists whose main quarrel with Friedman is whether in the real world, where there is no mechanism to insure that markets clear daily, a static equilibrium is necessarily quite as stable as Friedman Island.[4] This, however, is not the crucial weakness of his argument. Rather, it completely abstracts from the essential nature of a dynamic capitalistic system: a system of decentralized risk taking for assuring that, on the basis of positive and negative feedback, firms will try as best they can to seize new opportunities. Dynamic capitalism works because, when some firms undertake significant risks, penalties are simultaneously imposed on firms that otherwise might be inclined to maximize only their short-term profits. Consequently, when firms respond to such pressures, not only do they minimize their own risks, but a process is at work which internalizes risks for society as a whole: there is a far greater degree of constraint on price increases than there otherwise would be. Because in Friedman's world risk internalization is not allowed, it can perform no role whatsoever as an economic stabilizer. Dynamic competition also internalizes risks as far as workers are concerned. If unit wage costs (i.e., increases in wage rates divided by increases in productivity) are allowed to rise, the firm faces the risk of a local recession, and workers risk finding themselves unemployed. In industries where there is a low degree of constraint on raising prices, due to a lack of dynamic competition there will also be a low degree of constraint on raising wages and the adoption of highly inflexible union work rules. For example, before the rising tide of foreign automobile imports, wages in the U.S. automobile industry were not tied to increases in automobile productivity, but to increases in productivity in the economy as a whole. Only when pressed by foreign competition was this formula for determining wage increases abandoned, and the quality circle approach for improving productivity gains and reliability adopted. In a dynamic equilibrium the forces that determine wages are not completely independent of those that determine prices.

Friedman's argument is completely irrelevant to the real world. It ignores the role of negative feedback as both a deterrent to wage increases and as a stimulus to the productivity gains that insure the dynamic stability of the economy. According to Chicago's economics department, all these considerations can be safely swept under the rug by assuming that a static equilibrium is inherently stable. Inasmuch as the stability of a static equilibrium is, in part, an empirical question, I will leave further discussion of this point until the end of the chapter. On the basis of empirical evidence presented in the last two chapters, which industries do you think contribute most to economic stability—those operating under tight price constraints that, generally speaking, were responsible for rapid continuance of productivity gains; those operating under much looser price constraints and featuring declining productivity gains; or those moving away from or toward a classical equilibrium? The theoretical question: Do the mathematical properties of a static equilibrium determine its stability or is the stability the result of more fundamental properties?

A few classical, old-fashioned economists continue to believe that describing the economic world in completely deterministic terms is the very essence of scientific respectability! What they fail to recognize is that the validity of scientific theories is not demonstrated by providing them with a "scientific" appearance. In science the ultimate test of all knowledge is the ability to make predictions. When some scientists find others arguing that the physical world must behave in terms of their logical preconceptions, rather than the way it can be observed to behave, they describe the error as one of "imposing pompous preconditions on one's subject matter."[5] As far as the economics fraternity is concerned, there is absolutely no one who excels Friedman in laying down pompous preconditions: not only must there be a reserve army of the unemployed to prevent inflation, but, because the economic system was defined to be in a stable static equilibrium, the Great Depression was simply not permitted to occur in any other way than as a consequence of a monetary contraction!

By contrast, Keynes, who wished for the day when economists would become as humble as dentists, had a deep understanding of the basic meaning of science. Although the subject of his doctoral thesis was probability theory, Keynes was fully aware that in the real world uncertainties arise which cannot be described in probabilistic terms. As he observed in an article written in 1939:

> By "uncertain" knowledge, let me explain, I do not mean merely to distinguish what is known for certain from what is only probable. The game of roulette is not subject, in this sense, to uncertainty.[6]

Keynes was also aware that the principal failing of classical economic theory was its inability to deal with genuine uncertainties. "All these pretty, polite techniques," he said in the same article, "made for a well-panelled Board Room and a nicely regulated market, are liable to collapse." In his opinion, classical economic theory was "one of those pretty, polite techniques which tries to deal with the present by abstracting from the fact that we know very little about the future."[7]

Keynes was far more interested in finding a rationale to escape from the Great Depression than he was in reforming microeconomics. I suggest, however, that the main problem with the Keynesian revolution is that it did not go far enough; that is, neo-Keynesian economics leaves us standing with one foot on earth and the other in heaven. It does that by not providing an explicit connection between the micro- and macroworlds. To provide an answer to Friedman, it is necessary to make that connection and show in both theoretical and empirical terms why his argument is wrong.

According to the argument I am advancing, there is neither a trade-off between the rate of unemployment and the rate of inflation, such as that depicted by the Phillips curve (which assumes a zero rate of inflation), nor a natural rate of unemployment below which the economy can go without risking endless inflation. Both are static trade-offs, and neither is valid in the real world, because it is impossible to simultaneously fix the rates of unemployment and inflation. Suppose that via monetary and fiscal policies it were possible to keep the price level absolutely stable. Once supply shocks begin, such a policy cannot prevent large changes in relative prices and, as was pointed out in the last chapter, unless it is assumed that prices in other sectors of the economy are completely flexible, firms in the more competitive sector will fail and unemployment will increase. To say that prices are completely flexible implies firms have unlimited capabilities to make substitutions, an unlimited ability to deal with uncertainty, and that is absurd. Ironical as it may seem, a tight monetary policy can only insure that those industries contributing least to inflation will be among the main victims of a policy designed to stabilize prices! On the other hand, if the government pursues an easy money policy during downturns, aimed at keeping unemployment from rising above some predetermined level, prices will rise while there still is a substantial amount of unemployment.

Because neither kind of traditional policy (monetarist or neo-Keynesian) can succeed in generating prosperity without inflation, a genuine dilemma is involved—a dilemma that can be resolved only by measures either to prevent supply shocks from occurring or, if they cannot be prevented, to isolate the economy from their macroeffects.

THE 1960S IN HISTORICAL PERSPECTIVE

There are many people who regard the period from 1950 to 1970 (the 1960s in particular) as a "normal" period of economic activity. The main idea of dampening workers' expectations for higher wage rates is to restore the economy to the glorious "equilibrium" of the 1960s.

To understand how unique the 1960s really were, consider figure 9.2. Not only did the cycles dampen out between the 1950s and the 1960s, but, during the period from 1955 to the late 1960s, there was no recognizable pattern of leads and lags between the series. In terms of the previous discussion, if deadweight drag occurred during this period its impact was relatively modest. The dynamic stability of the economy was maintained because the balance of power favored the competitive forces.

However, by 1970 the relationships had changed. Note the downward trend in productivity gains before the 1970 downturn, and the slipping off in the rate of productivity gain while output was still rising before the 1974-1975 downturn. Though there was rapid improvement in productivity gains while the economy was recovering from the recession, soon afterward the rate began to decline again. This picture suggests a declining dynamic stability of the economy; that is, a shift occurred toward industries which generated deadweight drag.

To make an argument that the balance of forces is actually changing, it is necessary to have detailed industry data to show that the balance did in fact change. Unfortunately, such detailed data are unavailable for the period before 1959. However, if my basic argument is correct, it seems to be no accident that prior to all major downturns in the American economy—the Panic of 1908, the Great Depression, and the depression which occurred in the late 1930s—the trend in productiv-

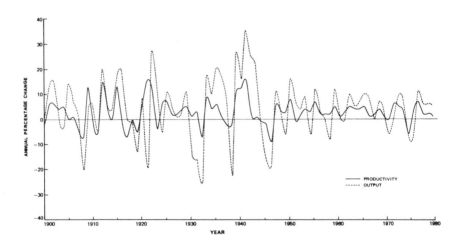

Sources: John Kendrich and Elliot Grossman, *Productivity in the Untied States: Trends and Cycles* (Johns Hopkins University Press); and John Kendrich, *Productivity Trends in the United States* (Princeton University Press).
Figure 9.2. Changes in Output and Productivity: Manufacturing Sector of U.S. Economy, 1900-1980.

ity gains was downward. This indicates that before each of these major downturns, production functions began to shift less rapidly, with the economy going toward a static equilibrium. This shift toward a more predictable economy indicates a declining ability to deal with negative feedback and, hence, a loss in dynamic stability. During each of these three major downturns, the money supply contracted, but only after the decline in dynamic stability was well underway. In other words, a contraction of the money supply occurred only after the economy had started to move toward a static equilibrium!

EMPIRICAL EVIDENCE FOR THE TRADE-OFF BETWEEN STEADY AND INTERMITTENT PRESSURES

In the following discussion, industries are divided into three principal groups, based on their price performance during the *entire* period 1959 to 1979. The best performers were those whose degree of price restraint placed them one standard deviation or more above the average; the worst performers were those industries whose lack of restraint in raising prices placed them one standard deviation or more below the average. Although the same industries were not involved in generating deadweight drag throughout the period, this procedure resulted in the inclusion of the major industries responsible for deadweight drag during the 1970s. One disadvantage of this procedure is that it resulted in combining the B and C industries discussed in the last chapter into a single group. The middle group of industries is not homogeneous. While this procedure was adopted to make it easier to read the charts, it does not seriously distort the overall picture.

Figure 9.3 shows the price performance for all three groups during the entire period. It will be noted that the price cycles for the worst group occurred during the early 1960s and, as cyclical deadweight drag became increasingly stronger, the average and best groups were pushed into a muted form of such behavior. It is not surprising that the average- and best-price groups began to cycle only during the 1974-1975 downturn. As we already have seen, during this period both the energy and steel supply shocks had a strong impact on manufacturing prices in general and, as the figure shows, they continued to push up other prices until after the downturn was underway. Even more surprising is that during the 1976-1979 time period, when the economy was again sliding into a recession and oil prices did not increase nearly as much as during the earlier period, the same pattern of price cycling continued.

Though the failure to increase tax rates during the 1960s undoubtedly contributed to inflation, the economy was highly vulnerable to the slightest increase in inflationary pressure. During this time the worst-price group, composed of a few basic materials and food-processing industries, was initiating price shocks; and except for the fact that President Kennedy's attitude toward the steel industry

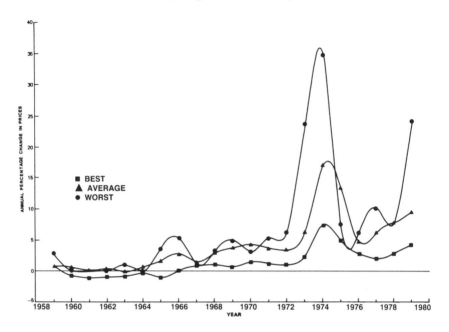

Figure 9.3. Cyclical Deadweight Drag, 1959-1979:
Price Performance of Worst, Average, and Best Groups.

differed from that of President Johnson's, the timetable for the supply shock in
steel might have been advanced by at least five years.

Turning now to a discussion of the trade-off between the fairly continuous
pressures to bring about productivity advances associated with dynamic competition and the highly intermittent pressures associated with business cycles: the first
general point is that economic downturns can evoke positive responses in productivity gains. For example, increases in total factor productivity in manufacturing
were greater during the Great Depression than during the 1920s (see figure 9.2).
The steel industry was the only major industry that did not generate rising
productivity rates during the Great Depression.

However, a great depression is not required to evoke a positive response to
negative feedback. For example, consider the behavior of the worst-price-performance group (figure 9.4). While, in the mid-1960s, prices and output moved
upward, the rate of productivity gain sagged and only increased significantly after
both price and output rates declined during the 1970 downturn. During the
1974-1975 downturn, the productivity and output series began to move in parallel
paths, indicating this group of industries was feeling the backlash from the
recession they had initiated by causing a huge increase in prices from 1972 to 1974.

When rates of output and price changes began to rise again in 1975, the rate of productivity advance declined, indicating that in these industries pressure to bring about productivity gains is highly intermittent. Note, also, that except during deep downturns, the rate of productivity gain was above zero. This meant that, due to the closing of unproductive plants and other measures, the main improvement in the absolute level of productivity performance was made while these industries were emerging from recessions.

To show the contrast between the worst-price-performance and the best-price-performance groups, consider figure 9.5. Notice how remarkably stable prices were until about 1972, when the oil and steel shocks began to drive all prices upward. This is precisely the price behavior we should expect in high-PERK industries. Notice, also, that until about 1970, rates of change in prices and productivity occurred concurrently. This is the kind of behavior we should expect in terms of the argument made earlier; it indicates that the causes of these cycles were originating outside of the industries in question.

It should be apparent that this pattern did not hold after the early 1970s. During the 1970 upturn, the rate of productivity gain soared to the highest rate it had ever achieved, with the productivity series anticipating the output series; and much the

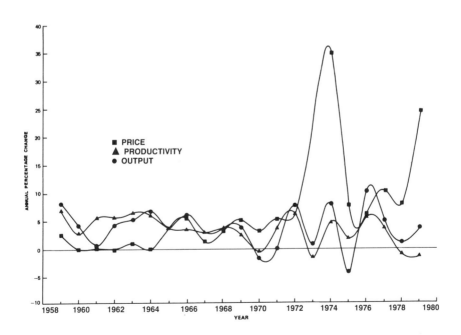

Figure 9.4. Worst-Price-Performance Group, 1959-1979.

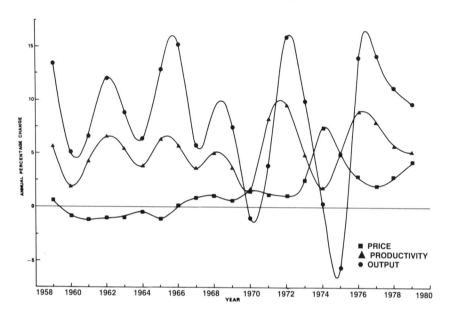

Figure 9.5. Best-Price-Performance Group, 1959-1979.

same happened after the 1974-1975 downturn. Figure 9.5 clearly illustrates the trade-off in question. The basic pattern changed because two forces were operating on productivity gains: a competitive force and a cyclical force. What was responsible for this change is quite clear: the worst-price-performance group was driving the entire manufacturing economy into a highly cyclical form of behavior. Notice the difference between the recoveries in productivity performance of best- and worst-price-performance groups: the best-price-performance group experienced a much sharper recovery because it had more experience in dealing with negative feedback.

As further evidence, consider figure 9.6 for the average group, which includes more than 200 industries. An examination of this figure will reveal that, during most of the 1960s, output and productivity changes occurred in a parallel fashion, with price behavior becoming unstable somewhat earlier than it did for the best-performance group (due mainly to the behavior of the C industries). In this entire group of industries everything that occurred in the best-performance group did so about one-half cycle earlier; and, when it did occur, the cyclical gains in productivity performance were not as pronounced. Inasmuch as the average-performance group had less practice in dealing with negative feedback, this is to be expected.

Ironical as it may seem, industries contributing least to the growth of inflationary pressures during an upswing suffer most in terms of output reductions during a downturn. The better-price-performance groups are subject not only to greater price elasticities, but also to greater income elasticities. This is illustrated by figure 9.7. During the 1960s output swings of the average- and best-price-performance groups were more volatile than those of the worst-price-performance group. In the 1974-1975 downturn, both the average- and best-price-performance groups suffered far more serious declines than did the worst-price-performance group. Because the real penalties resulting from the behavior of the worst-price-performance group are *externalized*, this form of behavior can continue. If those industries which raised prices the most during an upturn were to suffer the most during a downturn, then instead of becoming larger, the cycles would become smaller.

Figure 9.7 also shows that the prosperity of the late 1960s is to be explained more by the surges in production rates of the best-price-performance group than by the Kennedy tax cuts. The rate of output increase fluctuated between 5 and 15 percent annually. It can be argued that the tax cut had the effect of strengthening

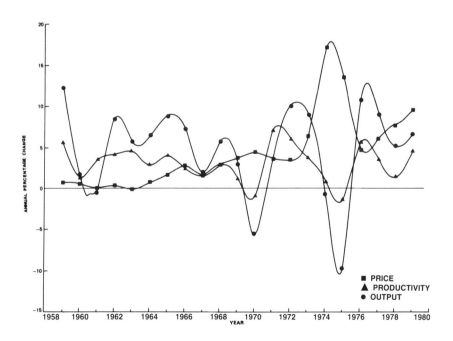

Figure 9.6. Average-Price-Performance Group, 1959-1979.

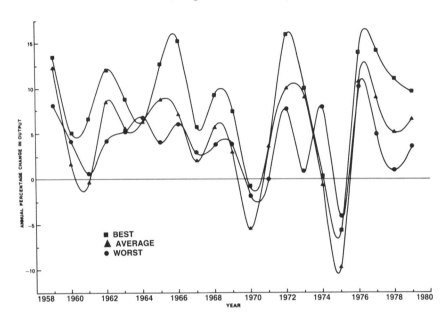

Figure 9.7. Changes in Output Rates, 1959-1979:
Best-, Average-, and Worst-Price-Performance Groups.

positive incentives. That argument does not take into account the impact of the tax cut on expectations. Instead of inquiring what they could do to increase their ability to weather downturns, industrial leaders in firms with a low capacity for dealing with risk and uncertainty were continuously asking what their government could do for them.

THE EXPERIENCES OF OTHER COUNTRIES

Unfortunately, I do not have detailed industry data for other countries. We do know that productivity growths in Japan (about 9 percent annually) and in Sweden and Germany (about 5.5 percent annually) were as high or higher than that of the best-price-performance group in the United States. If we assume that such productivity behavior can be roughly equated with a high degree of dynamic competition, then the relationship between prices, productivity, and output changes should be approximately the same: relatively small cyclical changes in prices and concurrent movements in the output and productivity indices. We also know that, from 1950 to 1970, Britain's productivity growth averaged only about 3 percent annually. If that rate of productivity growth is equated with a less competitive economy, then we should expect to observe a picture similar to that for manufacturing as a whole in the U.S. economy.

First, let us consider Germany, whose productivity performance during the post-World War II period was second only to Japan's (figure 9.8). In German manufacturing as a whole, productivity performance was somewhat lower than that of the best U.S. price-performance group, about 5 percent annually. Until about 1970, the picture was much the same for both the German economy and the best-price-performance group of industries of the United States; that is, prices were highly stable and productivity gains occurred quite evenly. There the comparison ends. Whereas the U.S. economy became more unstable from a dynamic point of view, productivity gains in Germany occurred at an even steadier rate than they had before. (Quite conceivably, this could have been accomplished by closing entire factories, particularly in the automobile and steel industries, and returning foreign workers to their home countries.)

It should not be assumed that the German economy is immune to being driven to the same behavior as the best-price-performance group in the United States. On the basis of the policies now being pursued by the United States government, this possibility cannot be ignored. Just as deadweight drag can affect the shape of cycles in the United States, so it can in other countries.

The case of Japan (figure 9.9) is somewhat puzzling. The swings in output and productivity occurred in a highly parallel fashion, indicating that the disturbances were coming from the outside. Although there was a considerable dampening in the cycles over time, with no reduction in the longer-term rate of productivity gain,

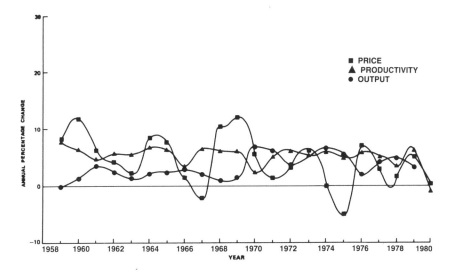

Figure 9.8. Germany: Manufacturing, 1959-1979.

it is by no means clear what caused such large cycles during the earlier postwar years. Conceivably, the cycles could have been caused by shortages of various materials; and it may therefore be true that the dampening represents a progressive elimination of such shortages. It also may be true that the dampening was the result of internal measures to make the Japanese economy less vulnerable to the cycles that were occurring in the United States. In particular, the interest of Japanese manufacturers, in shifting to production processes which place less emphasis on scale economies and more on types I and II flexibilities, may have played an important role.

Also puzzling was the movement in prices. Prices moved in a relatively narrow band, suggesting that competitive forces were continuously at work. In addition, price behavior was very sensitive to business conditions; note particularly the rapid reduction in the rate of inflation during the 1974-1975 downturn.

In conclusion: A very challenging question, indeed, is that of why, although the United States has been moving toward dynamic instability, Japan has been moving in quite the opposite direction? Did flexibility in production play a significant role? What other factors were involved?

During the post-World War II era, Sweden has been the third ranking country in the rate of productivity gain, which, from a monetarist's point of view, is almost unbelievable. The proportion of Sweden's GNP devoted to various social benefits was much larger than that of the United States or the United Kingdom. The long-held policy of pushing for equal wages in all industries to drive the least productive

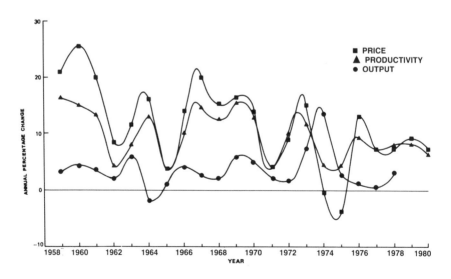

Figure 9.9. Japan: Manufacturing, 1959-1979.

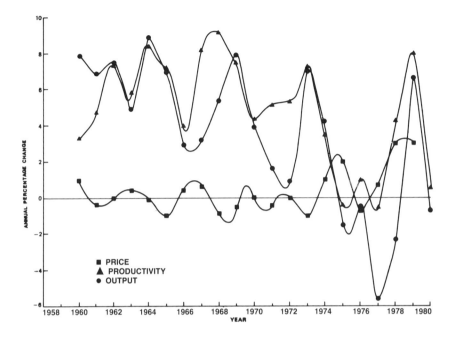

Figure 9.10. Sweden: Manufacturing, 1959-1979.

enterprises out of business also goes well beyond dependence on market forces. Nevertheless, as figure 9.10 shows, until the downturn in the mid-1970s, price and productivity behavior in Sweden moved in much the same fashion as it did in Germany. The cycles were caused by outside forces and, until the downturn of the 1970s, prices fluctuated within very narrow limits. The lesson is that, up to a point, there is no contradiction between having a highly competitive society and one based on humanitarian values.

Though very serious problems developed in Sweden during the 1970s, partly, because of calamities in its iron ore, steel, and shipbuilding industries and, partly, because of impressive increases in a variety of social benefits and higher tax rates, it would not appear that Sweden is developing the same problems as the United States. In Sweden, prices of metals rose little more than industrial prices in general. Though inflationary pressures abated substantially during the 1975 downturn, increases in wage rates were, before and during the downturn, the most rapid of any country in Europe. At the same time, the government adopted a very expensive subsidies program aimed at preventing Swedish firms from going out of business. Inasmuch as these measures lead to the development of powerful clienteles, they can make economies, once highly flexible, highly inflexible.

Because the Swedish economy recovered more slowly from the 1974-1975 downturn than other European countries, including Germany and the Netherlands, there is today a good deal of worry in Sweden that the vitality of its economy is declining.[8] There is an understandable tendency to place the blame for this on government policymaking. However, a more basic problem arises from its enormous resource advantages in the form of iron ore, forests, and cheap water power, plus closely patterning industrial development on the basis of these resource advantages. Inevitably such specialization has a negative impact on the dynamic stability of an economy—on its ability to adapt to new circumstances by generating new products for new markets. Sweden has been more involved in international competition than other industrialized countries, and this undoubtedly has played a major role in stimulating rapid advances in productivity gains. For the most part, however, these occurred in a slowly changing industrial structure.

By contrast, not possessing such resource endowments, and having to develop new lines of products (such as cameras and consumer electronics) which are skill intensive rather than resource intensive, Japan was much luckier!

According to the classical theory of trade, countries tend to have an export advantage in those commodities in which they excel at the moment. Countries in which firms base their expectations on the basis of an unchanging law of comparative advantage are likely to find their long-term stability jeopardized.

Finally, to turn to the case of Britain (figure 9.11). Britain's rate of productivity advance in manufacturing was more than 50 percent higher than that of the United

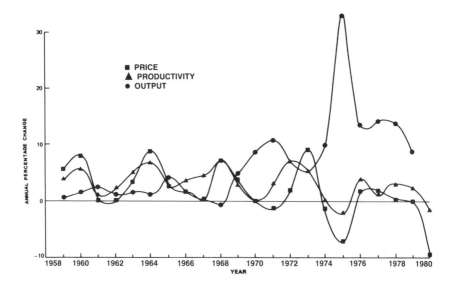

Figure 9.11. United Kingdom: Manufacturing, 1959-1979.

States during the post-World War II era. Considering the fact that British productivity gains began displaying cyclic behavior as early as 1960, this is not altogether surprising. Almost every time price increases approached a maximum rate, productivity gains began slipping, even though until the late 1960s fluctuations in output occurred within a very narrow range. In Britain, even a modest degree of positive feedback caused a slackening in the rate of productivity gain. Note also that in the mid-1960s, a few years before the United States, productivity declines began to anticipate declines in the rate of output. Still another similarity with the United States economy was that, in sharp contrast with the Japanese, Swedish, and German economies, there was no recovery of the previous rate of productivity gain after the 1974-1975 downturn. Although we cannot be sure, the British economy already may have exceeded its limits for dealing with negative feedback.

Without detailed industry-by-industry data, there is no way to know which combination of industries was initiating supply shocks in Britain. It will be recalled from the previous discussion that, in the United States, cyclical price changes occurred, first, in the least competitive industries, followed by smaller increases in the average group, with still smaller increases in the best group—an economic fugue in which the theme is initially sounded in very loud tones by the bass horns, taken up in somewhat muted tones by the violins, and carried in even more muted tones by the flutes. Regardless of which industries played the part of the horns, there is one good reason for suspecting that, over time, deadweight drag became increasingly more important in Britain. In each successive cycle after 1965, price increases did not begin to abate until an economic decline was underway. It seems safe to assume that, in Britain, nationalized industries played much the same role in generating deadweight drag as did protected industries in the United States. In industries such as steel and coal, excessive wage demands have not been as great a problem as have demands for stronger union work rules that invariably jeopardize productivity gains. Consequently, these industries generate deadweight drag in the form of monopoly costs.

Figure 9.12, showing manufacturing as a whole for the United States, will help to underscore the similarity with Britain, as well as the contrast between Germany, Japan, and Sweden. As the figure shows, the British were somewhat ahead of the United States in developing an economy in which business cycles became the main engine of productivity change. The tendency for prices to continue to rise after downturns were underway was also evident in Britain at an earlier date. The sharpest contrast between Britain and the United States and the more competitive industrialized countries was the tapering off of productivity gains soon after the recovery from the 1974-1975 downturn. There is nothing wrong, per se, with generating productivity gains in a highly cyclical fashion. The danger signal occurs when economies begin to show a relatively poor response to negative feedback. Since cycles occur because of an acute shortage of hidden-foot feedback, at least in a number of fairly critical industries, it can be said that the difference between Britain and the United States is the contrast between having

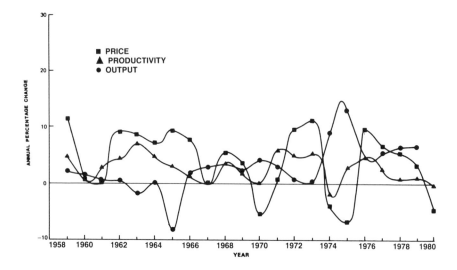

Figure 9.12. United States: Manufacturing, 1959-1979.

been a genuine colonial power and a neocolonial power: the former trades mainly with an empire, the latter, with itself.

Another difference, not shown by these figures, is that while wages and prices tended to move in parallel swings in Britain—thereby helping to strengthen the myth that the basic explanation for inflation was an underlying Phillips curve—this certainly has not been the case in the United States.

THE GENERATORS OF DEADWEIGHT DRAG

In table 9.1 are shown those industrial materials industries that raised prices the most during the periods 1971-1974 and 1976-1979, the most important of which are the steel and petroleum industries. In some cases, the industries engaged in raising prices were passing on increases of input costs. That was the case with respect to petroleum refineries, aluminum foundries, and cement. It was not the case, however, with respect to primary nonferrous metals, sawmills, and primary lead. The steel industry raised its prices by almost the same amount during both periods although, during the second period, input costs rose far less.

The lessons? No one can accuse these industries of being profiteers from inflation. They are better described as industries which exist on the basis of monopoly costs because, as the table shows, they incurred no penalties whatsoever in the form of a decline in total receipts (as measured by output) by allowing costs to rise so rapidly. The penalties such industries impose on the economy by way of cyclical deadweight drag are very substantial. It is surprising how small was the number of industries involved in making the cycles ever larger since 1970.

CONCLUSIONS

Do not the political leaders of the United States understand that, if nothing is done to deal with these problems, the result could be not only a very serious economic collapse in the United States, but a worldwide depression? Are their minds so ruled by their preconceptions that they somehow cannot bring themselves to understand what is happening? Is there so great a tendency to blame the government for all of the woes of the American economy that the political leaders are blinded to the fact that what is happening can be mainly explained by micro- rather than macrocauses? These are very perplexing questions. However, inasmuch as Milton Friedman's ideas have gained wide acceptance, I shall confine myself to a question that is easier to answer. Why is it wrong for a professional

Table 9.1. Generators of Supply Shocks: Industrial Materials.

	PERCENTAGE INCREASES					
	1971–1974			1976–1979		
INDUSTRY	PRICE	INPUT COST	OUTPUT	PRICE	INPUT COST	OUTPUT
Petroleum refineries	23	31	3	15	20	3
Blast furnaces & steel mills	11	19	7	9	11	2
Steel wire	15	20	5	7	13	6
Aluminum foundries	8	20	7	9	21	10
Plastic materials	14	22	5	7	20	12
Cement	9	18	5	10	16	4
Paving mixtures	16	17	0	8	15	5
Lime	10	18	4	10	12	0
Secondary nonferrous metals	18	20	7	13	7	1
Primary lead	0	13	2	27	19	0
Nonferrous rolling & drawing	15	19	2	13	18	1
Primary nonferrous metals	22	13	12	30	−2	1
Logging camps	18	17	3	21	23	3
Sawmills & planing mills	17	18	1	17	21	5

Source: Derived from Bureau of Labor Statistics data, 1982.

economist to say, "If only the money supply were kept stable, the economy would remain stable"?

From the standpoint of social justice, it is, of course, wrong to inflict unemployment on millions of people on the premise that their sacrifices will lead us back to a world of relatively minor business cycles. Providing that present economic policies do not result in a total economic collapse, the price paid by people who have absolutely nothing to do with bringing about serious downturns is one they will have to pay again and again. Not knowing, and not caring to know, with what disease the patient is inflicted, the physicians in charge have no alternative other than to prescribe ever-increasing doses of the wrong kind of medicine.

From a narrower technical point of view, what is wrong with such a policy is that investment in plant and equipment is not likely to proceed as scheduled when firms see on the horizon the indefinite continuance of unplanned cycles.

Figure 9.13 shows percentage changes in investment in equipment (measured in constant dollars) made by the various performance groups. Investment on the part of those industries whose price behavior was the worst increased substantially before the 1974-1975 downturn. Evidently, these industries were acting on the assumption that their pricing policies could not precipitate an economic collapse. These industries were then paying a relatively small price in the form of backlash. The average group, however, was more cautious both before and after the 1974-1975 downturn. Even the best group, whose increased investment outlays

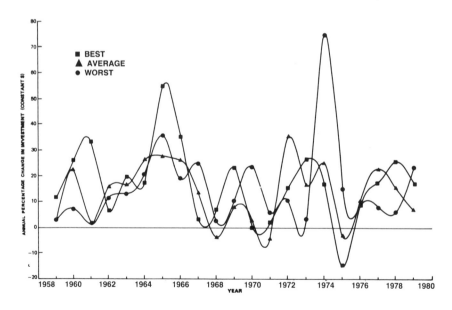

Figure 9.13. Investment in Equipment (Constant Dollars).

contributed most to the prosperity of the 1960s, displayed in the 1970s a degree of caution similar to the average group. Providing tax advantages for investment will not reverse this situation. Rapid recoveries in investment expenditures after downturns are likely to occur only if there is confidence that recoveries are not likely to quickly abort. Without dealing with the basic causes of the business cycle, present policies are destroying the basis for a sustainable prosperity.

Because data on output and productivity are not available, there is no way of providing a detailed explanation for the erosion of prosperity during the 1920s. We can say that with the faltering of productivity gains during the mid-1920s, the economy did exhibit a declining ability to deal with new circumstances. Apparently, the erosion of dynamic stability which led to Franklin Roosevelt's famous statement, "The only thing we have to fear is fear itself," was long in the making. Why it occurred, no one knows. Lacking a detailed explanation, we must agree with Paul Samuelson that the Great Depression was a statistical accident; not in the sense that with a revision in the data it would not have occurred, but that we are unable to explain the background of the macrostatistics.

Today a good deal more is known about the causes of business cycles. We live in a world in which price shocks from a relatively few industries can set in motion a chain of price increases which, when brought under control, will result in a ten or more percent unemployment rate. There is no reason to suppose that, under present policies, these price shocks will not be at least as important in the future as they were in the past. The steel industry has not changed its aversion toward risk taking. Anyone who believes that OPEC will not begin to live up to its reputation, once we have a moderate degree of prosperity, is whistling in the dark. Just as there were lapses of international competition in the petrochemicals industry during the 1970s, there will be lapses in other industries in the future. It can be assumed that politicians will not be able to resist the clamor to protect "vital" industries other than steel.

What is the danger in having unplanned cycles substitute for steady hidden-foot feedback? Part of the danger has already been discussed, namely, private investment will dry up and we will have to rely upon nervous consumers for the return of prosperity. The other and more serious part of the danger is that the cycles will become so large that the basic materials industries will not be able to recuperate from the backlash that they themselves generate. While the more competitive industries, such as semiconductors or farm machinery, have experienced larger cycles, they are not the industries that cause the greatest concern. As far as the less competitive industries are concerned, no one can be sure, at this time, that they have not generated more backlash than they can handle.

Now, to return to the monetarists' theoretical argument. According to Friedman, if the Federal Reserve Board were to keep the money supply absolutely stable, the economy would remain in a perpetual heavenly equilibrium—or if the Federal Reserve Board were to be abolished, the money supply stabilized, and the key thrown away, that would be even better. On the basis of empirical data, it should be apparent that when PERK is well above zero in particular industries, the rate of productivity gain will be high and steady, unless such advances are interrupted by downturns brought about by other industries. It is precisely these industries that are *moving away* from a static equilibrium that contribute least to inflationary pressures during an upturn. Equally apparent is that as PERK declines toward zero we approach a static Nash equilibrium. As the evidence clearly shows, industries only slightly above a static equilibrium (judged by their rates of productivity advance), or approaching such an equilibrium (judged by their declines in productivity performance), contribute most to economic *instability*.

How is this apparent paradox to be explained? Unfortunately, there are still a few economists, Friedman among them, who apparently believe that the mathematical properties of a system determine its stability. This simply is not true. An economic system, or any other kind of system, can remain stable in a static equilibrium only as long as its *boundaries are stable* (or the intrusions are highly predictable), which is to say, only as long as it is not subject to significant outside *unpredictable* influences. It is not the employment of profit maximization rules which makes an equilibrium stable, but rather, when, and only when, the boundaries of a system are reasonably stable is it permissible to employ maximization rules. Only the boundaries of industries that are protected from foreign competition, such as steel, or those in which there is little international competition, such as cement or glass containers, are quite stable. In order to have firms in general operate on the assumption that their boundaries were stable, a law would be required precluding the generation of new ideas, with such stiff penalties for violations that every entrepreneur in the world would have to go into hiding. The central problem with the argument of conservative economists is that they assume that such a law is already in effect!

The essential reason such a law should not be passed is that, while it might work in heaven, here on earth economic systems must constantly adapt themselves to deal with new circumstances, which means that it is impossible for society as a whole to conserve its predictability. The more that some industries are able to conserve their microstability— their predictability in the small—the more they dump uncertainty in the form of sharply rising costs on the economy as a whole. By attempting to preserve a way of life, they seriously impair the dynamic stability of the nation by increasing the amplitude of the business cycle. Those industries doing the best job generating and responding to negative feedback are making a positive contribution to the promotion of economic stability.

By expounding that the economy would remain in a stable equilibrium if only the money supply would remain stable, Milton Friedman is asking for a highly *unstable* economy. The more that industries behave in the eminently rational way he claims they should, the more unstable the economic system will become! That is nothing but common sense; but, apparently, there is nothing less common than common sense.

During the past ten years, Robert Lucas and others have combined Milton Friedman's key idea of a "natural rate of unemployment" with the theory of "rational expectations" to produce, as is often described, the "new classical theory of macroeconomics."[9] One of its main postulates is that aggregate demand and supply curves can be constructed for an entire economy; and it is assumed that whenever the effects of government policy are fully anticipated unemployment will remain at "the natural rate." (An anticipated increase in the money supply can cause prices to rise [but not output] and unemployment to remain at the natural rate.) While it is acknowledged that an unanticipated increase in the money supply can result in a temporary increase in the level of unemployment below the natural rate, it is also argued that the effect is likely to be short-lived.

According to the rational expectations school, supply shocks can increase the rate of inflation and lower the level of employment. But the only supply shocks that the "new macroeconomics" has legitimized to date are those brought about by OPEC or bad harvests. Indeed, only via the assumption of atomistic competition, in which every firm in a static equilibrium is looked upon as a microcosm of an economy in a general equilibrium, is it possible to construct aggregate demand and supply curves.

The new classical macroeconomics fails to recognize that only on Friedman Island, and not on the real world, is it legitimate to construct aggregate demand and supply curves. For the sake of the argument, assume that no supply shocks occur as genuine surprises. For example, people in the farm-machinery industry expect that at some point in the present recovery steel prices will again begin to rise very rapidly. In such a competitive industry no single firm may want to risk raising its prices in anticipation of an increase in the price of steel, because if it did, its products would become less competitive. Therefore, we can assume that, by so acting, the firm would be making best use of information *currently* available. When firms in the farm-machinery industry find that steel and other input costs have risen to the point that they can no longer compete on the same terms, it is irrational of them not to increase their prices, because their information has changed. Likewise, when steel and cement firms raise their prices rapidly, once an upturn is actively underway they, too, are simply recognizing that their circumstances have changed. The combined effect of such actions can greatly increase inflationary pressures during upturns. Even if the supply of money were held constant—if there were no unanticipated actions on the part of the monetary authorities—the ultimate effect of deadweight drag would be unemployment.

Curiously enough, the error in the reasoning of the so-called "new macroeconomics" is the same as that Keynes discovered when he found that the savings habits which favored the microstability of the individual did not favor the macrostability of a nation. Moving toward a highly predictable classical equilibrium tends to protect firms' microstability by jeopardizing the macrostability of the economy. While in an imaginary classical world microstability can be equated with macrostability, the error is one of assuming that what is true of the parts is true of the whole (i.e., the so-called "fallacy of composition error").

The preferences which result in oversavings on the part of individuals and myopic profit decisions on the part of firms are entirely different: in the former case, individuals may be overly concerned with their longer-run stability (hence, Keynes's famous statement, "In the long-run we will all be dead."). By contrast, in the case of firms, the obsession commonly takes the form of maximizing near-term profits. Both of these tendencies reveal an unwillingness to take risks. If my argument is correct, a greater unwillingness to take risks brings periods of economic prosperity to an end. There is no reason to expect that a decline in the propensity to take risks will be revealed in the same way in all countries. For example, during the 1920s, risk taking collapsed in Britain and the United States for entirely different reasons. Nor is there any reason to suppose that a lapse of risk taking within a country will always occur for the same reasons. For example, the economic movement of the United States during the 1920s was an entirely different story from that which is happening presently.

Unless we are prepared to acknowledge that static equilibria are inherently unstable and there is nothing automatic about the continuance of dynamic equilibria, we preclude ourselves from understanding the basic causes of economic instability.

Chapter 10
DETERMINANTS OF CHANGES IN WAGE RATES

In the last chapter I described in detail the thinking behind the so-called rational expectations school, the school that claims inflation is caused by workers (or others) bargaining or speculating in terms of further price increases. However, if the proposition about wage rates is correct, the evidence should show that increases in wage rates were actually driving up prices; and only some simple calculations are required to show that this is not the case.

The second point to be made is that Keynesians who argue for an incomes policy fail to recognize that dynamic competition does, in fact, provide just this kind of a policy. But I hasten to add that the argument to be made here is not inconsistent with that Keynes himself made with respect to wage rates.

An *incomes policy* is usually defined as a policy to keep wage rates in line with productivity gains. However, as will be seen, when it is working, dynamic competition performs just that function. And only when it is not working can it be assumed that increases in wage rates will outpace productivity gains. For example, as was already shown, wage rates in the automobile industry were tied not to increases in productivity in that industry, but to increases in productivity in the economy as a whole. The president of General Motors, Charles Wilson, may have felt that what was good for General Motors was good for the country; but executives from the United Automobile Workers union evidently felt that what was good for the country was good for them.

It may be noted, however, that the same does not apply to the role of the UAW in the agricultural machinery industry. For many years in that industry, workers have been paid bonuses for increasing their productivity. And special incentives are employed for assuring that workers will take a direct interest in repairing equipment when it breaks down. That is the difference between more and less competitive industries!

The nonstrike workers' agreement in the steel industry, which went into effect in 1974, provides not only a bonus for observing the nonstrike rule, but a three percent annual improvement in wage rates in the steel industry, quite irrespective of improvements in productivity in that industry! And there is no getting around the fact that, during the 1970s the steel industry played a major role in causing wage pressure on other industries.

It does not seem to be an accident that industries displaying little or no dynamic competition tend to feature both the most rapid increases in wage rates and the most restrictive labor practices. In 1979, hourly wage rates in the steel industry were more than 50 percent above the average for manufacturing as a whole. Hourly wage rates in the automobile industry ($14.24 per hour, including fringe benefits) were almost as high as wages in the steel industry ($16.24 per hour, including fringe benefits). By way of contrast, the comparable figure for the computer industry, which is far more competitive, was $10.68 per hour.

Not only are wage rates in industries such as automobile and steel extremely high relative to industries whose productivity has been increasing more rapidly, but, up until 1979, increases in wage rates occurred at a very rapid rate. Thus, from 1970 to 1979, hourly wage rates in the steel industry increased from $5.96 to $16.24; in the automobile industry, from $5.94 to $14.24; and in the computer industry, from $5.54 to $10.68.

It should be apparent, however, that once wage rates in the less competitive industries started to advance, it became virtually impossible for leaders of firms in the more competitive industries to hold the line on wage increases. If a firm desires to employ dedicated workers, it obviously must observe reasonable standards of

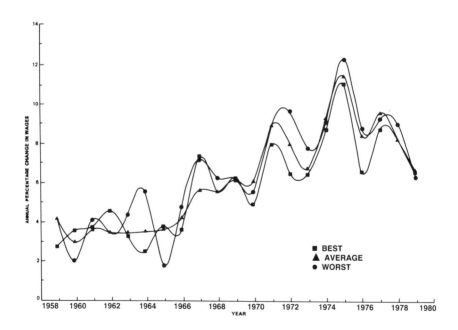

Figure 10.1. Wage Changes, 1959-1979.

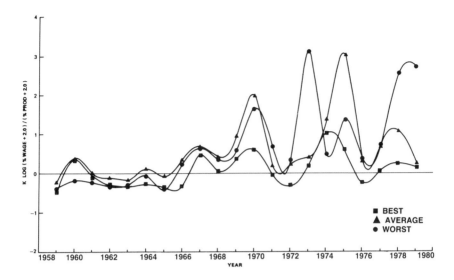

Figure 10.2. Log (Wage Changes/Productivity Changes) 1959- 1979.

fairness. Consequently, while wages may still be held in line with productivity gains, it is a relationship in which wages increase not less, but more, rapidly than productivity gains.

Consider figure 10.1, which shows changes in wage rates for all three groups of industries during the period 1958–1979. It will be noted that, up to 1965, movements in the three groups bore no relationship to each other, but beginning with the second half of the 1960s, movements of wage rates in all three groups of industries became more consistent, with accelerations tending to be most rapid in the less competitive industries.

In figure 10.2 is plotted the logarithm of increases in wages divided by increases in productivity. When wage rates increase less rapidly than productivity advances the number will be less than zero, and when they increase more rapidly the number will be greater than zero. Now, it should be clear that, while during the first part of the 1960s wage rates in the three groups of industries did not move together, they were, nonetheless, being held in line with productivity gains: wage increases in all three groups tended to increase less than productivity increases. So, if an "incomes policy" means keeping increases in wage rates in line with productivity gains, the United States did have one until rapidly rising wages in the automobile industry initiated its collapse. The automobile industry is the single most important industry in the average group; and, even during the 1960s, its wage rates doubled. By contrast, although union leaders in the steel industry would have liked to press for larger wage increases immediately after World War II, because it was felt that wage and price controls were operating in a manner that was grossly unfair to them during the war, not until the imposition of trade restrictions could they make the steel industry the wage leader of the country.

Nevertheless, while in the best-performance group of industries wages moved ahead of productivity increases during the late 1960s, competitive forces were still at work; that is, in relation to productivity gains they were the most constrained.

Finally, before concluding this section, there is one point to be made crystal clear. While many neo-Keynesians would like to have an incomes policy, as an old-fashioned Keynesian I would not want it in the form of a tax penalty for overly generous increases in wage rates or tax benefits for a niggardly increase in wage rates. The notion of a taxed-based incomes policy is naive, because it assumes a Congress that would be willing to provide the same penalties or premiums, as the case may be, as are provided by competition. The primary force involved in generating inflation is price increases and not wage increases. While rapid increases in wages in the steel industry affected union demands in other industries, this is not a problem that could have been dealt with by a tax policy.

However, there is no contradiction, whatsoever, in accepting Keynes's arguments and those given here. The argument that Keynes gave in his *General Theory* was strictly a *macro* argument; namely, reducing wage rates in general would not provide a way out of the Great Depression, because the affect would be to simultaneously reduce prices and workers' incomes. I agree entirely with that argument. On the other hand, it certainly cannot be argued that very large increases in wage rates in, say, the steel industry add to inflation only because they increase the real income of steelworkers.

Indeed, in this case the impact of aggregate income is so small that it can be safely ignored. But, there are two microeffects which cannot be safely ignored. One is that increases in wage rates in the steel industry can have an enormous impact on steel prices, and, thereby, on the prices of many commodities in which steel is used. The other is that fantastic increases in wage rates in one industry can have an impact on the demand for higher wages in others.

To be sure, the rational expectations people simply do not acknowledge this fact of life (any student at the University of Chicago who raised such a question would surely be severely reprimanded). On the other hand, when I asked a friend, who is in the chemical industry, why he did not use the same argument on the union officials with whom he dealt, his reply was that, while the argument might work at the University of Chicago, it did not work when dealing with labor union officials.

To control inflation it is necessary to either make competition work better (when it is not working as it should) or pursue policies that will have the effect of isolating the economy from the macroeffects of such behavior. The essential reason wage increases should be kept in line with productivity increases is that this is the only way to assure that workers will have a continuing interest in generating productivity gains. Competition not only does that, but it also holds prices in check!

Chapter 11
THE SECOND LAW OF DYNAMIC ECONOMICS

THE NEW PRIVATE WELFARE STATE

A public welfare state, as defined by its critics, is one in which people prefer to earn a living by remaining unemployed rather than by searching for jobs. Those who subject themselves to the iron discipline of the market, it is said, are carrying their weight in making capitalism work; and those choosing to remain on the public dole are, in effect, the main source of deadweight drag. Of course, in principle, if not practice, no American will be allowed to starve. Hence, the concept of a safety net has been developed to insure that the United States, while not completely oblivious to humanitarian issues, requires that the work incentives of private citizens will not be impaired.

A private welfare state is one in which the market is allowed to work so imperfectly that a safety net is created for important industries which are unable to withstand the rigors of competition. For example, restrictions on Japanese auto imports certainly do not completely remove U.S. auto firms from pressure to improve productivity and quality. Their impact has been to make Japanese cars more plush and expensive, with the consequence that the average automobile purchaser is obliged to spend an additional 1500 dollars or so to provide that industry with a safety net. Of course, the safety net for the steel industry is guaranteed to assure that even higher standards of safety will be observed. Hence, in this case, protectionist measures insure that, except in deep downturns, firms in the steel industry will not be saddled with losses.

According to the economics of the new private welfare state, the more indispensable the activity, the more protection must be provided. Consequently, it is not surprising that nowhere in the United States does the private welfare system thrive better than it does in the field of national defense. Suppose that due to some foul-up in military procurement, a defense contractor finds himself with engineers who are temporarily unemployed. What the contractor can do is loan them to another expanding company for which he receives 180% overhead plus profits! This, of course, is a more closely woven safety net than that provided the steel industry. When preparing the country to "safely" fight a nuclear war (i.e., the strategy commonly known as "we will not strike first unless they strike first"), absolutely nothing is more important than to assure that the task is undertaken with the utmost safety for those involved.

How, then, might the private welfare state be observed at the level of the firm? Let us say that union work rules forbid the firing of lazy or incompetent people, as they often do in industries which generate deadweight drag. Within the firm there is created a small-scale system of deadweight drag, because, as we have already seen, internal incentives tend to be mirror images of external incentives. Or let us suppose that you visit a research laboratory in an industry in which there is little or no dynamic competition. You will probably discover that, while some of the research people might have marvelous ideas for improving productivity, the people who want to get ahead have learned that the best way to do so is to publish articles in learned journals, rather than bother the operational people involved. When there is little or no pressure on the company, the operational people simply do not care to try new ideas, because if they succeeded no one would be greatly pleased; and if not successful, they would be fired. Hence, in the private welfare state the formula for getting ahead is to be a good politician and, above all, to look busy without rocking the boat. Bureaucratic managers go to uncommon lengths to impose all sorts of rules on themselves, so, if anything does go wrong they will not be blamed. This is another way in which the generation of deadweight drag is reflected in the internal workings of the firm. The consequence is fairly obvious. According to a recent *Fortune* article, "The Madness of Executive Compensation," the method of rewarding top executives in the private welfare state can be described as follows:

> In a totally rational world, top executives would get paid handsomely for first-class performance, and would lose out when they flopped. But to an extraordinary extent, those who flop still get paid handsomely.[1]

How can the consumer observe the workings of the private welfare state? If getting a bank to correct an error in your balance is an almost impossible task, you can be quite certain it is because you are dealing with one arm of the private welfare state. If the diesel engine in your automobile turns out to be a lemon, you must be prepared to receive comparable treatment when dealing with another arm of the private welfare state. If you have read about baseball players demanding unbelievable salaries, the reason is that, although dynamic competition is like a sport, baseball is a so-called sport with little competition.

The central feature of the private welfare state is a lack of self-responsibility, by which I mean, enlightened self-interest and not purposeful, benevolent behavior. Nevertheless, it also must be acknowledged that what may seem like self-responsible behavior from the point of view of a bank depositor, may seem like benevolent behavior from the point of view of a bank clerk. If you find a mechanic who actually manages to correct a problem with your automobile engine, you feel grateful for his benevolence because, statistically speaking, such behavior far exceeds the typical limits of self-responsibility.

This is not to say that the concept of the private welfare state is new in American history. Its origin can be traced back to the time of Alexander Hamilton, who wanted to protect those whom Jefferson described as the "artificial aristocracy." Even before that, when battling against mercantilism, Adam Smith was castigating the private welfare state. As far as American economic history is concerned, it can be observed that, while at some periods the role of the private welfare state was expanded, at other times it was contracted. Skipping over the period before the Civil War, it can be observed that regulation of the railroads was a victory for the private welfare state, as was the development of trusts prior to the passage of the antitrust laws—not so much because they charged monopoly prices, but because they permitted monopoly costs. By outlawing trusts, the antitrust laws brought about a temporary suspension of the development of the private welfare state, as did deregulation of the airlines. Before deregulation it was impossible for any major airline to go out of business; but, with a safety net no longer provided, failure is once again possible. However, there are so many competing airlines that one or two going bankrupt now and then does not violate the indispensability principle.

It now can be said that not only politicians but some economists, too, are in the service of the private welfare state. Divorced of all its trappings, the new supply-side economics is simply a means for assuring that those firms that succeed in raising prices the most are not unduly penalized. Or to make the point in another way, the supply-siders merely want to unbalance the federal budget so price increases can be financed without unbalancing the budgets of private firms. To be sure, they point to the wonderful effects of the Kennedy tax cuts. However, not only are the times now different, but the role the Kennedy tax cuts played in stimulating the economy has been greatly exaggerated. As was shown in chapter 9, the prosperity of the 1960s rested on the fact that deadweight drag was then quite unimportant, while at the same time the more competitive industries were going ahead full steam in expanding output and providing additional employment opportunities. Of course, the supply-siders have been dealt a temporary setback. But, it should not be assumed that the task of expanding the role of the private welfare state by socialization of the risk-taking function is not beset with problems.

Another sign that the role of the private welfare state is expanding is the willingness of the Antitrust Division of the Justice Department to allow firms in the same industry to engage in joint R&D undertakings. Quite obviously, if firms do not impose risks on each other, their freedom of choice to impose risks on the public at large is substantially greater. The allowance of mergers, on a larger scale than those which occurred during the 1920s, is still another sign that the role of the private welfare state is being expanded. The essential logic behind mergers and conglomerates is to insure themselves against uncertainty by engaging in a variety of activities; something they cannot do without weakening their own incentives to engage in risk taking. The better insured against risks any individual or firm is, the smaller will be its propensity to engage in risk taking. However, for quite understandable reasons, most of the legal profession is opposed to a law which would outlaw mergers.

It should not be assumed that only right-wing Republicans stand for the private welfare state. Inasmuch as shielding firms from either foreign competition or enforcement of the antitrust laws protects both union and company officials, doing away with a competitive society is one of the few points on which conservatives and so-called liberals are in solid agreement. Besides, one of the best friends of the new private welfare state is none other than John Kenneth Galbraith, who via price and wage controls would like to freeze the American economy into its present design. He also would like to see a larger fraction of the GNP allocated for public welfare, which is to say, he is for a mixed public and private welfare state.

The question raised by this discussion is the one that Schumpeter tried to answer: Can capitalism survive? Narrowly defined, capitalism is an economic system in which wealth is privately owned. But, considering the fact that large corporations are owned by thousands of stockholders who have little or no control over management, it is by no means clear that capitalism exists in the United States even in the narrow sense of the term. As has often been pointed out, American stockholders do indeed act like absentee landlords by demanding that, if they invest, corporations must pay regular dividends. How else should stockholders be expected to behave if they have no control over management? In Japan, when a petrochemical company failed recently, the stockholders ousted the management. A willingness to take risks in the absence of control is a contradiction in terms; and the real question is not why sensible people insist on regular dividend payments, but why they do anything other than sell stocks short.

Broadly defined, capitalism is a highly decentralized system of risk taking which will insure the generation of a wide diversity of ideas. But, while this system of capitalism exists in many industries engaged in making products not yet regarded as essential for our well-being, the question is, how long will it be before the list of essential activities is expanded? For example, while the machine tool industry has not yet been moved into the indispensable category, one can easily imagine that there are zealots in the government working day and night to do for this industry what other zealots did for the automobile industry. And, no doubt, semiconductors and computers are also on the list of industries to be saved. Consequently, while no one can be so dogmatic as to assert that capitalism will not survive in the doll, button, or smoking tobacco industries, it must be acknowledged that the boundaries of the private welfare state are likely to be substantially expanded during the next few years.

Granted, this line of reasoning does not entirely agree with Schumpeter's. The central problem with his analysis is that it left out of account the role of the hidden foot in providing for the dynamics of capitalism. Hence, he believed that one day progress would become so automatic that either capitalistic or socialistic bureaucrats would be able to do equally well in bringing about progress.[2] However, we now know that no matter how clever he was with some of his other arguments, this particular argument was wrong. The central feature of socialistic economies is that they generate almost no feedback, either from a firm's rivals or customers: if a Soviet automobile is not to one's liking, it is impossible to switch to a Japanese automobile. Nor do they generate the negative feedback associated with economic downturns. Consequently, even if completely shielded from other forms of negative feedback, the private welfare state cannot exempt itself from economic downturns; therefore, it has this advantage over socialism.

The Business Cycle

The widely held beliefs that inflationary expectations are now being cooled and we are entering a period of prosperity without inflation are more revealing of the psychological propensities of those who preach this sermon than they are of the economic status of the nation. Dampening inflationary shocks during economic upturns is not a mere matter of changing workers' expectations with respect to higher wage rates, but, rather, the recognition that protection of key industries from foreign competition has greatly increased the dynamic instability of the nation. Because of the absence of the hidden foot in some key industries, we are in a period in which there are no good macropolicies. Inflation can be held in check by keeping so much slack in the economy that all firms act as if they were facing elastic-demand curves. Even if interest rates were lowered further, there is no assurance that such action could insure an adequate volume of private investment: investment not only depends on interest rates; more importantly, it depends on expectations with respect to the likelihood of serious downturns. On the other hand, policies designed to stimulate a more rapid recovery will almost hasten the reemergence of supply shocks and the advent of another serious downturn. This basic dilemma occurs as a result of allowing a relatively few industries to hold the rest of the economy hostage.

What, then, might be done to escape this dilemma? Given the tendencies of politicians to appease the vested interests, and the basic lack of responsibility in the United States, the die is probably cast. However, it is certainly not too early to begin thinking about what might be done in the aftermath of a general economic collapse.

THE THREE ROLES OF DYNAMIC COMPETITION

It is no small wonder that competition has become a sadly neglected topic for study in economics. The attempt to make economics into an exact science like physics—a science in which all the laws are known precisely—has had the effect of making the static concept of competition both very precise and unimportant. Moreover, in the era after World War II, macroeconomics was made to seem too all-important and so completely mastered that no real emphasis was given to understanding better the relationship between micro- and macroworlds. Rather, the goal was to further refine a concept of competition unknown to business firms, no matter how vigorously they competed! Indeed, had E.T. visited the United States in the 1930s, and learned everything he knew about competition from reading the textbooks, and then revisited the United States after World War II, he undoubtedly would have concluded that, while competition was imperfect during the 1930s, it had reached an unheard-of degree of perfection after World War II.

Ironic as it may seem, it is only in the face of economic adversity that economists become somewhat more open-minded. During prosperous times all sorts of technical discoveries are made and entirely new industries come into being. However, the conservative economists will tell you, "All is going well, because the economy is in an almost, but not quite, glorious static equilibrium"; *not quite*, because it takes a little time before the automatic workings of the marketplace can wipe out monopoly profits. Indeed, it is a sad commentary on economic science that theories are not overturned because of the gradual accumulation of knowledge, but, rather, as a result of difficult economic times. It is, therefore, no exaggeration to state that economics, too, is a highly cyclical industry, with economists asking penetrating questions during difficult times and returning to "normal science" once good times return. What needs to be more generally appreciated is that, while dynamic competition can perform three very important functions, its role is by no means automatic.

Dynamic Competition's Role as an Economic Stabilizer. As of the time the Full Employment Act of 1948 was passed, a fundamental mistake was made; that is, it was assumed that economic stability would depend on only the *macro* policies pursued by the government. The argument between the neo-Keynesians and the monetarists was: How far should a ship be allowed to stray off course before corrective actions are taken? If one seriously believes the macroequilibrium concept proposed by the neo-Keynesians, he or she can rest easy: if the ship strayed more than fifty yards or so from a full-employment-without-inflation course, corrective actions could be promptly taken. On the other hand, Milton Friedman wants to set the heading in New York and not touch the wheel before the ship reaches Le Havre. In a nutshell, that is the argument between the neo-Keynesians and the monetarists.

What both sides are arguing about, essentially, is how the Great Depression might have been avoided—in much the same manner as generals argue about how the mistakes of the last war might have been avoided. However, both sides failed, and still fail, to appreciate that, if PERK is high enough in all industries to prevent deadweight drag, the seas will be so calm that it will not matter whether one is a Keynesian or a monetarist, because the actions or inactions of the Federal Reserve Board will be so unimportant that they will be noticed only by the financial analysts. On the other hand, if due to deadweight drag the seas really get rough, there is nothing fiscal and monetary policies can do to prevent another Great

Depression. In other words, the big mistake made in the Full Employment Act was to fail to appreciate the *microfacts of life*.

As we already have seen, when there is more or less continuous pressure upon industries to generate productivity gains, the industries in question play no role whatsoever in the initiation of business cycles. If the industries are relatively minor and receive feedback irregularly from other industries (as many do), productivity gains will cycle, but such cycling is unlikely to cause a business cycle. On the other hand, if the industries are major and receive feedback irregularly, this can cause serious business cycles. Hence, it needs to be recognized that a program to promote competition is vital to the promotion of economic stability.

The Role of Dynamic Competition in Increasing the Wealth of Nations. According to the first law of dynamic economics, costs are a function of firms' expectations with respect to their elasticity of demand, their ability to operate within tight price constraints (i.e., their dynamic efficiency), and luck. But as we have seen, and our common sense should tell us, output tends to increase more rapidly when demand is assumed to be elastic than when assumed to be inelastic. Consequently, when industries engage in such competition, they are adding to the wealth of the nation in question. No one will deny that competition between Japanese automobile firms was the most important factor in making Japan the number one automobile producer in the world, and that this accomplishment increased the wealth of Japan. Nor can anyone deny that even more robust competition between United States automobile firms during the early part of this century greatly increased the value wealth of the United States. If it were possible to measure the increased value of capital assets in that industry and a number of related industries as well, and add to that the discounted present value of automobile exports, we actually could put a figure on the degree to which competition increased the wealth of the United States; and, more recently, the same is true with computers and semiconductors.

There are people who actually say that, because wealth in the electronics industries is increasing far more rapidly than in other industries, resources should be shifted into them. If that argument is correct, fifteen years ago we should have shifted resources out of the scientific instruments and farm machinery industries, because, as of that time, the wealth of those industries (the discounted present value of their output streams) was increasing very slowly. In fact, who could have predicted that dynamic competition would reemerge in these industries to the extent that it has?

Nor is that all. Suppose that someone actually knew that the wealth of this or that highly competitive industry was rapidly increasing and chose to buy stocks from a random sample of firms in the industry in question. Would the buyer of those stocks be likely to increase his or her wealth? By no means. The chances are that anyone who gambled in that way would lose his or her shirt. When outcomes at the macrolevel of the industry in question are most predictable, outcomes at the microlevel of the firms are most unpredictable. It may be noted, however, that precisely the same is true of gold mining. There certainly was a period when California's increase in wealth was represented mainly by the increased value of gold mines. Yet there were many prospectors who were not lucky enough to discover a big strike, and many gold mining stocks became worthless. The old-fashioned notion that nations increase their wealth by individual thrift is pure rubbish. They do so because entrepreneurs engage in business activities which provide a great deal of fun and require a genuine taste for adventure!

If it is acknowledged that dynamic competition has had a highly predictable effect in increasing the wealth of a nation, how can it be explained why the fields in which such competition is likely to emerge are so unpredictable? The answer is that, in science as well as in technology, new fields are opened up by someone asking sharp questions. Why, then, do business firms not provide themselves with such a capacity? If they did, continuing increases in the wealth of a nation would be highly predictable.

There is one business firm which describes its main invention as a process of continually asking questions: The Minnesota Mining and Manufacturing Company. The organizers of this company bought, in northern Minnesota, a mine they believed to be a very valuable asset: a mine to produce the raw materials used for making sandpaper. However, the refusal of sandpaper companies to buy the material led to a decision to develop a capability for producing sandpaper to show the sandpaper companies how it could be done. The result of this experiment was to find that the mine was, in fact, a worthless asset. Nevertheless, it did help institutionalize the business of asking questions. When shortly after World War I, the company moved to Minneapolis under new ownership, the salesmanager, who at that time was in his 20s, insisted that the salesmen should not only call on the wholesalers to whom the sandpaper was sold, but also on the firms which actually used the sandpaper. This in turn led to the establishment of a small R&D laboratory to investigate various complaints; a procedure that resulted in a series of discoveries, particularly for the automobile industry. In fact, officials from the firm still describe the "invention" of the young salesmanager as their most important invention. For example, the wealth of the company was later greatly increased by the development of a process for making waterproof sandpaper. What led to that discovery was a letter, requesting samples of their grit, which piqued the curiosity of an employee who had the good sense to call on the requester personally to find out what he intended to do with the samples. This visit led to the discovery of a method for making waterproof sandpaper!

The moral of this account: If every company in the United States behaved exactly like Minnesota Mining and Manufacturing once did, there would be no concern about transferring resources from declining to prospering industries. Furthermore, it would not be nearly as difficult to make the connection between increases in the supply of knowledge, whether or not brought about by dynamic competition, and increases in the supply of wealth. The point about dynamic competition is that it is a more predictable way of increasing an industry's wealth—more predictable, because continuous challenges leading to new questions can be counted upon to produce a series of inventions or innovations no one could have predicted.

If individual industries can increase their wealth by engaging in dynamic competition, it follows that when the weighted average of such industries in a particular country exceeds that for other countries, that nation will be able to increase its wealth relative to other countries; that is, it can be predicted that real per capita incomes will rise, and the present discounted value of a stream of income will also rise relative to other countries. Thus, according to the second law of dynamic economics, countries possessing a relative advantage in dynamic competition will also have a relative advantage in increasing their wealth.

It must be emphasized, however, that both the first and second laws of dynamic economics are what scientists describe as *phenomenological laws* (i.e., seeing is believing) that cannot be deduced from other laws. As an example, if you did not know the impact of competition in, say, the computer industry, on increasing the total wealth of that industry—did not know beforehand the elasticity of demand for computers—there would be no way of deducing that fact from the classical laws of economics. According to classical theory, while all this may be very interesting, the wealth of nations is determined by exogenous factors.

On the other hand, as in the case of the other economic laws, the test of all knowledge is the ability to make good predictions. Assume that, during most of the nineteenth century, per capita income in Britain increased more rapidly than in other countries. If the theory is correct, we should expect that, at that time, Britain had a relative advantage in dynamic competition. Was this so? I honestly do not know. But one reason I would be willing to bet 5-to-1 in favor of this proposition is that during that period relative prices of almost all industrial materials were rapidly declining.[3] If PERK were not reasonably high, how is that to be explained? To take another case, I would be willing to wager the same amount that, during the period from 1860 to 1960, the United States had a relative advantage in dynamic competition, and now Japan is in the process of acquiring such an advantage.

Let us suppose that, on the basis of empirical research, it is discovered that the second dynamic law does make fairly good predictions; for example, predictions which would enable us to explain Germany's phenomenal increase in per capita income after World War II. Would such a finding invalidate the law of comparative advantage? By no means. The static law of comparative advantage assumes unchanging production functions—and the dynamic law, changing production functions. When the period is short, changes in production functions can be ignored, and the static law is the appropriate law to be used. For predicting the pattern of trade between Japan and the United States for the next year or two, it can be safely assumed that the static law provides a reasonable approximation of the truth. For making longer-term predictions it cannot be assumed that the same is true. If the static law held for Japan at each moment of time since 1945, it would still be an underdeveloped country! Consequently, the same proposition can be set forth regarding the second dynamic law as we did with the first one: the dynamic law of relative advantage is needed to protect the static law of comparative advantage.

There is no inconsistency whatsoever between nations becoming wealthier and more stable. Even a cursory knowledge of the facts should substantiate this. For many years per capita income in Sweden was increasing very rapidly, and yet at the same time her economy was remarkably stable. Conversely, at the same time as relative living standards in the British economy were declining, her economy was becoming more and more unstable. Steady competitive pressures both increase a country's wealth and lessen the likelihood of serious internally created downturns.

The Role of Dynamic Competition in a Democratic Society. George Stigler deserves a great deal of credit for being one of the first economists to discover that an economic system cannot be defined without reference to the political system in which it is embedded. His theory of economic regulation is based on this point of view.[4]

On the other hand, it seems to be no accident which particular industries will be regulated or protected by the government. The railroads became regulated because they were unable to attain a workable cartel without the support of the government. And it is not the computer industry that established a powerful protectionist lobby in the Congress, but, rather, the steel industry. The Smoot-Hawley Tariff Act, which undoubtedly played quite as large a role in deepening the Great Depression as did the monetary contraction, was also sought by the vested interests. The lesson, of course, is that anyone who would like to minimize the scope for intervention of firms in the political process ought to be a real friend of promoting competition, that is, unless firms are always seen to be ensconced in a static equilibrium—then it would not make any difference.

There is an even deeper reason for preserving a highly competitive society. Encouraging self-responsibility and promoting the generation of a wide diversity of ideas provides us with the best safeguards against totalitarian societies, a point also recognized by Keynes.[5] How can one stand for the freedom of the individual without favoring a competitive society—not in the trivial, but in the real sense of the word *competition*? *easy, alas... the 'free' person ought not face risks —???*

PROMOTING COMPETITION

The main way to promote competition is to reduce the barriers to international competition. For years, few countries in the world had laws to make particular anticompetitive practices illegal, and probably with good reason: U.S. firms acted as the agents of creative destruction. For example, until the 1930s, European automobile companies emphasized expensive cars for the rich; but competition with U.S. firms made them understand that demand was more elastic than they had earlier assumed.

Now, however, foreign firms have begun to repay the debt owed to U.S. firms, although it is unfortunate that they did not act nearly as promptly as they might have, from the point of view of the United States. For example, as of the time that Japanese television imports began to swell the market, the U.S. television industry had already begun to display all of the characteristics associated with a mature industry. If European and Japanese cars had entered the United States market in large numbers during the 1950s, U.S. automobile firms would have had a double advantage. In the first place, automobiles were almost two feet shorter at that time and seriously underpowered as compared with later models. Second, and more important, the 1930s can be described as a period during which U.S. automobile firms were at war with each other, and their operations were highly decentralized; for example, Oldsmobile and Buick operated as separate profit-making centers openly competing with each other. However, as of the 1960s, when foreign imports began to be regarded as a threat, except for minor skirmishes on the stylistic front, peace had been declared in the automobile industry—and when this happens, a much higher degree of centralization develops almost automatically. This, in turn, results in a high degree of inertia when dealing with hidden-foot feedback.

The single most important step that needs to be taken, if U.S. imports are to rise to something like 20 percent of the GNP, is to abolish the Department of Commerce. Started by Herbert Hoover as an effort to swing the balance toward Hamiltonian democracy, in recent years the department has led the effort to return the country to mercantilism. However, while this effort is no doubt well intentioned, its effect has been to simultaneously rob protected industries of the ability to achieve more rapid accumulations of wealth and to make economic downturns more serious. As we already have seen, when industries in the C and D categories are put under greater pressure, not all fail to respond: some end on the left side of the diagram and some on the right. There is good reason to suppose that the same would happen were the steel industry not protected; that is, small and highly efficient electric steel firms, located mainly in the South, would improve their productivity more rapidly if they had to deal with a greater degree of challenge. Thus, if they were provided with different incentives, it is likely that the discounted present value of their output stream would rise. The same is true of substitutes for steel, which are also protected by restrictions on steel imports. Hence, it is fair to state that the Department of Commerce is robbing this country of its wealth.

This is not to say that the only measure which is required to make the United States once again a country that exists for the living and not for the dead (i.e., Jefferson's concept of democracy) is the abolishment of the Department of Commerce. In addition to this measure, a two-pronged attack on the problem will be required. The first would consist of isolating those industries with serious or incurable diseases. If their recovery could not be guaranteed, at least the mac-roeffects of their microactions would not result in deadweight drag. The second would consist of changing the role of government policy to promote competition (under a new act to replace the Sherman Antitrust Act), to make the objective not so much the outlawing of specific wrongdoings as acting as a preventive medicine: a role of not allowing PERK to fall so far that entire industries would find themselves unable to respond to greater competitive pressures.

Needless to say, I would not favor a crusading effort in which the general goal was to drive up the rate of productivity advance in a wide variety of industries. There are many industries, such as the wood and metal caskets industry, whose price and productivity behavior need not be a matter of great national concern. The goal, rather, should be to prevent deadweight drag from occurring when the cost of the item in question affects the cost of many other commodities, and to prevent large price increases in entire classes of consumer products, especially when large price increases result in a tax on the poor.

DEALING WITH CONTAGIOUS DISEASES

Steel

It would, of course, be very optimistic to assume that all industries will always remain dynamic and, by so doing, conserve their ability to deal with unpredictability. Whether we like it or not, deadweight drag will develop in some industries. But, as with a communicable disease, the first obvious measure is to put the patient in an isolation ward. On this issue, nearly all economists agree. Consider, for example, the steel industry. If it were assumed that the present disease of the industry were one from which the patient might recover, the obvious way to isolate its microbehavior from its macroconsequences would be to let foreign steel into the United States at whatever prices it fetched, and pay to U.S. steel firms an outright subsidy amounting to the difference between market prices and their current costs. This would leave the steel industry as well off as it is today. Since increased steel prices would no longer be pushing up prices of many other commodities, the country would be rid of the supply shocks it has been causing.

On the other hand, if we were considering a case in which the recovery of the patient were highly questionable, then a direct subsidy would not be the appropriate remedy. As a purely hypothetical example, consider an industry producing commodity X. In industry X, wage rates are twice as high as its counterparts in other countries. And not only is industry X technologically lagging behind others, but Japan, which excels in the commodity produced by industry X, has begun to import that commodity from South Korea. Under such circumstances the appropriate policy would be to allow workers to retire with full benefits at the age of forty-five and provide for the retraining of younger workers. In this case, the cost to the taxpayer would be much smaller than with a direct subsidy.

It can be anticipated that there will be a huge cry that a large steel industry is needed for reasons of national defense. But can anyone imagine a conventional war fought across the whole continent of Europe without its turning into an uncontrollable nuclear war? If military measures ever need to be employed to prevent a nuclear holocaust, they will consist of the ability to get a brigade to the right place at the right time. And for that purpose, relatively competitive mini steel plants would provide far more steel than would be needed.

Farm Products

Another good example of where a policy of decoupling micro- from macroeffects could be used to good advantage is in the field of agriculture. Some years ago, Charles Brannan, who was Secretary of Agriculture during the Truman administration, introduced a plan which would have directly subsidized farmers, while permitting the price of food products to be sold at market prices. And today the country is paying an enormous price for not having adopted the Brannan Plan. Food expenditures still account for about 20 percent of total consumption expenditures, and upward of 30 percent for low-income households. This means that the average household is now paying more for its food than it would have under the Brannan Plan (it is now paying the equivalent of the subsidy plus the standard markups in food manufacturing and retail establishments on foodstuffs made more expensive by price supports). While conceived as a subsidy for farmers, the present price-support program is subsidizing a much wider variety of activities. Furthermore, the manner of subsidizing farmers has highly regressive effects. Making the prices of foodstuffs much greater than they otherwise would be only serves to increase the demand for food stamps.

An even more perplexing question is: Under what conditions would it not be appropriate to continue to subsidize farmers? If farm prices were lower, is it conceivable that the United States could export farm products to a wider number of countries than it does today, which would, in turn, encourage farmers to increase their yields? The fact that European countries aid farmers mainly through direct subsidies indicates that they are more sensible than we. However, according to the American interpretation of the Protestant Ethic, people must be kept at productive work until the day they die. Because a direct subsidy would destroy that image, the Brannan Plan was ultimately defeated.

Taxing Gasoline

As was already suggested, for all time to come, gasoline prices are likely to decline during times of recession, when the elasticity of demand is high, and to increase during periods of prosperity, when it is low. As a consequence, projects for conservation of gasoline (e.g., energy-efficient automobiles) and searches for new energy supplies are likely to be speeded up during business upswings and discarded during downswings, with the consequence that the overall rate of progress will be slower than it ought to be. It should be fairly obvious, therefore, that a sufficiently high tax on gasoline (about 50 cents a gallon) is needed to insure that, even in good times, there will be little leverage for further increases in the price of gasoline. By applying steady pressure, such a tax would make it possible to control our own destiny, while at the same time making the U.S. government, and not OPEC, the collector of monopoly rents. Moreover, there are a variety of ways for minimizing the impact of such a tax on the poor. From a political point of view the problem is that there is no ideal time to pass such a tax: when business is bad, politicians worry that it will slow a recovery, and when it is good, they worry that it will further increase inflationary pressures.

Why, then, has this not been done? It is one of the prices we pay for living in a private welfare state, where all public policies are calculated in terms of short-term benefits. Again, according to the American version of the Protestant Ethic, with a new gasoline tax the proceeds need to be used to put people to work at jobs which will increase the directly visible wealth of the nation. Nothing must be done to dispel the illusion that the private sector of the economy is not obeying the same code.

What this logic leaves out of account is that, unless action is taken to keep gasoline prices so high at all times that OPEC finds it unprofitable to bring about further increases during periods of prosperity, the effect of supply shocks during an upturn will be so great that it will be impossible to soak up the unemployment without doing such things as building useless bridges or, which is the same thing, increasing the size of the military budget. Is there anything wrong with extracting the rent from increased oil prices by increasing the tax by 50 cents a gallon? European countries have been doing this for years; and they have survived.

Promoting Competition as Preventive Medicine

I subscribe neither to that school of thought which proclaims that, because substitutes are so plentiful, there is no need to promote competition; nor to that school which proclaims that, because they are a far cry from the ideals of perfect competition, highly concentrated industries do not necessarily provide workable dynamic competition. The truth of the matter is that a high degree of concentration should not in itself be regarded as an evil. Some concentrated industries are characterized by a high degree of internal competition (e.g., farm machinery); others are engaged in fierce foreign competition (e.g., radio and television). On the other hand, there are industries in which international dynamic competition is precluded either for reasons of high transportation costs (e.g., cement) or high advertising costs (e.g., manufactured foods). Such industries do not necessarily generate workable dynamic competition.

To be more specific, the test for dynamic workable competition is in terms of results. When PERK in an industry becomes very small—when there is a high degree of similarity in prices and products in a concentrated industry—firms in that industry do not pass the test. However, the proposed test is not a new one. It is the same as was used in the Tobacco Case, which occurred because tobacco producers acted in concert by greatly increasing their prices during the Great Depression; this case was decided after World War II. As it happens, in the Tobacco Case no evidence of a conspiracy to set prices was required, because it was assumed by the courts that the actions of the firms during the Great Depression implied in themselves a conspiracy to raise prices. The essential change in the Sherman Antitrust Act that I propose is to remove the requirement for an overt conspiracy to set prices. It hardly can be argued that not until we are in another great depression can such a test be applied.

The main problem involved in applying such a test is this: On the one hand, if the law definitely indicates just how far firms can go to engage in parallel actions with respect to products and prices, we will no longer be engaged in preventive medicine. The basic idea of economic preventive medicine is not to tell the patient just how far he can go with respect to myopic profit maximization; it is, rather, to encourage firms to increase their economic wealth. For the same basic reason, our Founding Fathers refused to state precisely what would be an impeachable crime for a president; that is, they wanted to leave enough ambiguity in the laws so a president could not know beforehand just how far he could go with respect to unstatesmanlike behavior. And it is for this basic reason that a few teachers refuse to tell their students just how much they can get away with and still receive a passing grade.

On the other hand, it also must be acknowledged that a refusal to define laws in an almost completely unambiguous way is an open invitation to nonenforcement. Most lawyers are, as Jefferson described them, "Blackstone lawyers"; that is, they go by the book. And the only way to resolve this dilemma is to recognize that institutions must be changed to meet the needs of the times. In particular, the Antitrust Division of the Justice Department should be abolished for the basic reason that it has specialized in narrowing the interpretation of the antitrust laws. In fact, next to the Commerce Department, it is the greatest squanderer of this country's wealth.

By contrast, it must be acknowledged that the Federal Trade Commission has shown a great deal more enterprise in trying to promote competition from a broader point of view. Nevertheless, even in the Federal Trade Commission there is some room for improvement. In particular, a much wider diversity of people is needed to promote competition, including those who actually have been involved in fairly competitive industries. To really understand the benefits of risk taking it is absolutely essential to have been or be presently involved in an activity in which risks are taken—and neither law universities nor law firms are particularly noteworthy in that respect.

The more thorny issue is what penalties should be provided when firms engage in parallel actions with respect to prices and products? Should the firms be broken up? Should fines be imposed? Should the leaders of those firms be jailed? Or should the management be changed? Breaking up firms and then leaving the same people in charge certainly cannot be counted upon to change their character. When habits become second nature, neither fines nor prison terms are likely to have a lasting impact. From one point of view, requiring a new management team be brought in is the appropriate remedy. From another point of view, having the government involved in such actions could be extremely unfortunate.

When management of a firm needs to be changed, for whatever reason, the stockholders should undertake that responsibility. And when the stockholders no longer have that right, it is a government responsibility to find some way to restore it. There is nothing inherent in capitalism that requires the separation of ownership from control. The stockholders have little or no control because management wants it that way. Indeed, in many large corporations, even boards of directors have only a nominal voice in determining company policies. The restoration of stock-holders' rights requires, in effect, that they, and not management, be responsible for the selection of boards of directors, and for changing them and management when circumstances require. Perhaps what is needed is some procedure whereby they can elect a new board of directors which, in turn, will select new management teams every five years—or whenever such an election is required, because the firms in an industry are found to be guilty of actions tantamount to students copying each others' test papers.

Deregulating the Generation of Electrical Energy

Today, public utility companies are engaged in three activities: the generation of electricity, its long-distance transmission, and its distribution to the final consumers. If you, a consumer, have been wondering why your utility bills have escalated, the answer is fairly simple: private utility companies are to be regarded as still another arm of the private welfare state; that is, the manner in which public utility rates are set provides little or no incentive to search for ways to reduce costs. Utility companies are good at protecting their predictability in the small, while jeopardizing the economic stability of the country in the large. This subject comes under the heading of *preventive medicine* because something needs to be done to prevent soaring utility costs from becoming an even more serious problem than soaring food prices.

What should have been done years ago is fairly obvious: independent firms should have been allowed to sell energy into a grid on the basis of providing reliable energy at the lowest possible cost. This would not only have brought fresh blood into an industry where it is desperately needed, but it would have protected the consumer better. Moreover, the idea of having public utility companies engaged in operating nuclear power plants is quite as ludicrous as it would have been to allow the railroads to go into the business of building airliners. The operation of plants based on a new technology is an entirely different business from operating them based on a technology that is something like fifty years old.

POLITICAL RISK TAKING

Let us assume that our politicians were to consider the preceding proposals. One politician may not think it wise to press for the adoption of something like the Brannan Plan at the present time. Another might feel that this is not the time to press for deregulation of electric energy. But there can be no doubt that the measures discussed would make the American economy work far better than it is today for two rather obvious reasons: the theory behind them is a commonsense theory, and the proposals are directed toward the real, and not some imaginary, issues facing the American economy. By contrast, this country is now embarked on an economic course which *at best* can result in slow painful recoveries followed by very deep downturns.

Yet it must be acknowledged that, politically speaking, the chances of moving in directions other than the "New and Old Deals" are not very bright, and for good reason. By desiring, above all, to be reelected, politicians are quite as myopic as the business firms which seek to make their profits as large as possible during the next six months.

A more basic problem, as matters now stand, is the inability of our political leaders and many private citizens to face up to reality. The leaders of the United States desperately want to believe that we can reacquire a high degree of *absolute* military security (as contrasted with making poor investments to retrieve even poorer investments). In a nuclear world, however, there is nothing that is further from the truth. They want desperately to believe that we are about to enter a glorious period of prosperity without inflation, although it is simply not in the cards. Ruskin described the age in which Britain lost its technological superiority to the United States and Germany as an age of "decorative lies." And it is on such decorative lies that the new private welfare state thrives.

Chapter 12
CONVERSATIONS WITH ADAM SMITH

How did it occur to me to have a heart-to-heart talk with Adam Smith? It is well known that Adam Smith was born in the eighteenth century, when the scientific and technological revolutions were just beginning. But, to judge from the way he is quoted in the economics literature, Adam Smith seems to have been so deterministic in his thinking that one can well imagine that he lived not in the eighteenth, but in the nineteenth, century, when the essence of science consisted of providing every discipline with the appearance of Newtonian celestial mechanics.

Curiously enough, conservative economists, who claim to have a direct line to his innermost thoughts, say that there is an automatic hidden hand constantly at work to insure that the pursuit of self-interest will promote the general interest. For example, people may be praying for their deliverance when in a sinking boat, but, according to the doctrine of the automatic hidden hand, that only proves that the "general interest" consists of speeding their way to the world hereafter.

I must emphasize, however, that my motivation for this conversation was to ferret out his personal insights about the world *he* observed. As a matter of fact, throughout the ages scientists have made errors by uncritically accepting assumptions made by others. Adam Smith was no exception. In particular, C.D. Darlington, a British geneticist, has observed that Rousseau put forth a view that the differences between nations are original differences which have existed from the time of their creation.[1] According to Darlington, Darwin's views on this matter were, to say the least, highly ambiguous—and, no doubt, it was acceptance of this assumption that caused biologists to think of evolution in terms of a given environment for nearly a century; that is, the "environment" was assumed to be as free from outside influences as was the celestial system. Not until the 1920s, when biologists concluded that an environment cannot be defined without reference to the species of which it is composed, did the modern revolution in biology begin.

As far as economics is concerned, it seems that Adam Smith went wrong in the same way as did the biologists. By assuming that nations would trade in terms of some immutable characteristics they possessed, in effect, he apparently felt that they could not change their environments. Yet to his great credit, it must be acknowledged that, as far as Britain is concerned, he was not completely duped by his own theory. If he were really convinced that the relative advantage of nations to produce various commodities was immutable, why was he so concerned that by trading only with its colonies, Britain would ultimately jeopardize its ability to compete in international markets?

Adam Smith's international trade theory has survived, essentially intact, because it met the requirements of a highly deterministic age. Moreover, there can be no doubt that nineteenth-century economists began to think of all economic activities as trades which resulted in mutual advantages that would come about quite automatically. But did he really believe that the pursuit of self-interest automatically led to promotion of the general interest?

I began our exchange of ideas by asking Adam Smith what he had in mind when he wrote the following oft-quoted statement:

> It is not from the benevolence of the butcher, the brewer, or the baker that we expect our dinner, but from their regard of their own interest. We address ourselves not to their humanity, but to their self-love, and never talk to them of our own necessities, but of their advantage.[2]

I continued, "Did you mean to say that, if the butcher, the brewer, and the baker were allowed to follow their own interests, substitutes would be so plentiful that we would never need be at a loss to find a good dinner at a minimal price? Or, did you mean that, if the consumer were interested in protecting *his* self-interest, he should give the merchants the impression that demand for their products is very elastic— give them to understand, in other words, that selling a loaf of bread for a penny is better than selling none?"

Adam Smith seemed to be very surprised, indeed, that modern economists failed to understand that, at the time he wrote this statement, he was simply telling us how shrewd was the behavior of Scottish buyers.

"Well, then, in terms of your own observations, Adam Smith, how do sellers behave?"

His reply was to quote another passage from *The Wealth of Nations*:

> People of the same trade seldom meet together, even for merriment and diversion, but the conversation ends in a conspiracy against the public, or in some contrivance to raise prices.[3]

Now it must be remembered that this passage was written on the eve of the Industrial Revolution, long before the conception of dynamic competition.

The next question I put to Adam Smith was "What state were you describing when you said that the stationary state is dull, the progressive state hearty, and the declining state melancholy? Was your notion of a hearty state much like that held by dynamic economists, namely, one that can manufacture new technological recipes? And was it a world in which the brewer, the baker, and the butcher had to constantly adapt to new
ledge? Did the hearty state actually exist during your time; or was it a state which you, Adam Smith, hoped would emerge?"

Adam Smith's answer to the first of my questions was that he definitely was aware of the role that new knowledge can play in economic evolution. Moreover, he agreed entirely that this function of creating new knowledge was not a job for specialists, and quoted again from his treatise:

> Many improvements have been made by the ingenuity of the makers of the machines—and some by that of those who are called philosophers or men of speculation, whose trade it is not to do anything, but to observe everything; and who, upon that account, are often capable of combining together the powers of the most distant and dissimilar objects.[4]

It should be noted that this statement is inconsistent with Adam Smith's theory of international trade. Any nation that has a relative advantage in such "men of speculation"—as did Britain during the eighteenth and nineteenth centuries' scientific and technological revolutions—could change the industrial environments of many countries! Again, it should be apparent that economists, who consider all economic progress to be tantamount to increasing the degree of specialization, simply have not read *The Wealth of Nations* carefully.

Now, it is true that, as of 1776, the competitive spirit had not yet blossomed in Britain. In fact, it is conceivable that this spirit first emerged as competition between communities of inventors, and only later became the name of the game in industry. Consider Samuel Johnson's boast: "We work with our heads, and make the boobies of Birmingham work for us with their hands."[5] It should also be kept in mind that the cities which participated in the Industrial Revolution—cities mainly inhabited by people from Scotland and dissenters from the Church of England— were free of the religious superstitions which prevent competition in ideas.

With these thoughts in mind, my next query to Adam Smith was, "Did you really believe that there was an automatic hand at work which would lead to an acceleration of progress—or were you advocating a society in which the pursuit of self-interest would eventually become equated with the hearty state?"

According to Adam Smith, if competition were to work it had to be a game that people really enjoyed; that is, people had to understand that creativeness was equivalent to the pursuit of happiness. This he illustrated by again quoting from his writings:

> The state, by encouraging, that is by giving entire liberty to all those who for their own interest would attempt, without scandal or indecency, to amuse and divert the people by painting, poetry, music, dancing; by all sorts of dramatic representations and exhibitions, would easily dissipate, in the greater part of them, that melancholy and gloomy humour which is almost always the nurse of popular superstition and enthusiasm.[6]

It may be noted that not only Adam Smith took this attitude, but also Thomas Jefferson, who was constantly preaching that Americans did not listen to enough good music.

The similarity between Adam Smith and Thomas Jefferson does not end there. Both had remarkably similar views on education; that is, they believed that the purpose of an education was to add to the meaning of experience. But Adam Smith said that he certainly did not believe that, as of the time he wrote, education was achieving that purpose. He referred to the following passage from *The Wealth of Nations*:

> The discipline of colleges and universities is in general contrived, not for the benefit of the students, but for the interest, or more properly speaking, for the ease of the masters. Its object is, in all cases, to maintain the authority of the master, and whether he neglects or performs his duty, to oblige the students in all cases to behave to him as if he performed it with the greatest diligence and ability.[7]

In answer to the question, "What kind of rationality is required to make people adaptive in the face of new circumstances?" he had this to say:

> The man whose whole life is spent in performing a few simple operations, of which the effects are perhaps always the same, or very nearly the same, has no occasion to exert his understanding or to exercise his invention in finding out expedients for removing difficulties which never occur. He naturally loses, therefore, the habit of such exertion, and generally becomes as stupid and ignorant as it is possible for a human creature to become. The torpor of his mind renders him not only incapable of relishing or bearing a part in any rational conversation, but of conceiving any generous, noble, or tender sentiment, and consequently of forming any just judgement concerning many even of the ordinary duties of private life.[8]

This passage, which clearly indicates that there is no mechanism to insure evolution in the face of new circumstances, anticipates key ideas in both modern biology and modern economics. Biologists no longer believe that a high degree of specialization in the various species will favor evolution; on the contrary, unless their reproduction rates are very high, they face extinction. Survival depends on diversity in the gene pool, which can result not only in aggressive behavior, but also in altruistic behavior when survival is at stake.[9]

Like biologists, modern dynamic economists also believe that evolution can become virtually impossible when a high degree of specialization is involved. Specialists deal in such fine-grained distinctions that feedback suggesting the necessity of major adjustments is likely to be completely ignored. Hence, patterning of expectations on the basis of an unchanging world is likely to be a prescription for extinction.

Like Adam Smith, modern dynamic economists also believe that it is the ability of individuals and firms to deal with contradictions between theory and practice at the microlevel that leads to stability at the macrolevel. For example, which marriages are more likely to remain stable, those in which the marriage partners can be counted upon to never change their initial ideas, or those in which new "inventions" are constantly made to resolve matrimonial dilemmas? And the same is true in everything, from employing inventiveness to preventing a machine from breaking down often to constructing a new scientific theory. What Adam Smith saw, but neither David Ricardo nor Karl Marx could see, is that life could be something more than a zero-sum game. In a nutshell, that was the difference between eighteenth-and-nineteenth century concepts of rational behavior.

What prevents a positive-sum game from developing is a lack of dynamic competition; a class struggle can only develop in zero-sum societies. This led to a discussion of the most prominent feature of the new private welfare state: its managerial class. Ironic as it may seem, I told him, "This new managerial class puts a greater value on conspicuous consumption, and is more handsomely rewarded than, for example, those more competent managers of Japanese firms. While managerial salaries in our more competitive industries, such as farm machinery or scientific instruments, are not much out of line with managerial salaries in Japan, this is by no means the case in industries such as automobiles or steel." I also told him that university schools of business administration today emphasize teaching business executives how to get rich quickly by engaging in myopic decision making. But even the so-called management experts are beginning to feel highly nervous.

My next question was, "Am I correct in describing this as industrial feudalism? You lived in an age in which feudalism was only beginning to disappear—were the same tendencies also evident then?"

Adam Smith answered that, in feudalistic societies, badges of social distinction were quite as important:

> A man of fortune, for example, may either spend his revenue in a profuse and sumptuous table, and in maintaining a great number of menial servants, and a multitude of dogs and horses; or contenting himself with a frugal table and few attendants, he may lay out the greater part of it in adorning his house or his country villa, in useful or ornamental buildings, in useful or ornamental furniture, in collecting books, statues, pictures; or in things more frivolous, jewels, baubles, ingenious trinkets of different kinds; or, what is most trifling of all, in amassing a great wardrobe of fine clothes....[10]

Moreover, Adam Smith agreed that, although the practice of myopic profit maximization was not then as sophisticated as it is now, the basic idea was by no means an invention of American schools of business administration:

Masters are always and everywhere in a sort of tacit, but constant and uniform combination, not to raise wages of labour above their actual rate. To violate this combination is everywhere a most unpopular action, and a sort of reproach to a master among his neighbours and equals.[11]

CONCLUSIONS

In modern terms, mercantilism can be defined as a policy whose effect is to increase the momentum of the forces associated with deadweight drag, and it makes for results which are increasingly poorer than those associated with a positive-sum game. It is the kind of economy that Adam Smith wanted to avoid, not only because he argued for free trade for its own sake, but also because he saw in mercantilism practices which were morally repugnant.

What is ironical about the world in which we live today is that many so-called liberals are so anxious to protect their children and grandchildren from having to face new problems that, by pressing for more and more protectionism, they are seriously jeopardizing the creative process needed if nations are to survive in the face of new circumstances. A managerial mercantilistic society cannot survive, because it does not stand for competition in deeds. Rather, it encourages competition for personal power in which people are rewarded not to take risks, but to become highly skilled at manipulating the rules of the game to insure their own survival. In such societies, the system of values does not favor a liberal education designed for creativity. Rather, its role is to train technicians to engage in highly specialized tasks. Education, especially that geared toward inducing creative individual thinking, is given a much lower priority than the preservation of law and order. And, as Adam Smith deeply recognized, the promotion of such values does not lead to compassionate behavior toward one's compatriots, because without creativity all of economic life takes on the form of a zero-sum game.

The saving grace is that the private welfare state cannot endure. It will destroy itself by bringing about a very serious worldwide depression. And, as always happens in history, political leaders who were regarded as liberals by one generation will be regarded as the arch-conservatives of the next. The basic reason a dull state is likely to be succeeded by a declining or melancholy state is that, instead of generating economic stability, mercantilism generates deadweight drag.

NOTES

Preface

1. George Shackle, *Expectations in Economics* (Cambridge, England: Cambridge University Press, 1949).
2. Frederick A. Hayek, "Competition as a Discovery Procedure," in *New Studies in Philosophy, Politics, Economics and the History of Ideas* (Chicago: The University of Chicago Press, 1978); and Stephen C. Littlechild, "Equilibrium and the Market Process," in I. M. Kirzner, ed., *Method, Process, and Austrian Economics: Essays in Honor of Ludwig von Mises* (Lexington, MA: P.C. Heath, 1982).
3. Melvin W. Reder, "Chicago Economics: Performance and Change," *Journal of Economic Literature* 20 (March 1982):1-39.
4. Gunnar Eliasson, ed., *A Micro to Macro Model of the Swedish Economy* (Stockholm, Sweden: The Industrial Institute for Social and Economic Research, 1977).

Chapter 1

1. John W. Kendrick, *Productivity Trends in the United States* (Princeton, NJ: Princeton University Press, 1961), p. 482.
2. Gordon E. Moore, Intel Corp., "Are We Ready for VLSI?" Caltech Conference on VLSI, January 1979.
3. N.L.S. Carnot, *Reflections on the Motive Power of Heat*, trans. R.H. Thurston (New York: Wiley, 1890).
4. Ibid.
5. Richard P. Feynman, Robert B. Leighton, and Matthew Sands, *The Feynman Lectures on Physics* (Reading, MA: Addison-Wesley Publishing Company, 1966), pp. 52-53.
6. Ronald Miller, and David Sawers, *The Technical Development of Modern Aircraft* (New York: Praeger, 1970).
7. Joseph A. Schumpeter, *The Theory of Economic Development* (Cambridge, MA: Harvard University Press, 1934), p. 86.
8. Feynman, Leighton, Sands, *The Feynman Lectures on Physics*, p. 1.
9. Herbert Ginsburg, and Sylvia Opper, *Piaget's Theory of Intellectual Development and Introduction* (Englewood Cliffs, NJ: Prentice-Hall, Inc., 1969), pp. 99-103.
10. Frank H. Knight, *Risk, Uncertainty, and Profit* (Boston, MA: Houghton Mifflin, 1921), p. 223.
11. This information was obtained in a personal conversation.
12. Ralph C. Epstein, *The Automobile Industry* (New York: A.W. Shaw, 1928), pp. 353-354.
13. Alfred P. Sloan, Jr., *My Years with General Motors* (New York: Doubleday, 1964), pp. 71-94.
14. Burton H. Klein, *Dynamic Economics*, (Cambridge, MA: Harvard University Press 1977), pp. 126-127.
15. Niccolò Machiavelli, *The Prince* (New York: Mentor Books, 1952), p. 120.

16. W. Paul Strassmann, *Risk and Technological Innovation* (Ithaca, NY: Cornell University Press, 1959), pp. 122-123.
17. Ibid., pp. 118-119.

Chapter 2

1. See chapter 6 for further discussion.
2. Lawrence White, *The Automobile Industry Since 1945* (Cambridge, MA: Harvard University Press, 1971), chapter 13.
3. Bo Carlsson, "The Content of Productivity Growth in Swedish Manufacturing," *The Firms in the Market Economy* (Stockholm, Sweden: The Industrial Institute for Social and Economic Research, 1980), pp. 33-47.
4. Edwin Mansfield et al., *The Production and Application of New Industrial Technology* (New York: Norton, 1977), chapters 6, 7.
5. Ibid., p. 135.
6. Ibid., p. 137.
7. *Economic Handbook of the Machine Tool Industry, 1981-1982* (Washington, DC: National Machine Tool Building Assoc., 1982), pp. 100-102, 194, 198.
8. Mansfield et al., *New Industrial Technology*, p. 110.
9. Ibid., p. 110.
10. Burton H. Klein, "A Dynamic Theory of Regulation" (Caltech Working Paper 199; January 1978), pp. 42-43.
11. Simon Kuznets, "Modern Economic Growth: Findings and Reflections," *The American Economic Review* (June 1973), p. 247.

Chapter 3

1. Edward F. Dennison, *Accounting for Slower Economic Growth* (Washington, DC: Brookings Institution, 1979), p. 4.
2. Zvi Griliches, "R&D and the Productivity Slowdown," *The American Economic Review* 70 (May 1980).
3. Ibid., p. 347
4. Knight, *Risk, Uncertainty, and Profit*, p. 19.
5. C.D. Darlington, *The Evolution of Man and Society* (New York: Simon and Schuster, 1969), pp. 22-47.
6. Adam Smith, *The Wealth of Nations* (London: Everyman's Library, J.M. Dent & Sons Ltd, 1947), vol. 1, p. 72.

Chapter 4

1. See for example, Jennifer F. Reinganum and Nancy Stokey, "Oligopoly Extraction" (The Center for Mathematical Studies in Economics and Management Sciences; Discussion Paper 508, November 1981).
2. Louis D. Brandeis, *The Curse of Bigness* (New York: Viking, 1934), p. 115.
3. Ibid., p. 126.

4. Carl Kaysen and Donald Turner, *Antitrust Policy: An Economic and Legal Analysis* (Cambridge, MA: Harvard University Press, 1959), chapter 1.
5. *Encyclopaedia Britannica*, 1968 ed., vol. 12, p. 989.
6. White, *Automobile Industry Since 1945*.
7. Klein, *Dynamic Economics*, pp. 193-195.
8. See chapter 5.
9. Hiroto Ohyama, "The Current State and Future Course of the Japanese Automobile Industry" (International Policy Forum on the Automobile Industry, Eagle Lodge, PA, June 18 - July 1, 1981).
10. Adam Smith, *Wealth of Nations*, p. 99.
11. For a summary, see F.M. Scherer, *Industrial Market Structure and Economic Performance* (Chicago, IL: Rand McNally Economic Series 1970), pp. 366-367. For more detailed accounts, see S.G. Sturmley, *The Economic Development of the Radio* (London, England: Duckworth, 1958); Robert Schlaifer and S. D. Heron, *Development of Aircraft Engines and Fuels* (Cambridge, MA: Harvard University Press, 1959); John E. Tilton, *International Diffusion of Technology* (Washington, DC: Brookings Institution, 1971); Burton H. Klein, *Dynamic Economics*, pp. 89-140.
12. Strassmann, *Risk and Technological Innovation*, p. 66.
13. The Center for Policy Alternatives, MIT, *Technology and Industrial Innovation in Sweden* (Cambridge, MA: CPA W/P 81-06 Sept. 4, 1981), p. 17.
14. Erik Dahmnén, *Entrepreneurial Activity and the Development of Swedish Industry, 1919-1939* (Homewood, IL: R.D. Irwin, 1970).
15. Simon Kuznets, *Economic Growth and Structure* (New York: W.W. Norton, 1965), pp. 304-328.
16. James M. Utterback, "The Dynamics of Product and Process Innovation in Industry" in *Technological Innovation for a Dynamic Economy*, eds. Christopher T. Hill and James M. Utterback (New York: Pergamon Press, 1979), pp. 55-57.
17. Ann F. Friedlander, *The Dilemma of Freight Transport Regulation* (The Brookings Institution, Washington, DC, 1969), p. 97.
18. Joseph A. Schumpeter, *Business Cycles* (New York: McGraw-Hill, 1939).
19. Klein, *Dynamic Economics*, p. 125.
20. Sturmley, *The Economic Development of the Radio*.
21. Klein, *Dynamic Economics*, p. 97.
22. Ibid., p. 125.
23. For a detailed account of these threats see Bruce M. Owen and Ronald Braeutigam, *The Regulation Game* (Cambridge, MA: Ballinger, 1978), pp. 195-239.
24. Epstein, *Automobile Industry*, p. 213.
25. Moore, "Are We Ready for VLSI?"
26. Lester C. Thurow, *The Zero Sum Society* (New York: Basic Books, 1980), pp. 146-150.

Chapter 5

1. Koichi Shimokawa, "Entrepreneurship and Social Environment Change in the Japanese Automobile Industry," (Working Paper, 1981); "Automobiles: Groping for Coexistence Rather than International Rivalry," *Japan Quarterly* 20 (1981); "An Innovator Succeeds: Honda's into the Worldwide Automobile Industry" (Harvard Business School Working Paper, September, 1978).
2. Charles G. Burck, "Can Detroit Catch Up?" *Fortune*, 8 Feb. 1982, p. 35.
3. William J. Abernathy, Kim B. Clark, and Alan M. Kantrow, "The New Industrial Competition," *Harvard Business Review*, (September-October, 1981), pp. 72-73.

4. Peter Payne, *Colvilles and the Scottish Steel Industry* (Oxford: Oxford University Press, 1979).
5. Utterback, "Dynamics of Product and Process Innovation," pp. 40-50.
6. Smith, *Wealth of Nations,* vol. 1, p. 115.
7. Ibid., vol. 2, p. 101.

Chapter 6

1. Alfred Marshall, *Principles of Economics* 8th ed. (London, England: Macmillan and Co., 1920). It may be noted that the theme of the book is contained on the opening page: *natura non facit saltum;* and that the idea that nature does not move by leaps was the central idea in Darwinian biology. However, in defense of Marshall it certainly can be said that, with relatively few exceptions, British industry does not move by leaps.
2. H.J. Habakkuk, *American and British Technology in the Nineteenth Century* (Cambridge, England: Cambridge University Press, 1967), p. 58.
3. Klein, *Dynamic Economics,* pp. 141-175.

Chapter 7

1. Joseph A. Schumpeter, *Capitalism, Socialism, and Democracy* (New York: Harper and Brothers, 1942); John Kenneth Galbraith, *The New Industrial State* (Boston, MA: Houghton Mifflin, 1967); and Richard Nelson and Sidney Winter, *An Evolutionary Theory of Economic Change* (Cambridge, MA: Harvard University Press, 1982).

Chapter 8

1. For an interesting article, see Walter S. Measday, "The Petroleum Industry," in *The Structure of American Industry,* ed. Walter Adams (New York: Macmillan Co., 1982).
2. For an excellent article on this subject see Walter Adams and Hans Mueller "The Steel Industry," in *The Structure of American Industry,* ed. Walter Adams (New York: Macmillan Co., 1982), pp. 73-136.
3. Ibid., p. 101
4. Ibid., p. 102
5. Payne, *Colvilles and the Scottish Steel Industry.*
6. Adams and Mueller, "The Steel Industry," p. 102.
7. *1982 U.S. Industrial Outlook* (Washington, DC: U.S. Department of Commerce, January 1982), p. 1.
8. Ibid., p. 153.
9. Adams and Mueller, "The Steel Industry," p. 122.
10. Ibid., p. 123.
11. Ibid., p. 120.
12. *1977 Census of Manufacturers,* Special Supplements on "Fuels and Electric Energy Consumed" and "Steel Consumption" (Bureau of the Census, 1977).
13. *Economic Handbook of the Machine Tool Industry, 1981-1982.*
14. Ibid.
15. Ibid.

16. Ibid.
17. See, for example, *1982 U.S. Industrial Outlook,* p. 176.

Chapter 9

1. Milton Friedman, "The Role of Monetary Policy," *American Economic Review* 63 (March 1968):7-10.
2. Ibid., p. 8.
3. Leonard J. Savage, *The Foundations of Statistics* (New York: Dover, 1972).
4. See, for example, Guillermo A. Calvo and Edmund S. Phelps, "A Model of Non-Walrasian General Equilibrium," in *Macro Economics, Prices and Quantities,* ed. James Tobin (Washington, DC: Brookings Institution, 1983), pp. 135-161.
5. Richard P. Feynman, *The Character of Physical Law* (London: British Broadcasting Corp., 1965), p. 147.
6. J.M. Keynes, "The General Theory of Employment," *The Quarterly Journal of Economics* (February 1937), p. 209.
7. Ibid., p. 215.
8. Gunnar Eliasson, et al., *Policy Making in a Disorderly World Economy* (Stockholm, Sweden: The Industrial Institute for Economic and Social Research, 1983).
9. Robert E. Lucas, Jr., "Some International Evidence on the Output-Inflation Trade-off," *American Economic Review* (June 1982).

Chapter 11

1. "The Madness of Executive Compensation," *Fortune,* August 1982.
2. Schumpeter, *Capitalism, Socialism, and Democracy,* see especially pp. 165-200.
3. Thomas Tooke and William Newmarch, *A History of Prices* (New York: Adelphi, 1928).
4. George J. Stigler, "The Theory of Economic Regulation," *Bell Journal of Economics and Management Science* 2 (Spring 1971).
5. J.M. Keynes, *The General Theory of Employment, Interest, and Money* (New York: Harcourt Brace, 1936), p. 380.

Chapter 12

1. Darlington, *Evolution of Man and Society,* pp. 544-546.
2. Smith, *Wealth of Nations,* vol. 1, p. 9.
3. Ibid., vol. 1, p. 117.
4. Ibid., vol. 1, p. 9, 10.
5. Darlington, *Evolution of Man and Society,* p. 512.
6. Smith, *Wealth of Nations,* vol. 2, p. 278.
7. Ibid., vol. 2, p. 249.
8. Ibid., pp. 263, 264.
9. See for example, R.I.M. Dunbar, "Sociality," in *Current Problems in Sociobiology* (London, England: Cambridge University Press, 1982).
10. Smith, *Wealth of Nations,* vol. 1, p. 310.
11. Ibid., vol. 1, p. 59.

INDEX

Abernathy, William J., 53, 57
Adams, Walter, 122
agriculture, 16. *See also* farm products
air conditioning industry, 119
aircraft carriers, 66
aircraft technology, 3-4, 9, 13-14, 19, 20, 21, 39, 60
airline industry, 13, 14, 21, 39, 40, 60-61
  costs per mile, 9, 12, 40
  deregulation of, 163
  productivity increases, 21
  tooling in, 60-61, 62
  See also Boeing
aluminum industry, xv, 118-119
  prices, xv, 122
American Iron and Steel Institute, 121
anti-trust laws, 44, 163-164
  See also Justice Department, Anti-trust Division)
Anti-trust Policy, 32
AT&T, 2, 40-41, 51
Automobile Industry, The, 41
automobile industry, U.S., 1, 3, 13-14, 19, 21, 23, 34-36, 41, 53-54, 75, 86, 135, 145, 161, 164, 167-171, 173
  assembly line flexibility, 55-67
  compared to Japanese, 34-36, 53-54, 55, 56-57, 75, 87-88, 125, 161, 167, 171
  foreign competition and, 135, 167, 170-171
  and machine tools, 19, 125-126
  in private welfare state, 121
  productivity of, 13-14, 23, 34-36, 53-54, 87-88, 161
  rivalry in, 34-36, 41, 167
  wages in, 23, 135, 157-159
  See also individual brand names; wages; UAW
automobiles, 3, 16, 21, 23, 39, 55-67, 161, 173
  cost of, 1, 3, 16, 39, 161
  front wheel drive, 39, 70

Japanese, 34-36, 39, 53-54, 75, 161, 167, 171
  quality of, 1, 3
  size and horsepower of, 16
  time needed to produce, 53-54
  See also individual brand names
Avery, Clarence, 7

Baldridge, Malcolm, 122
"Bandwagon Effect," 17
Bayesian probability theory, 4, 134-135
Bell Telephone Laboratories, 2, 40-41, 53
Bessemer steel process, 103-104
"Blackstone Lawyers," 175
Boeing, 13, 39-40
Brandeis, Louis D., 32-33, 37
Brannan, Charles, 173
Brannan Plan, 173, 177
Buick, 171
Business Cycles, 39
business cycles, vii, 127-156, 164-165
  dynamic theories of, 132-137
  independent, 129
  "pea coat," 129, 130
  static theories of, 132-137
button industry, xv

Cadillac Company, 3
Canada, productivity of, 14
capitalism, 47, 111, 164
  defined, 164
  dynamic, 135
  feudalistic, 33, 65
Carlsson, Bo, 16
Carnot, Sadi, 2-3
carpet and rug industry, 68, 87
Carter, Jimmy, administration of, 121
chemical industry, 38
Chicago School (University of Chicago Economics Department), v, 134-135, 136, 160
Chevrolet, 9

United Automobile Workers (UAW), 157
utility companies, 176
  utility costs, 176
Utterback, James, 39, 57

Vietnam, war in, 128
Volkswagen, 9, 39
wages, xi, xiii, 23, 24, 65, 96, 116, 128, 135-136, 147, 157-160, 162, 183
  in automobile industry, 23, 135, 157-159
  changes in, 157-160
  executive, 162
  in industries with little dynamic competition, 157
  prices and, 116, 124, 157-158
  and productivity, 157-160
  reasons for changes in, in steel industry, 121, 124, 157-160

The Wealth of Nations. 29, 36, 66-67, 179-180

welfare states, 161-177
  private, 161-165
  public, 161
Western Electric, 2, 51
White, Lawrence, 35
Whitney, Eli, 3, 12, 37
Wilcoxon's Signed Rank Tests, 84, 100-101, 116-117
Wilson, Charles, 157
Winter, Sidney, 111
wood product industry, xv

zero sum
  defined, 42
  game, xiv, 29, 41, 42, 182, 183
  society, 182
  world, 44
The Zero Sum Society, 44

ABOUT THE AUTHOR

Prior to becoming a Professor of Economics at Caltech, for fifteen years Burton H. Klein was involved in numerous empirical studies of research and development at the RAND Corporation. Insistently piquing his interest was, what strategy in business was necessary to succeed in research and development? When one firm might operate in text-book fashion by carefully optimizing its products for the market at particular points in time, another might never engage in such a seemingly rational strategy, yet, in five or ten years time will completely outdistance the first firm.

In all disciplines, dynamic considerations were brought into play by trying to understand phenomena which did not agree with a static paradigm. Biologists, for example, found that characteristics which permitted species to adapt to a given environment were by no means the same as those required for survival in a rapidly changing environment. So, with help from science majors he has taught, Klein has attempted to learn as much as possible about the lessons learned in the fields of physics, chemistry and biology as they were weaned from their devotion to understanding reality in terms of Newtonian celestial mechanics.

In his book, *Dynamic Economics*, published in 1977, Klein contrasted a static concept of stability (microstability) with a dynamic concept (macrostability); and he argued that unpredictable behavior at the microlevel leads to smooth progress at the macrolevel. This book, *Prices, Wages, and Business Cycles*, provides a statistical demonstration of the importance of these concepts by showing that the quest for microstability—for behavior associated with an unchanging world—ultimately leads to increasingly serious economic downturns.